D1060318

REMEMBERING THE GREATEST COACHES AND GAMES OF THE NFL GLORY YEARS

REMEMBERING THE GREATEST COACHES AND GAMES OF THE NFL GLORY YEARS

An Inside Look at the Golden Age of Football

Wayne Stewart

ROWMAN & LITTLEFIELD
Lanham • Boulder • New York • London

Published by Rowman & Littlefield
An imprint of The Rowman & Littlefield Publishing Group, Inc.
4501 Forbes Boulevard, Suite 200, Lanham, Maryland 20706
www.rowman.com

Unit A, Whitacre Mews, 26-34 Stannary Street, London SE11 4AB

British Library Cataloguing in Publication Information Available

Library of Congress Cataloging-in-Publication Data

Names: Stewart, Wayne, 1951– author.
Title: Remembering the greatest coaches and games of the NFL glory years : an inside look at the
golden age of football / Wayne Stewart.
Other titles: Remembering the greatest coaches and games of the National Football League glory
years | Greatest coaches and games of the National Football League glory years | National
Football League glory years
Description: Lanham, Maryland : Rowman & Littlefield, [2018] | Includes bibliographical references
and index.
Identifiers: LCCN 2017060391 (print) | LCCN 2018021178 (ebook) | ISBN 9781538101599 (elec-
tronic) | ISBN 9781538101582 (hardback : alk. paper)
Subjects: LCSH: National Football League—History—20th century. | Football coaches—United
States—Biography. | Football players—United States—Anecdotes. | Football teams—History—
20th century.
Classification: LCC GV955.5.N35 (ebook) | LCC GV955.5.N35 S725 2018 (print) | DDC 796.332/
64—dc23
LC record available at https://lccn.loc.gov/2017060391

♾ ™ The paper used in this publication meets the minimum requirements of American National Standard for Information Sciences Permanence of Paper for Printed Library Materials, ANSI/NISO Z39.48-1992.

Printed in the United States of America

To those closest to me—
my wife Nancy,
my sons and their spouses,
Sean and Rachel, Scott and Katie,
and to my grandson Nathan.
Also to the memory of my parents,
O.J., who taught me to love words,
and Margaret, who taught me the pleasure and
importance of reading.

CONTENTS

Acknowledgments   ix

Introduction   xi

PART I: THE GREATEST GAMES OF THE GLORY YEARS   1

  1 The Greatest Game Ever Played: "Good Grief, I've Never Seen Anything Like That"   5

  2 The Ice Bowl: "I'm Going to Take a Bite of My Coffee"   23

  3 The Heidi Game: A Swiss Miss Takes on Pro Football   49

  4 Super Bowl III: "No Brag, Just Fact"   59

PART II: THE GREATEST COACHES OF THE GLORY YEARS   79

  5 George Halas: The Bear Who Never Hibernated   81

  6 Paul Brown: "Act Like You've Been There Before"   97

  7 Weeb Ewbank: The Short Coach Who Stood Tall   111

  8 Vince Lombardi: Dynasty Builder   125

  9 Tom Landry: The Man in the Funny Hat   155

10 Hank Stram: Dapper Mentor   179

11 Don Shula: King of the Hill   193

12 George Allen: "He Wanted to Win at All Costs"   217

13 Bud Grant: "He Understood Every Player"   233

Notes   247

Bibliography	251
Index	255
About the Author	263

ACKNOWLEDGMENTS

Sincere and huge thanks go out to the following people: Stephen Russell, general chairman of the Mid Mon Valley All Sports Hall of Fame; Ron Paglia, a longtime newsman and writer from Charleroi, Pennsylvania; Chad Unitas; Paige Unitas; Joe Unitas; Leonard Unitas; Sandy Unitas; John Ziemann, former deputy director of the Sports Legends and Babe Ruth Birthplace Museum, and president of Baltimore's Marching Ravens (formerly the Baltimore Colts Marching Band); Rich Erdelyi, Carnegie Mellon University football coach; Ron Main, chairman of the Larry Bruno Foundation at Carnegie Free Library of Beaver Falls, Pennsylvania; Pete Fierle and Chris Schilling of the Pro Football Hall of Fame; and John Vorperian, host and executive producer of *Beyond the Game*.

Thanks also to the people who gave up their time to do interviews with the author, with special appreciation extended to the former players and coaches who generously gave several and/or lengthy interviews: Mike Ditka, Jackie Smith, Floyd Little, Mel Renfro, Chuck Mercein, Don Maynard, Charley Taylor, Manny Fernandez, Gino Marchetti, Tony Benjamin, Sam Havrilak, Fred Cox, Myron Pottios, Doug Crusan, George Belu, Bob Hyland, Tom Matte, Dave Robinson, Rick Volk, John Isenbarger, Paul Warfield, Lenny Moore, Chuck Bryant, Mike Lucci, Joe Walton, Andy Nelson, Bill Malinchak, and Raymond Berry. The quotes in the book, unless otherwise noted, are from interviews conducted by the author with the aforementioned men.

Finally, a huge show of gratitude is owed to my editor, Christen Karniski, for helping make the book better and having faith in our two-book project, *Remembering the Stars of the NFL Glory Years*, and now this companion book as well.

INTRODUCTION

This book stands alone but is a companion book to *Remembering the Stars of the NFL Glory Years: An Inside Look at the Golden Age of Football.* That book focuses on the game as seen through the eyes of the men who played in that era, the 1950s and 1960s. *Remembering the Stars* contrasts the way the game was back then with the NFL today, while also featuring the greatest, toughest, and funniest players of that time period.

This book recalls and pays tribute to the greatest coaches, for example, Vince Lombardi, Don Shula, Paul Brown, George Halas, and Tom Landry, and four of the most interesting, noteworthy games of the era: the Greatest Game Ever Played, the Ice Bowl, the Heidi game, and Super Bowl III—games that conjure up magical memories. The 1950s and 1960s truly were golden decades of pro football's history.

One final note: The quotes in this book are from exclusive interviews conducted by the author unless otherwise indicated (and there are no endnotes provided for widely quoted items that can be found in many, various sources).

PART I

The Greatest Games of the Glory Years

The Golden Era of the NFL, defined here as the 1950s and 1960s, featured more than its share of outstanding, unforgettable games. Decisions made by some of the greatest, most memorable coaches in the annals of the league featured prominently in those contests.

The 1958 NFL championship game is a must for inclusion in any discussion of great NFL contests. After all, more than a half century later it is still labeled the Greatest Game Ever Played for many reasons.

Weeb Ewbank took a 7–5 team from 1957 and helped the Baltimore Colts capture the championship, knocking off the New York Giants, who employed two assistant coaches who were destined for greatness, Tom Landry and Vince Lombardi. The New York head coach was the much more obscure Jim Lee Howell, but even he gained fame by winning the 1956 NFL championship and registering a highly laudatory win–loss percentage of .663 over 84 regular season games spread out over seven seasons.

Howell's coaching forte was his willingness to give power to Landry and Lombardi, who were in charge of the Giants defense and offense, respectively. By his third year on the job, Landry's defense helped win the championship and had crowds, perhaps for the first time, enthusiastically shouting, "Dee-fense! Dee-fense!"

Howell once stated, with just a bit of hyperbole and humor, "With Tom and Vince, all I have to do is make sure the footballs are blown up, send in the punter on fourth down, and decide whether to kick off or receive."[1]

Hall of Fame receiver Don Maynard, who was on the 1958 Giants team, commented, "To me Jim Lee Howell was just a head coach in name—he had two assistants that were as sharp as any who ever coached the game of football."

Maynard said of his one year (1958) as a New York Giant, "Lombardi was a great coach, and I was fortunate enough to play for him on the offensive part of it, and over on defense where I was a backup defensive back I had the privilege of playing under Landry also."

The Giants head coach never realized Maynard's potential, but later Weeb Ewbank would. "A lot of situations are like that," began Maynard. "A lot of guys became a little more famous after a year or two, and you just have to keep plugging away. I was fortunate to be under Lombardi and Landry. It worked out perfectly for me. Then, as my career went on later, the same thing [worked out with Ewbank]."

Maynard recalled Howell's delegating authority to Landry and Lombardi, saying that among other duties, they even "did their own bed checks. They had top of the line ballplayers and you didn't have to really worry about somebody breaking curfew." Part of that was the respect the players had for both Landry and Lombardi.

The combination of the two contrasting assistant coaches, who did share the traits of being driven and dedicated coaches, worked. There was Landry, the calm, soft-spoken, controlled one, and Lombardi, the emotional, brash, explosive one. He could be moody—at times after a tough defeat he wouldn't talk to his players. Ultimately, though, the two coaches liked and respected each other and, above all, knew they would do all they could to help the Giants succeed.

As for Ewbank, he was fired by the Colts after the 1962 season even though he had coached Baltimore to a second consecutive NFL title just three years earlier. Then, in his sixth year with the New York Jets, Ewbank took his new team to Super Bowl III, a game featured here because it was such a shocker, with the upstart Jets outplaying the Baltimore Colts who went 13–1 during the regular season. The game was the biggest, most stunning upset of the era, and it changed the complexion of the sport.

In Super Bowl III, Ewbank not only faced his old team but also went toe to toe against one of his former players in Don Shula, who had succeeded him as the Baltimore head coach. Shula's greater days were ahead of him.

As a matter of fact, there were many times legends butted heads during this time frame. For instance, Lombardi and Landry, former coaching colleagues, went at each other in the classic NFL title game dubbed the Ice Bowl.

The inclusion of the Ice Bowl is based primarily upon three factors—the importance of the game; the dramatic ending; and the horrific, unforgettable weather conditions.

Finally, there's the 1968 Heidi game, another classic game featured here, a contest famed for its dramatic (for many reasons) conclusion. In that gem of a game, one head coach was John Rauch, perhaps not a famous figure, but his Oakland Raiders posted a 13–1 record in just his second season ever as a head coach in 1967, good for a trip to the Super Bowl. He then chalked up a 12–2 record the following season, which took his Raiders as far as the AFL championship contest. He was fired the next season when the Raiders chose to go with a young John Madden.

Opposing Rauch in the Heidi game was, once again, none other than Weeb Ewbank, a man whose name pops up over and over again throughout the history of pro football. It's as if Ewbank was the prototype for Kevin Bacon's fame with his six degrees of separation.

The Heidi game was memorable mainly for two reasons: a scoring frenzy and a questionable call made not by a ref but by a television network. The game featured the Oakland Raiders scoring two touchdowns in the game's final 50 seconds to storm back and knock off the New York Jets after NBC decided to cut away from the game in order to air the movie Heidi.

It's little surprise that the majority of the six coaches who were involved in the four great games featured here made it to the Pro Football Hall of Fame—only Rauch and Howell didn't earn that prestigious honor. Collectively the four who are inducted in Canton, Ohio—Shula, Lombardi, Ewbank, and Landry—accounted for 12 championships and racked up a colossal total of 804 wins in regular season contests.

By way of comparison, Bill Belichick is number one with his eight trips to the Super Bowl as of the one held in 2018, while Shula (6) ranks second. Landry with five and Grant with four follow (tied with several others). Furthermore, only Belichick and Chuck Noll have won more Super Bowls than Lombardi, Landry, and Shula.

Without a doubt then, the classic games that follow were influenced by truly legendary coaches. Some of their decisions panned out, others simply didn't work, but a study of the games and the coaches provides deep insight into not only the greats involved but into a sterling era of pro football as well.

Admittedly, such choices are subjective, but all four certainly do reflect and represent the Golden Age of the NFL.

I

THE GREATEST GAME EVER PLAYED

"Good Grief, I've Never Seen Anything Like That"

Experts almost universally contend that the 1958 NFL championship contest between the Giants and the Colts was the best/most important game of its era. It was also a contest that forever changed the world of pro football and turned out to be a game that spawned a slew of books, documentary film footage, *and* legends.

Incidentally, even though their exhibition games were meaningless, the Colts had gone 2–3 in the 1958 preseason schedule, with the two wins coming against the Giants. Weeb Ewbank's team outscored the Giants by a combined 68–42 score even though he cleverly, cautiously refused to use any of the offenses or defenses he would employ once the regular season opened.

Even the 1958 title game's venue was part of the reason the contest was so important, as a throng of 64,185 fans packed the House That Ruth Built, venerable Yankee Stadium. That figure was about 3,000 spectators short of a sellout, but this crowd was still in the holiday mood just three days after Christmas had passed, ready for more festivities and a belated bonus Christmas gift. An estimated 15,000 of those on hand were faithful, rabid Colt fans who made the trip from Baltimore to New York to support their team.

The Colts and Giants, three-and-a-half-point underdogs at game time, posted identical 9–3 records during the regular season, but Baltimore had staggered down the stretch, coming off a two-game losing streak. Of course, those games also seemed almost meaningless because, as Hall of Fame receiver Raymond Berry recalled, the Colts, who began the season at 6–0, wrapped up their conference title right around Thanksgiving. In fact, before their final two games, their only defeat had come in a 24–21 loss to the Giants on a late field goal in Yankee Stadium during a game when John Unitas was hospitalized. The way Berry saw it, the loss to the Giants was the only one that came in a meaningful game all year long.

When the Colts first learned they had mathematically nailed down their West Division title, they were delighted. Another Baltimore Hall of Famer, defensive end Gino Marchetti, recalled the joyous pandemonium, saying, "We were running around, going crazy, you don't know who to tackle or what to do. We just really enjoyed the moment. That was my first professional title, our first big title, and that is the most important one, I think."

Meanwhile, the Giants peaked down the stretch, winning eight of their last nine games. Both teams were star-studded, with 15 future Hall of Famers, including 12 players who played that day. The Giants featured such greats as Frank Gifford, Sam Huff, and Andy Robustelli. Across the field, the Colts standouts included Marchetti, Lenny Moore, and two 25-year-old men, born about two months apart—the Colts main passing combo, quarterback Unitas and his superb favorite target, Raymond Berry. Furthermore, in 1994, four Colts, Unitas, Berry, Jim Parker, and Marchetti, would be named to the NFL's All-Time Team.

It had truly been a golden year for both teams, with eight of the Giants being named to the All-Pro team and an even dozen of the Colts earning such honors, tops in the league.

The Giants also had two future Hall of Famers on their coaching staff in Tom Landry and Vince Lombardi. They would go on to amass 346 regular-season wins when they later became head coaches (250 for Landry alone).

Ewbank, yet another future Hall of Famer, prepared for this game with almost single-minded precision. Having a viable pregame plan is a coaching essential, of course. Ewbank had prepared two sheets of paper prior to the game, folded them twice, and placed them in his pocket, easily accessible. The plans were succinct and covered every angle he could imagine, along with every flaw the Giants had he felt the Colts could exploit.

Ewbank had Unitas scrutinize the defenses he likely would face and memorize the plays he wanted to run against the Giants' usual 4–3 defense. Ewbank believed such study would help Unitas quickly recognize what he was facing each time he broke from his huddle.

Every Colt on the offensive unit was given special instructions, with great attention given to the pass routes designed for Ewbank's deep threats, Moore and Berry. Delving deeper, getting as specific as possible, Ewbank wrote down both the strong and weak points of the individual Giants, all the way down to players' particular habits, which, like a "tell" in a poker player, might give an edge to his players. One such example was his notation it would probably be better to throw the football in one passing lane rather than another because defensive tackle Dick Modzelewski, being five inches shorter than the other tackle, the 6-foot-5 Rosey Grier, would be easier to throw over. No detail was too minute for Ewbank.

Before games, when possible, he plastered the Colts locker room with clippings that contained disparaging quotes about the Colts from writers, opposing players, and coaches. He also directed his players not to talk to the press, fearing a Colt might slip up and say something to provoke their opponents.

Just as Don Shula would do prior to Super Bowl III, a move his Colts would regret, Ewbank had permitted his players' wives to make the trip to New York for their regular-season road game against the Giants. The team stayed in a Manhattan hotel where things were hopping. For the championship game, however, wives were banned, and Ewbank housed the Colts in the Bronx, far from the bright lights, glitter, and temptations of downtown.

The Giants–Colts matchup was an intriguing one. The Giants' defense was stingy, having surrendered the lowest point total in the NFL, 183. The Colts' defense was no slouch, either, ranked second in the league, permitting just 203 points. The Colts' offense purred with mechanical efficiency, sitting atop the NFL with 381 points scored, an average of almost 32 points per game. On the other hand, the Giants had scored just 246 points, or 20.5 points a game. The Giants had playoff experience on their side, having won the championship two years earlier, while the Colts were only in their sixth year of existence.

Prior to the game, Ewbank gave a locker room pep talk, naming every Baltimore player, followed by such comments as, "Unitas was cast off by the Steelers, and Berry didn't go in the draft until the 20th-round draft pick. Nobody wanted you but the Colts." Ewbank even included himself as an example of being unwanted, saying the Colts had originally wanted to hire Blanton Collier, not Ewbank, to become their head coach in 1954. Berry said the rah-rah talk did inspire many, but not all, of the Colts.

The Giants opened the scoring in the first quarter on a 36-yard boot by Pat Summerall, but the Colts roared back with two second-quarter touch-downs. Alan "The Horse" Ameche scored on a two-yard run, as if to foreshadow his later heroics on an even shorter carry.

In the final moments of the game, the Colts would cap off two long drives, both etched into NFL archives; however, there was another key 15-play drive of 86 yards on their last possession of the first half with time elapsing that seems to be mentioned only rarely.

Much like the famous fourth-quarter drive to keep the Colts alive, this one also heavily featured the irrepressible Unitas and Berry combination. They made good on a five-yard completion, a look-in pass for 13 yards to move the chains, and a 15-yard touchdown bullet with 1:20 showing on the clock. On that pass, Berry found a crease between defensive backs Jimmy Patton, a five-time Pro Bowl honoree, and future Hall of Famer Emlen Tunnell. This play seemed to signal bigger things for Berry, too, as he would wind up with two new championship game records: most recep-tions, 12, and most yards on catches, 178 yards.

On the Berry score, the Colts, who were trying to add to their scant 7–3 lead, were expected to run an off-tackle play, but Unitas almost invariably defied convention and expectations. He went with a formation in which Berry came in a bit from his wide receiver slot, giving the impression the Colts planned to run with the ball. Unitas carried out a fake, taking the snap, then spinning and sprinting to a spot behind where Berry had lined up, decoying a handoff to Ameche. Berry picked up the account:

> Ameche started in to the left tackle area, while I acted like I was blocking. Then John put the ball in Ameche's belly and pulled it out. In the meantime, after I had faked the block, I slipped between the linebacker and the defensive back. I was standing in the end zone, wide open, and John hit me for a touchdown.

With time almost expired in the half, the Giants ran three meaningless plays after taking the kickoff. The teams sprinted to the locker room with the Colts holding a 14–3 lead.

Early in the second half, the intensity of the game became apparent when Berry snagged a pass in front of the Baltimore bench and linebacker Sam Huff belted him with a dirty, late shot, right in front of Ewbank, who said he saw Huff knee Berry while they were out of bounds. Berry said his coach may have been rather short and dumpy, but he was a true competitor. Instantly after the hit, Ewbank lit into Huff, but it wasn't much of a skirmish.

Berry said, "Sam was sort of humoring him. He outweighed Weeb by 100 pounds, but Weeb got real hostile—I think he tried to throw a punch, but there's Huff, he's got his helmet on with his mask. All Weeb could do was hurt his fist." Fellow Colt Art Donovan insists the 51-year-old Ewbank never really got close to making contact with Huff—and *that* was a good thing. Huff was eight inches taller and perhaps 35 pounds heavier than Ewbank and, needless to say, in a lot better shape than the roly-poly coach.

On their second possession of the third quarter, the Colts had the ball in a first-and-goal situation but put nothing on the board because of a crucial Ewbank decision. He instructed his Colts to go for it on fourth down from the one-yard line, but, on that occasion, Ameche, thrown for a four-yard loss, failed to hit pay dirt.

The score soon got as tight as a balled-up hand when the Colts lead melted away. Coming off their goal line stand, New York made Ewbank pay for not kicking a field goal. The Giants made it 14–10 with a one-yard run by Mel Triplett late in the third quarter. The score was set up on a fortuitous bounce of the ball. Charlie Conerly connected with Kyle Rote on a deep slant pattern. Rote darted to the Colts 25 before safety Andy Nelson tackled him from behind. Rote fumbled, but an alert Alex Webster grabbed the ball on the run and scooted for 24 yards before defensive back Carl Taseff knocked him out of bounds.

The Giants soon snatched the lead from Baltimore, going up 17–14, when Conerly connected with Gifford on a 15-yard pass to the sideline just 53 seconds into the final quarter. In their drive for the score, Conerly and Bob Schnelker pulled off their best Unitas–Berry imitation, coming through with damaging passes of 17 and 46 yards.

Lombardi had prepared the Giants offense to try to negate the Colts ferocious pass rush of Marchetti and Art Donovan by having Conerly roll out to his left, away from the future Hall of Famers, and his strategy was paying off brilliantly.

New York had the chance to drain the clock and win by that 17–14 score, but on a third-and-four with about 2:50 to play, Marchetti stopped Gifford on a sweep. A ref spotted the ball one foot shy of a crucial first down, sparking controversy. In 2008, the controversy, stemming mainly from Gifford, who always claimed he made the necessary yardage, ended when modern technology proved that he, in fact, did not earn the first down, which, of course, would have allowed them to keep the ball and kill more time.

While tackling Gifford, Marchetti was hit by a 284-pound human avalanche when teammate "Big Daddy" Lipscomb entered the picture, breaking two bones right above Marchetti's ankle. Marchetti recalled the play during an interview in 2016, closing in on 60 years after it occurred:

> They were somewhere around midfield. If they make the first down then, naturally, they can control the ball, the game is over, and the Giants would win. But what happened, and I think their coach made the right decision, they ran the ball around the left side of the line, at me. I made the tackle on Gifford. When I went down, Big Daddy was coming from the right—he wanted to make sure Gifford was going to stay where he was stopped, so he kinda' piled on, I don't call it piling on, but helped make the stop, and they missed the first down.
>
> The funny part of it is when I'd see him years later, Gifford kept saying, "We made that first down." I said, "No you didn't." He said, "Yes, we did," and I said, "Frank, who's got the ring?" That kind of shut him up.
>
> Then they had a decision to punt or go for it on fourth-and-one. I think they made the right decision to punt the ball. We got it with little time [2:20] and 86 yards to go, and no timeouts left. That's a pretty tough chore. So it was a good decision.

Perhaps, but it was one Gifford vehemently disagreed with and one Howell would be grilled about later.

So, the Giants gave up the ball, deciding to rely on their rugged defense to cling to and maintain their slim 17–14 lead. The Colts were faced with the prospect of moving the ball almost 90 yards for a game-winning touchdown, and only slightly less than that distance away from being in striking range for a tying field goal. Just before the drive began, Berry peered down the field at the goalposts and said it looked as if they were in Baltimore.

Still struggling for the first Baltimore score of the second half, Unitas began to engineer the two-minute drill, one Ewbank had efficiently trained his offense to execute. Berry later said it was the best two-minute execution Unitas had ever carried out.

However, it began with two incompletions. They were followed by a vital pass to Lenny Moore, good for a first down at the Colts 25-yard line. Gambling a bit, Unitas decided to go deep but wound up with another incompletion.

Then he turned his attention to the always reliable Berry. What followed was a barrage of three consecutive Unitas-to-Berry passes. Berry later observed Unitas made a highly unusual decision—he threw all three of the passes to the inside of the field, on a slant, a square-in, and a hook pattern—none near the sidelines, where Berry could have made his catches and then stepped out of bounds to kill the clock. So, it was a case of Unitas calling several rather unexpected plays in the huddle: throw a completion, hustle to the line, and run another play with little wasted time.

Berry related the backstory for his first reception of the drive, which took the Colts to midfield. The play was supposed to be a 10-yard square-in, but something occurred to make Unitas and Berry rethink the call. The Giants outside linebacker, Harland Svare, went over to cover Berry head on. "I knew he walked out on top of the split end, but just occasionally," said Berry. "John and I had reviewed and rehearsed what we were to do on the slant pattern *if* the linebacker came out and stood right on my face. I told John, 'If he does that to me, we have to come up with an adjustment. I can't run my route with him right on me.'"

Berry and Unitas had arranged to run a slant, with Berry making an outside fake then cutting underneath Svare's coverage, which would be focused on a pass toward the sideline. In theory, this was a wise, clever ploy. The only problem was Unitas and Berry had discussed the need to use a counteracting tactic long before the situation came up in the title game. Said Berry, "When I lined up and Svare walked out on me I thought, 'Does John remember what we agreed on?' And John was looking at me, thinking, 'I wonder if Raymond remembers what we agreed on?'"

They both had. Berry continued,

When the ball was snapped, I did what we had planned—I took two quick steps outside, Svare came out there to knock my head off, hold me up, and keep me from getting into my pass route. I slanted underneath him clean as a whistle, and John backpedaled, watched me, waited, then drilled me with the ball.

Berry said he can't recall for sure, but some say that just prior to running the ad-libbed play, one which required no audible being called, Unitas and Berry's eyes met, and the quarterback flashed a smile at Berry as if to say, "Here we go. Time to make our plans pay off." At any rate, their telepathic communication worked.

Berry went so far as to say, "If we don't run that play, we may never have earned our championship ring," and he called it the "most important single play of my entire career because that was the start of our three completions." He added, "We went on a roll: Go to the line of scrimmage and hit one, go to the line and hit another one, and another one. The play ultimately led to the tie and the eventual win."

The clock had wound down to 1:04 after the historic slant. The duo clicked again on a 15-yard square-in. Still working without a huddle, Unitas threw to Berry, who had run his inside hook pattern. Eluding the cornerback, using a quick inside fake and a spin to the outside, Berry gained 22 yards to the 13 before right safety Jimmy Patton brought him down.

The Colts were buoyant, but the clock was still running, dwindling down to about 20 seconds. Ewbank had trained his players to get a field goal attempt off in very little time, so his troops hustled out, lined up, clock still ticking, and prayed their erratic kicker, Steve Myhra, could nail a 20-yard field goal. With just seven seconds left, the ball sailed through the uprights—game tied, 17 all.

At the start of the drive, Marchetti, who knew how difficult it would be to march and score against the Giants as the clock wound down, looked back and said proudly, "But John Unitas, Raymond Berry, and Lenny Moore took it right down the field like it was nothing."

Don Shula once said he felt as if Unitas had virtually invented the two-minute drill. Even though the Colts certainly were not the first team to use that strategic tactic, the Colts of Unitas became synonymous with the drill after running it to perfection in this high-profile contest.

Berry pointed out that he and Unitas were in sync like never before. Discounting the game-tying field goal, on the seven-play drive the two men were responsible for 62 of the 73 yards the Colts compiled before Myhra's kick tied things up. Berry noted,

> You just don't see anything like that. Three plays in a row where you just keep on going, keep on going, keep on going. It's unheard of. And there was so much at stake and so big a payoff. You couldn't help but kind of shake your head and say, "Good grief, I've never seen anything like that."

Nobody had, and it caused the collective jaws of the Giants to drop.

Berry said he once asked Unitas about their game-tying drive, asking him to explain why he went to Berry three straight times. Unitas basically said he just knew Berry would catch the football, that he kept throwing them simply because Berry kept catching them. He was, of course, correct—three passes capped by the field goal sent the game into overtime.

Other Colts chimed in on the two-minute drill. Defensive back Rick Volk noted,

> If we were down by a couple of points, or whatever, towards the end of the game, we had confidence that John knew what he was doing, that he was going to win the game. Raymond often would work on that out pattern, going down, making an out move, and then working that sideline. And John would throw it out to where only Raymond could catch it and go out of bounds so the clock stops—and they could work it down the field that way and not take a lot of time off the clock. Then we could set up and go again.

Volk said he and his teammates always had confidence Unitas would mastermind and execute drives for their Colts, especially with time trickling away. He commented, "Whether it was just the way our offense was set up at that point or whatever, we felt we had a chance to always win the game even if were down by a few points."

So, while the fourth quarter two-minute drill didn't lead to a win in the 1958 title game, it did take the Colts to a tie, and in this case, as the old football line goes, a tie wasn't at all like kissing your sister. That's because, even though many were unaware of the rule about a playoff tie, this game would not end knotted up.

Marchetti said, "I didn't realize it was going to go overtime until it came down from the press box. It was a big surprise to me. Of course, being hurt, I wasn't in a mood to worry about overtime at that particular time. Even the coaches said, 'We didn't know there was an overtime clause in the rulebook.'"

Andy Nelson and Sam Huff were others who were unaware this game would go beyond the regulation four quarters. Huff thought the teams would split the playoff pot. Players were so conditioned to quitting after regulation play some had an almost-dazed look on their faces.

Actually, the overtime *rule* for postseason games was not all that new—it had been established in 1955—but it simply had never come up before. Being a "first," playing into sudden death to decide a championship was obviously another enormous reason the game is considered a classic. As a matter of fact, for half a century it remained the only sudden-death NFL championship game played until Super Bowl LI (2017) was won by New England.

Berry said that going into overtime, after cashing in on the field goal, he just sensed Baltimore would prevail. There was a strong, intangible feeling of confidence that came over him and, he believes, permeated throughout the entire team. Lenny Moore agreed, saying the Colts "knew when that thing went into overtime, what we could do. We felt that way against *any* of the other teams, even the teams that we lost to."

After a three-minute break to sort things out and give everyone a rest, historic sudden-death play commenced. The Giants won the coin toss to resume play. Don Maynard became the answer to an obscure trivia question as the first player ever to take the football on offense in a sudden-death championship contest. "We won the coin flip in overtime," he said, "and they kicked off, and I received it and ran it back about 18 yards. So I was the first guy to ever touch the ball in a playoff, overtime game." Maynard actually took the kickoff at about the 10-yard line and fumbled it on the run right away but recovered and advanced the football to the 20 before being brought down.

Maynard continued, "Everybody was wound up for it. They knew that to get the extra payoff money was important; it would be extra money in our pockets."

On New York's only overtime possession, their offense fizzled, managing just nine yards on three plays. Playing it safe, Howell ordered his team to punt the ball on yet another fourth-and-one. The Colts got the football on their 20, faced with another long-distance trek to the goal line.

Berry was optimistic, stating,

One big thing—there were no time constraints. We were in overtime and didn't have a clock to work against. We could do what we wanted to, and take the time we wanted to use, and run whatever we wanted to. Of course, we did have to keep making first downs against a tough defense.

Unitas mixed things up, pounding the ball on the ground and brilliantly mixing in passes, always trying to do the opposite of what the Giants were expecting. What made his execution easier was, as Berry commented, "He had great players to call on, no matter who he handed the ball to." Berry continued,

We had a totally balanced attack, and this was a real huge part of the whole Baltimore Colt story.

It was also what you need to win a championship. What a totally balanced attack does is it makes the defense play honest. That was one of the big problems the Giants had—they had to defend the entire field, and that was not an easy assignment at all.

The Giants had to cope with Lenny Moore, who was a threat as a runner and receiver; tight end Jim Mutscheller; Berry; and Ameche. "They couldn't gang up in one place or another because they don't know what the heck you're going to do," said Berry, "and Unitas played this to the hilt. He was totally unpredictable in dealing from his deck of cards."

So, the game-winning drive unfolded with precision. It began with an 11-yard run by L. G. "Long Gone" Dupre. That was followed by an incomplete pass to Moore, which, if nothing else, served to remind the Giants to play Unitas honestly and respect Moore, who wound up with six catches for almost 17 yards per reception. During the season, he had led the NFL with an average of 7.3 yards per carry.

Four plays later, right after Unitas was sacked, the Colts were in a gloomy third-and-14 situation from the Baltimore 37; however, Unitas and Berry came through once more, clicking on a 21-yard pass to the Giants 42-yard line. On the play, Berry was actually the third receiver Unitas looked to. Berry said he believed that was the only time he had ever caught a pass from Unitas while he was considered to be his third option.

Ameche then took the ball up the gut for 22 yards on a trap play. Unitas deserves much of the credit for this dash. He knew Dick Modzelewski had been putting on a fierce pass rush, so when Unitas got to the line of scrimmage and saw Sam Huff was cheating away from the line, no doubt to help cover Berry, he audibilized, shunning the play he had called for in the huddle, instead going with the basic trap play.

Tom Landry would later say that, anticipating a pass, they were double-teaming both Lenny Moore (with Harland Svare and Cliff Livingston) and Berry (with Carl Karilivacz and Jimmy Patton). He also verified that Unitas was correct—Huff was also guarding against a pass. It was a beautiful example of Unitas's football intelligence paying off.

With Ameche's run, the longest by a Colt all day, Baltimore was now within striking distance for a score, setting up on the Giants 20-yard line. Two plays later, Unitas and Berry teamed up for the last time on the afternoon, good for 12 yards, advancing the ball to the eight-yard line on a slant pattern.

That's when NBC lost its television signal—the image of millions of fans banging the sides of their television sets springs to mind. But they missed nothing because someone, probably just a drunk fan, spectators assumed, went onto the field. By the time he was escorted off the field, NBC had fixed their live feed. Later, it was discovered the man who disrupted play, Stan Rotkiewicz, actually worked for NBC and had created a time-consuming distraction while workers corrected the broadcasting issues.

After a one-yard run by Ameche on first down, Mutscheller took a pass on the right sideline for a gain of six yards before he slipped on the icy turf and tumbled out of bounds at the one-yard line.

Berry recalled Ewbank had instructed Unitas to run at that point, aware that if runs didn't result in a score, a fourth-down field goal would do the trick. Unitas, having seen the Giants stymie Ameche on the previous play, had instead gone to Mutscheller, going against his coach's wishes *and*, more importantly, against what the Giants were looking for.

When Unitas was asked why he had elected to throw a risky pass so near to the goal line, he replied there was no risk at all because he knew exactly where he would put the ball, including out of bounds if his tight end had been blanketed.

In an interview conducted almost 60 years after the pass, Marchetti remembered the media's concern with the play selection:

They asked him after, "Weren't you worried?" He said, "No, when you know what you're doing, you do it. I wasn't going to throw an interception."

John wasn't afraid of hard work, and he wasn't afraid to take chances. If you check back on that championship game of 1958, we're down practically in the end zone, and he throws a pass. How many quarterbacks would have enough guts to do that—to throw to Jim Mutscheller. But when they asked John about it, John just said, "You're not taking a chance if you know what you're doing."

But that's John. He was the coolest guy under pressure you ever want to play with. The truth of it was one of the main reasons we wanted to go for the touchdown was because Myhra played most of the game because one of our regular guards got hurt and Myhra was a reserve guard. When a guy plays quite a bit and he's not used to playing, his legs get a little bit tired, and maybe he won't be as accurate. If I was going to have a kicker, I'd much rather have a kicker with fresh legs than a guy who's being plowing around on that field. The coaches decided to run the ball. Myhra did make the one kick we were most worried about.

Another factor in the decision not to go for a game-winning gimme field goal was that Myhra was not a dependable kicker. On the year, he was just 4-of-10 on his kicks, and earlier in the game he had missed two kicks. That included a blocked first-quarter kick when the game was still scoreless, wasting the Colts' longest pass play of the day, a 60-yarder to Moore.

Yet another reason not to rely on the foot on Myhra? The Colts believed in Unitas, confident it was Johnny U who would guide them to the win.

He did. Unitas called the play; the blocking was effective; and, at 4:51 p.m. in New York, with six-and-three-quarters superfluous minutes remaining in overtime, Ameche plunged into the end zone. Final score: 23–17.

Berry stated the Colts truly believed if a game came down to the wire, they would walk away victorious. This time they did so after running off 13 plays, methodically marching 80 yards. The Colts and the city of Baltimore had secured their first NFL championship.

Marchetti said that when the Colts elected to run the ball to win the game rather than try for a field goal, it was, unlike one fallacious story, the coach's decision, not one Unitas made. "I just don't think it would have been John's decision," he reflected. While Ewbank did allow Unitas to call his own plays (pretty standard practice then), going for the game-winning run rather than try a chip shot of a field goal was Ewbank's decision.

Marchetti stated that going for six points was, of course, the popular decision among the Colts. He opined that had it been entirely up to Unitas, "I don't think he would have wanted to kick a field goal." He added,

> Personally, I think he wanted, like the rest of us, to go for the touch-down. You got to remember one thing: In those days, a field goal kicker wasn't as reliable as, for example, Johnny throwing the ball on the one-yard line because a field goal kicker had to be a position player.
>
> Nowadays, a field goal kicker, all he does all week long is practice kicking; therefore, they're probably more relaxed and are able to han-dle it more than, say, Steve Myhra. I can still visualize Steve kicking the field goal that tied it, but we didn't have much confidence in him making it.

Andy Nelson said Unitas was businesslike on the final drive, relating, "John just took them right down in there." Nelson added that Unitas's behavior after the game also made a deep impression on him, stating, "I dressed next to him, and he didn't show any emotion at all." Often, even after an exciting win, Unitas concluded his day as if he was simply punching the clock, finally off duty.

Nothing ruffled Unitas. Nelson commented,

> He walked off the field after that game and he wasn't turning backflips or jumping up and down. His eyes were focused straight ahead. Like it was just another game. I thought, "This man just played the greatest game of his life, and it's like another game to him." He just casually walked off. He took it all in stride.

Unitas's daughter Paige watched film of the 1958 title game with her father and remarked,

> When you watch him at the very last second before they won, after he handed the ball off, he is out of there. I asked him what he was doing. He said, "Getting the hell out of there. If I didn't get out of there, they

would have killed me." People were going crazy. He was probably showered and changed before they even got off the field.

Unitas's son Joe said his modest father spoke about the game only when he asked him a question about it. Joe stated,

> I did ask him one time about the 1958 game. I said, "After Mr. Ameche scored, what did you do? I mean, you guys had just won this awesome game, overtime, and you were finally the world champions—what'd you do?" He said, "I turned around and walked off the field. The game was over." He was a very matter-of-fact person. Black and white—you're right or you're wrong. I probably should have expected that [answer from him] to be honest.

In fact, in Baltimore, after Nelson rode home with Unitas, the star quarterback didn't speak until they parted, when he simply said to Nelson, "I'll see you tomorrow." Nelson remembered, "It was as if he were saying so long to a buddy, leaving a factory after putting in an eight-hour shift."

Throughout it all, Unitas exuded self-confidence. John's brother Leonard once ran into a referee from the 1958 title game. He remembered,

> He told me that when the Colts had the ball and were driving for the field goal to tie the game, John asked how much time he had left. The ref said 58 seconds and John said, "Well, that's plenty of time." The ref said he was thinking, "Man, he's a smart ass." But then he said John made a believer out of him.

In dissecting the game, the media was fascinated with the Colts' two-minute drill, and Nelson said it was not only the key to the game, but also something Berry and Unitas perfected by sheer talent and countless hours of hard work. "We worked on it in practice every day—between Raymond Berry and Johnny Unitas," said Nelson. "That's what made the game so famous. They knew what they wanted to do. They had worked on the pass routes they wanted to run. That just didn't happen, it was planned."

As mentioned, Berry's 12 catches and 178 yards on receptions set records for an NFL championship game, and almost half of Unitas's 26 completions were to Berry. Furthermore, more than half of Unitas's 349 yards came when he hit Berry. Through 2015, Berry's 12 catches still ranked number two for an NFL championship game. The Colts set a new record for 17 passes going for first downs, and Unitas's passing yardage also established a new record.

Simply put, the game gained classic status mainly due to the two long, vital drives and because it went into sudden-death overtime. The fact that it was just the third title game to be broadcast nationally helped spread its fame and helped the popularity of the NFL grow enormously. Even though New York City was blacked out, an estimated 40 million people watched the game, making this the most widely watched football broadcast to date.

Marchetti's take on the game was interesting. He said, "It was quite a game. They say it was the best game ever played, but I doubt that. There were a lot of mistakes made, like Gifford fumbling." In all, the Giants set a record by fumbling six times, and the Colts added two more. Marchetti added,

> I thought at times it was a little sloppy, but I will say this: It was probably the most important game the NFL ever played.
>
> From that point, with all the publicity about the first sudden death and everything, everything just blew up.

He said that prior to that memorable game, teams would play in stadiums that were "maybe three-quarters full, but after that game, stadiums were full," continuing,

> The next season every stadium was packed—people were looking for tickets. And it hasn't stopped to this day. When you say something is the first time it's ever happened, that puts some importance to it.
>
> And they always called it the most important game in pro football or the Greatest Game Ever Played, a lot of terminology, but, again, the way I feel about it, that probably was the most *important* game ever played. That was the first sudden death, and we won it in sudden death, and it was played in New York. If we had won that game in Baltimore, it would've been exciting, but not like New York, not like Yankee Stadium.

In short, Marchetti, well aware of the impact the 1958 title game had on the NFL, perceived the game to be the start of a new era in football.

Former NFL player and coach Joe Walton agreed, saying, "It may not have been the greatest game, but it is the most prominent game. It did so much for television. That was the booming part of television."

Art Donovan also felt the game was not the greatest one ever, saying the Colts made it a tight game because they didn't play well early on despite being the superior team. Thus, after the game, he felt relief more than elation.

Minor carping about the sloppiness of the game aside, Marchetti stated, "The 1958 championship game remains the highlight of my career, and it came against the number-one defense in the NFL. It was my biggest professional achievement." He could well have been speaking for the entire Colts team. The game will never be forgotten.

Despite the importance of the contest, players of the glory years were paid an inglorious pittance for their participation in such games. The winning Colts paychecks were for $4,718.77 per man, while the Giants earned $3,111.33 per player.

Exactly one month after game's end, Vince Lombardi departed from the Giants staff and agreed to a five-year deal to take on the duties of head coach and general manager of the Green Bay Packers.

Landry briefly stayed in New York. Having already impressed everyone, he was destined to become a head coach. Don Maynard reflected on the two great coaches from his rookie season with the Giants, remembering, "I was fortunate that I was under Lombardi on offense as a backup to Gifford, and over on defense, why, I was kind of the fifth defensive back and Landry had been there himself as a great player there, so that made it extra important and [helpful]."

Maynard said Landry did have his defenders well prepared for the Colts. "I'll tell you what," he began, "with Landry on defense we were really *always* prepared for every team we played."

Landry, said Maynard, always knew what it took to stop other teams. "Like when we played the Colts [for the '58 title], you always set up your defense to stop their best player in the passing attack. You'd overplay the coverage on Raymond Berry, and then you'd kind of let Lenny Moore go a little. But the main thing would be to stop their main star."

Unfortunately for the Giants, said Maynard, it didn't work that day. He reflected, "No. I'll tell you what, they had a great line. We knew we were in for an extra tough game, and we had to make sure that we didn't make any mistakes. In the meetings everything was set up so that we had to be very careful—no mistakes." Of course, the Giants did make mistakes, especially their six fumbles (four of them turned over), and Ewbank and the Colts outlasted the Giants.

The following season, the Colts repeated, again knocking off the Giants. It is regrettable that so many fans neglect the 1959 championship, but the reasons the 1958 title game overshadows virtually every other game (especially in Baltimore) are obvious. Plus, it's a simple fact of NFL life—some games go down as classics, while others get glossed over. And the 1958 duel was, and remains, a classic.

2

THE ICE BOWL

"I'm Going to Take a Bite of My Coffee"

Obviously, due to unique circumstances, some games become so famous they are endowed with a special, descriptive nickname. That was certainly the case with the NFL Championship Game played on New Year's Eve 1967, between the Green Bay Packers and Dallas Cowboys.

From November 6, 1966, until October 15, 1967, counting preseason contests, the Packers had run off a streak of 17 games without a loss. On the other hand, the Cowboys were cold, having lost three of their final five regular-season contests. Due to absolutely unbearable weather conditions at Lambeau Field, the game became known as the Ice Bowl. The already floundering Cowboys were destined to become even colder.

As far back as early August, Vince Lombardi had begun to prepare his Packers for the NFL title contest, exhorting them to excel. "There's no room for second place here," he emphatically told them. "There's only one place here, and that's first place. I've finished second twice in my time here, and I don't ever want to finish second again."[1]

On August 28, the Cowboys hosted the Packers in an exhibition game. The temperatures in Green Bay when the team had boarded their plane for Dallas nudged the 40s; during the game, the thermometer read a sizzling 93 degrees, and many Packers felt ill by halftime.

The classic Ice Bowl game remains the coldest contest (based on temperature, as opposed to wind chill) ever played in the annals of the

league, and it made players sick for a totally different reason than had
been the case in Dallas.

The game featured a future legendary coach in Tom Landry, who was
coming off his first two winning seasons, both resulting in a trip to the
title game. Across the field was a coach who had already earned god-like
status, Lombardi, whose game-winning call with precious little time left
to play in the Ice Bowl would prove that he had ichor—the golden blood
of the Greek gods—or, more fittingly considering the weather condition
that day, that he had proverbial ice water running through his veins. What
a marquee billing—a classic game with two legends matching wits and
their incomparable coaching savvy.

The clash also featured some of the golden age's best players executing vital plays despite icicles figuratively dangling from their noses and
every extremity. Eight of the Packers had made the All-Pro team one year
earlier, and nine Cowboys were headed for the Pro Bowl in three weeks.
In addition, the Packers had experience galore—14 of their players went
as far back with the team as their 1961 championship season.

Dallas sported a 9–5 record, and Green Bay, who, despite having lost
running back Paul Hornung, who had retired, and Jim Taylor to the expansion draft after the 1966 season, finished the 1967 regular season at
9–4–1.

In 1960, Hornung accumulated 176 total points, forever the record for
a 12-game season. LaDainian Tomlinson broke the record, but it stood
until the 2006 season, and even then Tomlinson required four games
beyond what Hornung had played in to score a paltry 10 points more than
the Golden Boy. Meanwhile, Taylor was just the second runner ever to
amass 1,000 yards rushing three years in a row. Somehow, despite such
losses, Lombardi and company never missed a beat.

The weather was the main story line of the game, and many of the
participants' accounts of the Ice Bowl begin the day before or the morning of the game. Packers running back Chuck Mercein remembered game
day vividly, saying, "I couldn't even believe it, because it was so beautiful the day before. A balmy day in Green Bay with sunshine and maybe
in the 30s. To think that polar vortex or something happened overnight—
came down from Alaska, north of us. It was shockingly freezing." In fact,
two days before the game, the Cowboys rode into town, informed they
could anticipate decent weather.

Bob Hyland, the ninth overall player drafted in 1967, mainly played at the center position for four teams, one of which was the Packers, for his first three seasons. He said that during the Ice Bowl, he "played special teams, all the kickoffs, and kickoff returns," adding, "I believe I also snapped the punts. So I got a little bit of playing time—I made the first tackle of the game and was involved in a couple of other tackles, but that was really about it. I was disappointed that I didn't play much but, obviously, elated that we did win."

He also remembered (who can forget) the weather from that day. "It's funny how different things were back then," Hyland began, continuing,

> Now you get these long-range forecasts to know what's going on, but I remember that Saturday before the game. We had a quick workout, I guess around 9:00 or so in the morning. Jim Flanigan and I were about ready to leave when we saw the Cowboys' buses come in. We thought we'd hide behind the pillars and see them out on the field. That day was kind of comfortable. We had no idea what was in store for us the next day. I don't think anybody did. It was quite a surprise to me and a lot of the players how cold it got overnight.

The day of the NFC championship contest began with ominous signs of things to come, and it resulted in many Johnny Carson-like, "How cold was it?" incidents. It was *so cold*, the Cowboys hotel operator's morning wake-up calls informed people that it was already well below zero.

It was *so cold*, Dallas defensive end George Andrie threw a glass of water against his hotel room window and it froze before it had the chance to run down the pane and onto the windowsill, despite the fact his room was heated to a cozy 70 degrees.

And it was *so cold*, a TV broadcaster put his cup of coffee on the press box ledge and it froze. He quipped, "I'm going to take a bite of my coffee." Media members who sat near the press box windows had to use ice scrapers and windshield deicer to clear the windows.

Mercein said,

> I awakened to my little clock radio alarm next to my bed, and the first thing I heard was, "Good morning, Green Bay. Happy New Year. It's 16 below zero outside." I said, "This can't be right. I must have misunderstood that, or I must be dreaming or something." I called somebody, maybe the radio station, and said, "I just heard this. Is it possibly true?" They said, "Yeah. This polar thing came down, and it's going to

be even colder." I got up, went to Mass, prayed that no one would get hurt, and prayed to survive the day.

Different reports, even from the game's participants, attest to somewhat different temperatures and wind-chill factors for the game. Hyland, with just slight exaggeration, said,

> I usually had dinner with one of the guys the night before a home game. The next morning my clock radio wakes me up and says the temperature was, like, 25 below zero. I couldn't believe it. The cold front just wreaked havoc.
>
> I immediately called up the stadium and asked, "What are we going to do?" They said, "Come on out. We're in Green Bay. We play these games." I got to tell you, it was some test to try to play that day. It really took everything you had to put up with that discomfort and still try to win a game.

There were other backstories before the opening 1:10 p.m. kickoff. The Packers made it to the Ice Bowl game by cruising by the Los Angeles Rams, 28–7, in postseason play. Then, a short time before they met the Cowboys, Lombardi informed the media that the team had installed an $80,000 heating system a half-foot beneath Lambeau Field that would guarantee good playing conditions even in subfreezing weather. Because the local television stations were predicting the high temperature for the game would only reach 12 degrees, the importance of the heating system was obvious.

Lombardi had prepared his men by driving them toward a common goal. Mercein said that during the week prior to the Ice Bowl, Lombardi had repeatedly stressed to his team that another championship would give the Packers an unprecedented three titles in a row, something he positively craved. Actually, he had begun that refrain as early as September, after he made his final cuts. He told his men that repeating as champs would be difficult because every team on their schedule would be gunning for them, ramping up their game.

The Packers had won it all in 1961 and 1962—in '61, exactly half of their 22 starting players went on to become Hall of Famers, a record for one team. Then they lost only one of those men to retirement, retaining a potent '62 roster; however, they didn't make it to postseason play in

1963. Part of the reason for that failure was the team was without Hornung, who was suspended for the entire season for betting on NFL games.

Since the Packers attained their three-peat goal for their leader, no NFL team (through 2017) has managed to match that accomplishment. Technically, the Packers had been declared NFL champs three successive years from 1929 through 1931, but prior to 1933, there was no playoff system in place. The same was true for Guy Chamberlin, who won three titles in a row coaching from 1922 to 1924, again before playoffs (with teams in Canton and then Cleveland). Lombardi felt those accomplishments didn't count. In addition, through 1967, only five other teams had won two straight title games, and no team aside from Green Bay had done that twice.

Another key to Green Bay's success in this game (and many others) was Lombardi's offensive philosophy. He believed in keeping things basic—nothing so complicated that any player with even a modicum of intelligence and experience couldn't handle easily. Instead of creating a playbook the size of an unabridged dictionary, Lombardi went with the staples.

Take, for example, the Packers' patented sweep. Lombardi had trained his men to execute it so well the play was foolproof and highly effective. When told on a few occasions he should try to deceive opponents or not run the sweep because everyone knew it was coming, he countered by concisely saying, "They may know it's coming, but they still can't stop it."

Lombardi also felt his teams would win consistently because he worked so hard at keeping human mistakes to a minimum. By and large, he had run-oriented teams, and stressing ball control and avoiding fumbles and interceptions tied in with that philosophy.

For instance, with Bart Starr at the helm, Lombardi didn't have to fret much about interceptions, allowing the Packers to play keep-away football. During a stretch from 1964 to 1965, Starr set a record by putting the ball in the air 294 consecutive times between interceptions. In postseason games, Starr threw 15 TD passes and was picked off just three times, which helped him establish the highest postseason quarterback rating ever. He finished in the top ten 11 times for the lowest percentage of passes intercepted, which represented virtually every season in which he started at least half of his team's games. In addition, he led the league in that realm three times, one of which came in 1964, when his percentage of 1.5 intercepted throws set a new NFL low (since broken).

Lombardi once said he would have Starr go deep on fly patterns once in a while just to keep defenses honest, but possessing the ball and figuratively owning the clock by rattling off long drives was the way to go.

Lombardi was almost obsessive about not turning over the ball to his opponents. In 1959, when Starr was playing in his first scrimmage under the recently hired Lombardi, he threw an interception. Even though Starr had been with the Packers for three seasons and started 19 games for them, Lombardi didn't care. He snapped at Starr and basically said if he threw another poor pass like the one he had just witnessed, Starr was kaput.

Going into the Ice Bowl, Starr, with a dozen seasons under his belt, was in no peril of being kaput. He and his fellow Packers, however, did have two enemies to combat—the Cowboys and the cold. Still, before the game began, Lombardi told his players, "We've got Jack Frost on our side."[2]

Green Bay defensive tackle Henry Jordan would later joke that he assumed Lombardi had gone down on his knees, praying for bad weather before kickoff, but that he must have stayed down too long, hence the atrocious weather.

The Cowboys were coming off a Christmas Eve 52–14 trouncing of the Browns to win the Eastern Conference in the Cotton Bowl. There, the temperature at the opening kickoff seemed quite chilly to Texans, at 44 degrees. The Cowboys had no way to imagine the wild temperature swing they would experience just one week later when they would make the trip to Green Bay for the title game.

Mercein stated,

> The upshot of the whole thing is it was colder for the Cowboys than for us. I think they were even in more shock than we were. They didn't know what to do. They were wearing all kinds of different crazy stuff underneath their equipment to try to keep warm. Some guys used Saran Wrap, some used sweatshirts underneath their pads, and [things] almost like the stockings you put on when you have a knee injury, very flexible, light cotton [material] over their faces with holes cut in for their eyes, nose, and mouths. They looked kind of Halloween-ish, like monsters—it was goofy looking, and it didn't help a damn bit, I'm sure.

Landry was bundled up with so many layers of clothes he said he "moved around like a bear with arthritis,"[3] but before leaving the locker room he remained optimistic. Once he felt the first blast of icy wind, he changed his mind, realizing his wide-open style of offense, which relied heavily on speed, was not as conducive to winning as the Packers' grind-it-out style.

Mercein picked up the narrative:

> Some wore gloves, but Lombardi wouldn't let us, especially anybody who touched the ball, like running backs—not that the gloves were any good anyway. The only gloves I saw were the ones you'd wear when you're out gardening, the brown ones, like golf gloves. We didn't have the technology that you have now.
>
> We didn't have thermals or stuff on the sidelines to help you warm up. We had a lean-to on the sideline—they put plywood holding up a tarp. It was scary to get into. It was something a homeless shelter might look like. It was totally ineffective. It was such a jerry-rigged kind of makeshift thing. Guys got into that once in a while to get away from the wind a little bit, but there was not much you could do. It was just as cold in there as it was on the outside. You had to discipline yourself to realize it was as cold as ice, and that was just the way it was going to be. Even the ball was freezing. It felt like an ice cube.
>
> Players were affected to the degree that they were ineffectual. Remember Bob Hayes? The world's fastest human, their wide receiver. When Bob was not going to be "hot," or a target in a play, let's say it was going to be a running play, he'd come out of the huddle with both of his hands tucked down in the front of his pants to keep his hands warm. Well, that was a pretty good "tell," right? I mean, if he had his hands out, that means he was going to be in a pattern. Our players figured that out pretty quickly—when he had his hands in his pants, you could pretty much ignore Bob Hayes and play 11 men on 10.

Hyland put it this way, "Bob Hayes was telegraphing the plays when he wouldn't be a pass target. He was giving a pretty sure indicator that he wasn't going to be receiving the ball."

Discovering Hayes's revealing habit (caused, in part, by Landry's insistence that his men not wear gloves) was mainly the job of corners Herb Adderley and Bob Jeter. Hyland said,

They knew they had to cover the guy. Anybody is going to try to keep his hands warm until he really has to put them to use. I can't blame him. So Hayes was keeping his hands there [in his pants], and they had muffs around their waist to keep their hands warm.

With cold hands, you're just not going to catch the ball. So they had to do everything they could to give themselves a chance by keeping them as warm as possible. During the three or four seconds that a play occurs, you would like to have your hands warm enough to catch the ball and hold on to it.

Don Maynard said the coldest game he played in was at Denver and that he could relate to the difficulties of trying to perform in adverse weather conditions. He commented, "You'd put on the long flannels and put on the gloves, and get close to a fire or the heaters they had. Then you'd be warm so when you went in the game you were comfortable and you had to do your job. In cold games I used gloves. All the guys did."

Even though Maynard's coldest days couldn't compare to the Ice Bowl, Hayes might have benefited from doing as Maynard did by donning some gloves. "It didn't hurt my ability to catch the ball," continued Maynard. "No, not really, because the gloves were the type that were real limber or flexible and you'd be okay."

Mercein said he has no idea why a member of the Cowboys personnel didn't notice Hayes was guilty of, to use baseball parlance, tipping his pitches. "They had to have guys upstairs who could see what was developing," he said, continuing,

Bob was Florida-bred, too, so he was used to the heat, and he went to Florida A&M, then Dallas was his pro team. He probably never came north to have weather like that—nowhere within 50 degrees of that. So I can imagine how freezing he must have been.

There were other guys, too, on that team that were Southern guys, but they weren't as affected as he was.

Dallas quarterback Don Meredith, also a Southerner for all his football days, was similar to Hayes. Mercein remembered, "Some Dallas guys I've talked to say he had a hard time in the huddle voicing the plays. His mouth got frozen, almost. He was kind of slurring his words, and the guys said it was hard to pick up what he was saying."

Meredith, who was nearly perfect the week before, when he put 52 points on the board, certainly was visibly, terribly impaired by the weather. Fingers barely able to bend, he suffered through a 10-for-24 afternoon for a minuscule 59 yards. He threw soft, wobbly passes and one interception, and his longest pass went a measly 14 yards.

Hyland stated,

> I can just imagine what those Cowboys felt—probably the coldest day they had dealt with. In Dallas they probably never saw anything under 50 degrees. It's amazing how well they responded to it. The Packers deserve a lot of credit for winning, but the Cowboys deserve a lot of credit for making a very competitive game out of it.
>
> When you become familiar with the elements, you can deal with them somewhat. I think we had an advantage over the Cowboys, for sure. As a rookie, I was just so damned excited to be in that game I don't think anything would have affected me. I was just so thrilled to be there, to take part in it, I wasn't really thinking about the weather that much. I know we had to deal with it, but, hey, you felt as though you were the luckiest guy in the world playing in that game.

Mercein grew up in Wisconsin and felt he could handle the severe weather, although he said he had never before experienced a day like this one. He added,

> There were some guys on our team, too, who were from Southern climes or California. I remember Willie Wood, who went to USC. He said, "I'm sure the commissioner is not going to let us play this game." As it turns out, obviously he did because everything was set up for the game. There were rumblings of, "Are we really going to do this?" You couldn't really postpone it, but Willie didn't want to play.

Mercein realized that joining him in the starting Green Bay backfield would be Alabama-born Bart Starr and Texan Donny Anderson. Would that be a problem, he fretted? Then it hit him—if his teammates were discontented about the conditions, grumbling about having to play, what would the Cowboys of Texas be thinking? Later, at least one Cowboy confided that at times his team was thinking more about the cold than the game.

Temperatures never reached the predicted 12-degree mark, and thermometers took a precipitous nosedive to 13 degrees below zero, making it the coldest final day of a year in the city's history. The game is also said to be the coldest football contest ever played. In such conditions, even the innovative heating system failed to do its job, and ice quickly formed on the field, turning it into a veritable ice skating rink. The heat from the system had caused the ground to dampen due to condensation, and when the tarp was removed, the moisture had frozen.

Clumps of grass and dirt froze, sticking to the field, so that one player said running on it was like running on a hard, stucco field. He commented, "It made AstroTurf feel like a pillow."[4] Falling to the turf resulted in many an abrasion and worse. In the final quarter, for example, Boyd Dowler was knocked unconscious.

Mercein noted that the day was actually pretty sunny, reflecting, "The elements were so severe. I've never been so cold in my life, and I think nobody else who played in the game or was there had been. It was like being inside a meat locker or a freezer for two and a half or three hours."

Nevertheless, the Green Bay fans, unable to move around like the players and not afforded an indoor halftime break, had still showed up, and by and large, they stuck it out. The game drew a full house of 50,861 brave and/or foolhardy spectators.

The Antarctic-like conditions worsened, of course, due to winds that whipped through the city of Green Bay, through the field, and almost literally through the players and fans alike, howling at about 15 miles per hour. Mercein continued,

> The wind chill was around 48 below, and it got colder—I think it was 50-something below by the end of the game with the chill factor. We were just frozen and so was the field.
>
> Conditions could not have been more difficult for the players and fans. That's what also made the game so memorable—to be able to persevere under those conditions and to come out victorious made it all the more dramatic and historic. It was the coldest game played ever, period.
>
> Since then there was a game in Cincinnati [the January 1982 AFC title game versus San Diego] when they said the chill factor was in the minus 50s also, but I don't think the actual temperature was as low as it was for the Green Bay game. I've never heard of a game played in the temperatures that were that cold. Then again, I don't know how sophisticated wind chill was at that point. Maybe people have gone back and just sort of extrapolated what the wind chill might have been depending upon the temperature and the wind, but I didn't know what a wind chill was. All I knew is it was freakin' cold, man.

Prior to the game, a helicopter was brought in to blow snow off the stadium seats. CBS cameramen placed electric blankets around their cameras, fearing they would freeze. The halftime show had to be cancelled because during the band's warm-ups, some instruments froze, and the mouthpieces of the musicians who played brass instruments stuck to their lips.

Referees had to make their calls by shouting them out because their lips would freeze to the whistle's metal if they tried to use them, not unlike the character Flick, whose lips stick to the flagpole in *A Christmas Story*. In fact, one ref who did blow his whistle at the start of the game discovered his lips not only froze to the whistle, but also when he removed the whistle, some skin from his lips was torn off. Whistles cast aside, refs had to yell things to players and coaches in an era long before officials wore microphones (which may also have been rendered useless).

As touched on, there was some doubt as to whether the game would go on, as officials feared for the health of everyone involved; however, Hyland said, "When you have a TV audience and the press, which had traveled there, it's pretty hard not to have the show go on." Furthermore, with another miserable weather forecast for the next day and the scheduled Super Bowl looming on the horizon, the decision to play was made. "They didn't have much of a choice," Hyland commented. Also, if such conditions were to come up again, Hyland said the game probably still would go on. "If we could perform, I think that the current-day players can. God knows they're being paid a helluva' lot more than we were. They'd be able to suck it up as well."

This begs another question: What would it take to postpone such a game? Mercein said,

> The only thing I can think it would take is if it was dangerous, like a natural disaster happening—like if an earthquake was predicted, something where we shouldn't be outside. I've seen them delay games and cancel practices for lightning because that's really lethal, but as far as weather conditions go, unless it was a tornado or something, no.
>
> The Ice Bowl was freezing, not healthy for anybody, and I was told later there was a fatality in the stands, probably weather induced. But it wasn't a life-threatening game, like a natural disaster.

Sam Havrilak of the Colts, who averaged 14.9 yards per catch lifetime, could *almost* relate to the plight of the Packers and Cowboys. He remembered playing a game in Kansas City when the temperature, with the wind chill factored in, was about 20 below:

> Back then, nobody had heated benches, nobody had heaters on the sidelines. We just had capes [parkas] to wear when we weren't on the field.
>
> They gave you mittens to warm your hands, but by the time you got back on the field, your hands were freezing again.

The ball stings the hands and is slippery, too. Havrilak continued,

> Very difficult to catch, and nobody wore gloves then. You were allowed to wear Stick'Em, but that didn't work when it was that cold.
>
> The traction and the footing were horrible because everything was frozen, so it was hard to get leverage if you're blocking, and it was hard to run and cut. Plus, every time you get hit, the force of the impact feels greater because your body is cold. The hits, even the small ones, hurt worse than they should hurt.

If that's what the game in Kansas City was like, imagine the wind chill plummeting an additional 28 degrees, then picture going out onto an NFL field to run, cut, block, and get belted by some behemoths.

Despite the conditions in the Ice Bowl, some basics, surprisingly so to some, remained the same. Hyland said during such games, a center does not try to snap the ball softer. Some people may think such a snap might better prevent the exchange, done with nearly frozen fingers, from resulting in a fumble. Hyland explained,

> No, I really don't think there's much of a difference. Basically, the ball is harder and it's more difficult to grip, but it's just a matter of trying to keep your hands warm the best you can. You do have to be a little more careful to make sure that [all goes well], whether it be a direct snap to the quarterback or snapping a punt or extra point. Not so much gentle, but you just want to make sure it's there. You've got to snap the ball as quickly as you can and get into your block or else you're going to be beaten. You're just hoping that it's going to be a secure snap so Bart Starr or Zeke Bratkowski, or whoever the quarterback is at the time, will be able to handle it okay.
>
> Also, you've got wind that you're dealing with—you've got to put a little bit more on the ball, I think, for a long snap. Ken Bowman did a heckuva' job that day. I don't think we had a bad exchange, so he

deserves a lot of credit, and Starr, too. Under the circumstances, he also did a heckuva' good job.

Hyland said Starr didn't soften his passes, either, remembering,

> If anything, you might be trying to put a little more on it because there were around 15-mile-an-hour winds. You have to get the ball there quickly. I'm not a quarterback, but I assume it's pretty much the same motion. You're not going to throw the ball a lot under those circumstances, but when you do, the mechanics still have to be there.

On the day, Starr threw 24 times and hit on 14 of his tosses for 191 yards and two scores.

The Packers, in their attempt to become the first team in the 35-year history of NFL title games to win the big one in three successive seasons, got off to a 14–0 lead on a pair of Bart Starr-to-Boyd-Dowler hookups of eight and 46 yards.

However, it wasn't to be an easy day for Starr, who was hounded by the highly touted Doomsday Defense and sacked eight times for a loss of 76 yards. One sack would result in a fumble that defensive end George Andrie scooped up and scored on, lumbering into the end zone from seven yards out. Green Bay's lead was slashed to 14–7.

Frigid hands led to yet another score, a 21-yard field goal by Dallas placekicker Danny Villanueva to close out the first half scoring with the Cowboys trailing, 14–10. The Villanueva boot came after Willie Wood lost the football on a punt return shortly before the end of the half. It was one of six fumbles during the game. Former Vikings kicker Fred Cox believed the use of Stick'Em could help during such contests but summarized, "The balls *are* slippery. A lot of fumbles are caused by the cold."

Make no mistake, kicking in freezing conditions is, like handling a slippery football, a difficult task. Cox, who set a record for the longest field goal at Lambeau Field when he once boomed a 52-yarder in the month of November, shook his head, stating, "When I did that, it was a major feat, because it was like kicking an ice chunk. I have no idea what possessed Bud Grant to tell me to kick that day." Cox also said horrid weather conditions always make a "kicker wake up and have shakes in the morning. I guess it's mostly psychological. You have to be able to convince yourself that you know you can still kick it."

It clearly wasn't an easy day for either offense. At one point near the end of the second quarter, Dallas had not yet rung up a first down. In all, there were only 172 yards gained on the ground throughout the day (92 by Dallas), and it took 65 carries to do that, resulting in an average of fewer than about 2.6 yards per rush.

As mentioned, the usual longball threat, "Bullet Bob" Hayes, was a nonfactor. He caught a pass on the first play of the game for 10 yards. It would prove to be his longest gain of the day. In fact, he wound up catching only three passes. The Olympic medal winner whose longest catch ever went for 95 yards was limited to 16 yards.

After getting a modicum of the chill out of their bones at halftime, the third quarter was scoreless. Offenses severely impaired, the Packers had to be hoping they (and the weather) would ensure the Cowboys would fail to score again, and that they would win it with their vaunted defense.

Such optimism was quickly stifled when Cowboys coach Tom Landry called for a halfback option on the first play of the final quarter, just eight seconds into that period. Dan Reeves was no secret weapon. He had completed four passes in 1967, resulting in two TDs and 195 yards, almost 50 yards per completion. Thus, it was hardly surprising for Dallas to run the play. Reeves hit Lance Rentzel for a 50-yard score to grab the lead from the Packers. The Cowboys' 17–14 advantage would hold almost to the final play of the game. Almost.

With six ticks short of five minutes to play, and with the thermometer icicled over at about 18 below, the Packers got the ball at their own 32, still trailing by those three points. With neither team exactly lighting up the scoreboard, no one could be sure Starr, frigid fingers and all, could move the ball well enough to score on either a field goal or a touchdown. During a stretch of 25 plays beginning after Starr hit Dowler on their first drive of the second quarter to take the score to 14–0, and extending until the 20th overall play of the third quarter, Green Bay had "gained" negative yardage and failed to register a single first down. They had run their 25 plays for a net minus 12 yards. Given that, moving the ball 68 yards seemed an impossibility.

After they manage their first down in an eon on their next-to-last possession in the third quarter, they took a 16-yard loss on a sack, which was their 10th play resulting in no gain or a loss over their previous 29 plays. Six- and nine-yard runs, and a punt, followed.

Still more futility followed in their next possessions. The ineptitude began with four plays that resulted in minus two yards. Then came the first possession in the fourth quarter, which featured a gain via pass interference followed by no gain on a run, a five-yard sack of Starr, and an incompletion. Finally, a 19-yard completion, a one-yard gain, a pass batted away by Chuck Howley, and another incompletion ensued. Again, the prospects of winning seemed as dead as a cold, clammy cadaver.

But Starr seemed to exude confidence, at least on the surface. Mercein, who would soon become vital on this final possession, said that when Starr came to the huddle prior to the last drive, he simply told his teammates to get the job done, and following his lead, the team became convinced they could do just that.

One year earlier, Mercein was with the 1–12–1 Giants. Even though he had led that team in rushing, they cut him six games into the 1967 schedule. Both the Cowboys and Packers tried to acquire him—Green Bay succeeded.

Starr, relying on short passes and mixing in several key runs to Mercein and Donny Anderson, guided the Packers march down the glazed tundra. He did it even though he was banged up pretty badly for much of the season, and his 210 passes attempted and nine TDs were his lowest output since 1960—he didn't even throw a touchdown pass until October 22. Furthermore, his 17 interceptions still stand as his single-season worst. Soon, none of that would matter.

Starr's final drive opened with a six-yard gain on a pass to Donny Anderson in the right flat after he had swung out of the backfield. Mercein made good on a seven-yard run, and then Starr hit Dowler for 13, invading Dallas territory. Next, Anderson was dumped for a nine-yard loss by Willie Townes.

Landry then adjusted his defense, having his backs play deep to take away any long throws. Starr gained 12 on a pass to Anderson, exploiting the Cowboys formation and their linebackers' inability to get their footing. That brought up a third-and-seven from the Dallas 39.

After the two-minute warning, Starr came through once more, hitting his fourth pass of the drive, a nine-yard toss to Anderson to move the sticks. Starr would soon finish his role as a passer in the drive, going 5-for-5, and his final throw was one key to the win. With about 1:30 to go came the play Mercein will never forget. He reflected, "Another interesting part of that drive was a big catch I made over in the left flat. It was probably the only time I ever spoke up in the huddle and called my own play. It was so crucial to keep our drive going."

Mercein said that a bit earlier, after he had checked to see if he'd have to block a blitzing Cowboy, he made his way out into the flat and noticed how the Cowboys were defending Starr:

> I realized the linebackers were taking a straight drop, back into coverage. So I told that to Bart. "If you need me, I'm open in the flat," and he hit me there. It was a hard catch. The ball kind of floated in behind me, and it was freezing anyway. I had to jump up and twist around, and catch it, which I was pretty good at doing.
>
> I outran a linebacker or juked him out, and I got 19 yards, went out of bounds, and stopped the clock. Coach Landry said that was the killer in the drive. Normally, nobody spoke in the huddle except for the quarterback, but it was just too important. I realized I could get open and make the play.

The clock read 1:11, with the Packers on the 11. Starr sprung a play, "65-Give," on Dallas, one he hadn't used all day. Mercein blasted through a hole tackle Bob Skoronski opened, moving the ball to the three-yard line.

Mercein, so instrumental in the drive, later said the one aspect of his career he was most proud of was his "contribution to the Packers victory in the Ice Bowl." He elaborated,

> That was very important to the history of the Green Bay Packers and Vince Lombardi, our coach. He emphasized all year about how important winning three in a row was—about how unprecedented it would be. And my moment came in that game. I was able to come through, and that's what it's all about, getting the opportunity and producing. On that last drive I got half the yardage, 34 of the 68.

An Anderson plunge for two gave Green Bay a first down at the one-yard line.

Packers Hall of Fame linebacker Dave Robinson said during one of the reunions held many years later by participants from both teams in the Ice Bowl,

> A couple of guys from the Cowboys said Donny Anderson scored on first down—he went over the goal line and scored, but the referee

marked it on the one. But I want to tell you this: In 1967, back in those days, it was very common for an official to mark where your knee hit, not where the ball was. Today, we've got instant replay, and it's, "Watch the ball. Watch the ball." If your knee hit on the one and you fall down, and the ball was over the goal line, they marked it at the one.

And here's something else, as a defensive ballplayer, we knew on first and second down that if it was real close, they gave it to the defense. On third and fourth down, they gave it to the offense. As a matter of fact, if you watch when he runs that first play, you watch the reaction of the players—they have their hands up like it's all over, and then the referee comes over and marks the ball on the one. Donny scored, so he couldn't believe it when he watched the referee mark the ball on his first-down run.

Two more dive plays by Anderson, who slipped on both runs, went nowhere. The Packers spent their last timeout, and Starr and Lombardi conferred on the sideline.

So, it all came down to one play. Throughout the afternoon, with each exhale, Green Bay fans saw their breath billow out in front of them. Now, with 16 seconds left in the game, they held their collective breath. With the Packers in a third-down and goal-to-go situation from about a foot and a half shy of the goal line, quarterback Bryan Bartlett Starr trotted back onto the field.

For obvious strategic reasons, the Cowboys had to be thinking, "Pass to the end zone," perhaps on a rollout. That made sense—a completed pass could win it, and even if it went incomplete, the clock would stop, and a field goal of about 18 yards would at least tie things—*perhaps*. Given the weather, however, there were no sure things that day. Being a scant 18 inches short of the goal line, Starr had suggested a quarterback sneak to Lombardi. After all, he reasoned, right guard Jerry Kramer, in his 10th pro season, had told him he believed he could get his footing to execute a block on Jethro Pugh, an agile tackle who was in just his third NFL season. Additionally, who wants to run at superstar Bob Lilly? The Packers would run their "31-Wedge" play and attack Pugh.

The play actually called for the quarterback to hand off to Mercein for a dive up the gut; however, Starr felt a sneak—although, technically, the Packers didn't have a "quarterback sneak" in their playbook—was probably a better call than handing off to a running back set farther back from the goal line than Starr.

Hyland said,

> When Chuck lined up, he thought he was going to be carrying the ball. Bart knew right from the start that he was going to carry it himself. He just went to the hole that Chuck would have been going to. He didn't want to take a chance of fumbling the ball or having an exchange problem, so he thought he should just hold on to the ball and get behind two blockers, and get in there. And he did.

Sam Havrilak said in such situations, the offense and blockers, like Kramer, have the advantage "because, number one, he knows where he's going and the defensive guy does not. So if you catch the defensive guy just a bit off balance, then the offensive player has the advantage."

Starr told his head coach he also believed the sneak would work because he, standing upright at the snap, would be able to shuffle his feet, hit the hole, and score. He also said they'd run the play on a quick count to minimize the amount of time Dallas would have to dig in.

Lombardi naturally considered all the factors, too. He believed if a team couldn't come up with one measly yard, they didn't deserve to wear the NFL crown. So, he responded to Starr's suggestion, in a quote later widely repeated: "Let's run it and get the hell out of here."

Starr did just that, and the Packers offensive unit exited the field, freezing but elated, on the winning side of a 21–17 score. Lombardi may have been trembling inside when Starr broke huddle in their last play of the game, because taking such a risk was certainly out of character for him, but he had the fortitude to make that call.

After the score, a desperate Dallas team had time to throw two long passes, but both fell harmlessly to the frozen field, the final one intended for Bob Hayes. Game over. Soon the goal posts also fell to the turf.

Postmortem examinations and discussions of the game abound. Landry, always pragmatic, said, "I can't believe that call, the sneak. It wasn't a good call, but now it's a great call."[5] In fact, he also went so far as to call it a horrible move but said it was so unexpected that the sneak, the most fundamental of all football plays, got the job done. He expected Starr would roll out and find a receiver or fire the ball away to kill the clock, setting up a game-tying field goal. He said if the run had failed, time would have run out, that there would not have been enough time to get his kicking crew onto the field. Landry was, of course, 100 percent correct.

Mercein recounted his part in the Starr sneak, which capped off a 68-yard drive in a dozen plays:

> We called what I thought would be the "31-Wedge," which was what the call was—the "3" back through the "1" hole, myself through the hole between the center and the right guard. But Bart Starr kept the ball because he almost had a bad exchange to Anderson on the previous play because Donny slipped.

Hence, believing he would get the ball, Mercein went through his normal movements. Then, seeing Starr dive into the end zone, ball tucked tightly into his belly, Mercein did something smart:

> I go over the top on the play thinking I can't stop. The ice was such that I couldn't stop, so I threw my hands up in the air—not to show touchdown, because it *was* a touchdown, but to show the referee I wasn't assisting or pushing Starr. That would have been a penalty and a terrible mistake.

No flags were thrown. Instead, the refs threw *their* hands in the air, signaling touchdown.

Mercein, who in a matter of a few months had gone from being waived by the Giants, who would finish the season at 7–7, to wearing the Packers championship ring, says today's refs don't seem to call the "Bush Push" penalty for a player shoving or in any way aiding a ballcarrier to advance the ball. He said, "But back then I think they would have. I was always aware of all the rules. I realized you couldn't push or pull a guy into the end zone. Now I've seen them do both of those things, but at that point it was more clear that you couldn't do those sorts of things."

Lombardi greeted the media in the locker room with a line that pretty much summed up his thoughts on going with the quarterback sneak. "All the world loves a gambler," he grinned. "Except when he loses."[6] Starr confessed he could not remember the last time he had run a quarterback sneak.

Jerry Kramer got most of the credit for the play, deservedly so for handling Jethro Pugh, but center Ken Bowman helped out, double-teaming the Cowboys defensive left tackle, and Starr slipped between those two blockers.

It's not at all rare for a quarterback to be a hero in a big game, but for his iconic block thrown on Pugh, Kramer became famous—not bad for a guard out of the University of Idaho whose signing bonus was a microscopic $250. In fact, that play even spawned a classic book, *Instant Replay*.

George Belu, a college coach and NFL scout for more than 40 years, recalled the play: "You talk about rising to the occasion and knowing that you have to do something—it's one of the great moments in sports. Kramer had really good movement. He got underneath the pads, and once you do that to a defensive player, you know you're going to win."

Kramer said after the snap he immediately plowed into Pugh, who had lined up inside Kramer's left shoulder, admitting he may have actually been a microsecond offside. With that play, Dallas was done, left with only 13 seconds to play.

Hyland came up with another insight into the game-winning play, something Kramer had spotted two days before the Ice Bowl:

> The guy who was villainized for the final touchdown that Starr scored, Pugh, was a disciplined player. That's one of the reasons why they went over there. From watching film Jerry realized that [the 6-foot-6] Pugh didn't get quite as low as a guy like Bob Lilly would. So they thought there was a vulnerability there that they took advantage of.
>
> Every one of those guys on the Dallas defense was very disciplined and played according to the total scheme of the defense, and not individually. I really thought that the ice affected Pugh more than it did Kramer and Bowman, and they were able to dig in, and anticipating the count, they were able get into him before he could react. One of the big plays in NFL history, of course.

The aftermath of the game was ugly. Several people had to be treated for hypothermia, and some of the players wound up with frostbite, mainly linemen who had to place their hands on the field as they got down and took their three-point stance. Hyland concluded, "It's no wonder. The defense was out there a great portion of the game." Reportedly, 4 fans suffered heart attacks, 14 had to be treated for exposure, and 6 of Ray Nitschke's toes were frostbitten. Hyland also said he caught a flu bug and wound up losing between 10 and 15 pounds.

Mercein reported, "There were guys that were hurt more than others. You just had to persevere, hunker down, and suck it up, play hard." Hyland said, "I'm not sure anyone lost toes, but they lost sensation in their toes." Cowboys owner Clint Murchison commented succinctly, "If I owned Green Bay, I'd dome it."

The weather so dominated the story of the day, columnist Jim Murray observed, "I don't know why they scheduled this game here—I guess the top of Mt. Everest was booked."[7]

Hyland said,

> We were kind of slow getting out of the locker that day. I know I spent a lot of time in a hot shower. After a big game like that you have more of the TV people and a lot more sportswriters around. Jerry Kramer always had a good line for the guys so he probably spent some extra time with the media sportswriters, as did Bart and Chuck, who did a super job for us on that final drive. There was such a great feeling and a sense of accomplishment. We all knew it was something special, that the conditions were so difficult.
>
> We went out that night and really celebrated—it being New Year's Eve and one of the most important games of our lives.

Even now, a half-century later, Hyland said the glow from that game lingers, despite how time naturally has also changed some things adversely for the Packers. He related,

> Sometimes it's kinda sad—you can see we're not physically what we used to be, sometimes mentally as well. It's amazing what winning a championship together can do. The game really takes its toll, but nobody can ever take the Ice Bowl and the Super Bowl win two weeks later away from us.
>
> I know that I, and all the other guys who played in the Ice Bowl, whenever it comes down to playoff time [each season], the first thing you do is look at the conditions that there might be, whether it be in Minnesota or wherever there's an outdoor stadium. And you're hoping that there's never going to be a colder day than when we played. I think we still like to revel in the fact that we put up with some very difficult circumstances and were able to win.

Lombardi soon made news. Gutsy decision behind him, and yet another NFL title behind him as well, he told his son shortly after the Ice

Bowl that he had just coached his next-to-last game ever. After the ensuing Super Bowl win, he did retire from the Packers.

Later, craving to be back on the sidelines, he returned to the coaching ranks, but this time with the Washington Redskins, and just for one season. He went 7–5–2, finishing in second place in their division behind the Cowboys. That record, and his 7–5 record in his first season, were the closest he ever came to a posting a mediocre, break-even season—he never had a losing season in NFL play.

It's probably safe to say many fans would be astonished to learn Lombardi was only an NFL head coach for nine seasons, but what an impression those nine years made.

In the Ice Bowl, Green Bay had endured the unfathomably brutal weather and a talented Cowboys team. Both teams survived, but only the Packers would thrive. While the Cowboys were in no mood to ring in the New Year after this bitter defeat, Green Bay would go on to outclass the Oakland Raiders by a score of 33–14 in Super Bowl II. That contest was played in Miami in mid-January, under blue skies and a temperature of 60 degrees—a whopping 73 degrees higher than what the thermometer read in Green Bay at the start of the Ice Bowl. With the win against Oakland, the Lombardi-led Packers had won his three straight championships and fifth title in a seven-year span.

Another aftermath of the Ice Bowl illustrates the intense pride of a valiant but defeated warrior. Bob Lilly, a consummate pro for Dallas, can never forget that contest. He and Mercein talked about one play from the game many years later, the "65-Give," which, although risky, worked, with Mercein carrying for eight yards to move the ball to the three-yard line shortly before the Starr sneak won the game. Mercein recalled,

> Bob wanted to make a very serious point to me. He said, "Now, Chuck, on that 'Give' play you ran, you were not my responsibility."
>
> That was a big play we ran right after I caught a pass for about 19 yards, when I ran up the middle for another eight. It was a "Give" play, but is also sometimes called a "sucker" play, where your guard [Gale Gillingham] pulls and, in this case, the defensive tackle, Lilly, would follow him down the line of scrimmage trying to disrupt what looked like the Green Bay Sweep. The fullback was supposed to block Lilly, replacing the guard who had pulled because both our guards pulled on our sweeps. Lilly was so fast and he was such a good reader, as soon as that guard would pull, he would just follow him down the line. As the

fullback, I [often] had to block him, and I ended up almost clipping him because he'd be going away from me. He wouldn't stay at home.

So what we did was run our "Give" play; they just gave me the ball and let him take himself out of the play. Basically, I ran right up the middle.

Had Lilly not followed Gillingham, the play would have broken down.

Lilly made sure Mercein understood that he had not goofed, that he had done his job. "Oh, yes," said Mercein. "All these years later. It was so important to him. He is a very nice man, very humble, but also very proud."

Mercein told Lilly, "Bob, the only reason the play worked as good as it did was you were such a great player. You were so hard to block. We knew you'd read the play and try to disrupt it down the line of scrimmage, which you did, trailing."

Then, said Mercein, "Of course, Donny didn't get the ball—the handoff went to me instead of the halfback. Interesting play."

The Ice Bowl remains an unnatural disaster in the minds of the Cowboys and their fans. The plane ride back to Texas dragged on and on with hardly a word being spoken. If there had been a soundtrack to this somber scene, it would've been a dirge—perhaps Chopin's *Funeral March*.

To this day, the Cowboys, said Mercein, "don't like to talk about it much," continuing, "I think it still pretty much sticks in their craw. I think Lee Roy Jordan is still a little bit bitter about that Ice Bowl game. Whenever I've see him, he doesn't like to talk about that thing at all. Donny Anderson tells me that he's in the same club as Jordan, and he's still pissed off about losing."

Dallas linebacker Chuck Howley realized the frozen field and bitter weather presented the same challenges for both teams but said he wished he could've taken on the Packers in normal conditions. Myriad Cowboys feel the better team lost that day.

Mercein realizes that if, say, Starr had slipped on the ice and failed to score, the Packers would be the bitter ones. He said,

> Of course! Dallas had every reason to be bitter because they had also lost the previous championship in the last seconds, on almost the last play in the Cotton Bowl, when they had the home-field advantage. They were driving down and were intercepted by Tom Brown in the end zone after great pressure by Dave Robinson on Meredith. So they

lost two times at the very end of games against the Packers. I don't blame them for being bitter.

One Packers defensive player looked back on the game, offering quite a different take on the victory, an observation seldom chronicled. He said he'd rather not have his name used because he feels his comments would get him "in trouble with the people in Dallas." He stated,

> But here's something for you. I like to take things that no one else discusses. I don't know how many times I've heard people from Dallas, and some players, say that if it hadn't been for the frozen field, they would have kicked our ass. I've had people go so far as to say that they think Vince Lombardi turned the heaters off so that the field would freeze, which is ridiculous—he didn't.
>
> When that tarp came off that field, because the tarp was on the electrified field, the field had been kept warm—the tarp kept the warmth [trapped] in the field, but the condensation on the tarp came back down on the field and it was muddy, just like it had rained. The field was very playable, just muddy to start of the game.
>
> They knew they weren't going to have a halftime show, but a halftime at a championship game is longer than in a regular game. When we went in at halftime, that field was still very playable. Now, hindsight is 20–20, but they should have rolled out the tarp because there wasn't going to be any band or anybody on the field, and cover it and take it back up when we came back out for the third quarter. If they did, I think we'd have had a playable field the whole game. But when we came back out the field had started to crust over a little bit. As the game went on and on, the crust got deeper and deeper, and by the end of the game the crust was only about a quarter of an inch thick, but it might as well have been a foot thick because you couldn't break it with your feet.
>
> Now here's the interesting part about it. When the field was wet, we were dominating, going out to a 14-point lead before you know it. When the field froze, Willie Wood dropped a punt, which led to a field goal, and they sacked Bart Starr and he fumbled—they picked it up and ran in for a touchdown. Then they threw that halfback option pass to take the lead.
>
> Also, if you checked the box score, their defense shut out our offense down to nothing. Their defense was superb when the field was frozen—in the third and fourth quarters. Jerry Kramer says that on the last play before the last drive, the offense had a total of something like

10 yards—that's all we had. They shut our offense down the whole second half until that last drive, the last 65 yards.

What I'm trying to say is this: When the field was wet and playable, we dominated. When the field froze, Dallas had their best moments. Everybody thinks it was the other way around, that we did everything after the field froze. I've always been one to stick to the facts, and that's what I remember.

One final, obvious, and irrefutable fact about the Ice Bowl to tie in with the players' memories: Both teams did play the entire game in identical circumstances, and as close as the game was, Green Bay was the team that came out on top—case closed.

Like survivors of any ordeal, the Packers can look back and delight in the fact that they not only emerged with a win, but also struggled with and overcame their tribulations. To this day, they relish the fact that they shared a grueling, yet ultimately rewarding, experience. Also, thanks to the passage of time, they can *almost* minimize how taxing and dangerous it was to play in the Ice Bowl.

Today, for example, Mercein can fondly reflect on the experience: "We prevailed. It was gratifying. I was able to pay back Coach Lombardi for bringing me there to Green Bay to begin with. It was wonderful to be with those great teammates and to be a part of NFL history, which is what it amounted to, right?"

3

THE HEIDI GAME

A Swiss Miss Takes on Pro Football

There's a basketball cliché about coaches of teams that are so good they can blow everyone out of the gym on sheer talent alone. The saying goes that such coaches don't even need to design plays or fret about practice sessions—they merely roll the ball out on the court and let their players loose. Now, the old AFL was a pass-happy league, rife with wildfire scoring rampages, and teams were stocked with quarterbacks who unleashed many a bomb, making some uneducated fans feel as if there was little need for coaching in that league. Want to rack up points—just give a Joe Namath or a Daryle Lamonica the football and watch passes rain down on the field to create a point explosion.

That, of course, is nonsense. Make no mistake, going into the Heidi game, or any game for that matter, coaches like New York's Weeb Ewbank always had a solid game plan. Ewbank had a long history of keeping things relatively simple, but, again, a well-thought-out plan was definitely in place.

As a matter of fact, both Ewbank and Oakland's head coach, John Rauch, simply *had* to have a great plan because so much was at stake for their clash. Both teams stood at 7–2 on the season. The Jets wanted to keep their momentum flowing, their aspirations of traveling to the Super Bowl entrenched in their mind, while the Raiders, despite a great record, were a half-game behind Kansas City in their division.

Furthermore—although, of course, no one knew it going into the game of November 17, 1968—due to the game's dramatic finish after NBC suddenly stopped their broadcast of the game for the TV movie *Heidi* (and with horrendous timing on their part), this one was destined to become an instant classic, one that would forever change the way pro football was broadcast.

Both Ewbank and Rauch wanted to feature a balanced attack. The Jets runners carried the ball 32 times, one more than the Raiders. Moreover, both teams passed the ball only slightly more often than they kept it on the ground. Namath threw 37 passes, while Lamonica put the ball up 34 times. The big difference between the teams is that when it came to scoring, the Raiders relied more on the pass than Ewbank's Jets—four of Oakland's five touchdowns came on passes, while New York scored two TDs running and just one on a throw.

Prior to the game and other games Ewbank coached against the Raiders, he suspected Oakland of spying on his practice sessions. If he saw a helicopter fly overhead during a team workout, he would stare and shake his fist at it, convinced espionage was afoot.

It seemed as if there had always been bad blood between the teams from 1960, when they entered the AFL as charter members (when the Jets were named the Titans). Both teams didn't exactly tear the league apart at first. During Oakland's first three seasons, their record was abysmal, at 9–33, and from 1960 to 1967, the Jets never finished a season above the break-even mark. Ewbank finally hoisted New York to a record above .500, at 8–5–1, in 1967. Of course, in 1967, the Raiders also had a bulked-up record. They lost only two games all year, one to Lombardi's Packers in the Super Bowl and one to Ewbank's Jets, one more reason for Oakland's animosity toward New York.

Before the beginning of the Heidi contest, Namath reflected on a game between the two teams from one year earlier, the second of their two head-to-head contests in 1967. In that contest, 6-foot-8, 275-pound defensive end Ben Davidson was said to have broken Namath's cheekbone, drilling him to the ground with a vicious right-hand shot to the head that sent his helmet airborne during the Raiders' 38–29 win. The defeat cost the Jets a chance to win their division, dropping them out of a tie with Houston, who went on to win the East by one game over the Jets. This was yet another reason for Jets players to detest the Raiders.

Furthermore, after the game, Namath stated he had been hit worse by girls, prompting Davidson to say Namath was just begging for more punishment, issuing a Ralph Kramden–like threat to, in effect, send him to the moon. For the record, the truth is, Namath's broken bone actually took place on a previous play, when he was hit by defensive end Ike Lassiter. Nevertheless, a picture of the mugging of Namath by Davidson is what's forever remembered.

A few days before the Heidi affair, a game some observers still believe was the most violent game in Jets annals, it was discovered that a photograph of Davidson's wicked hit of Namath was displayed on a wall in the Raiders offices. One reporter approached Namath prior to kickoff and asked if he felt Oakland would again zero in on him. Namath replied, "If they want to win, they'd better be."[1] Indeed, the Raiders' decision to go all out after Namath resulted in four sacks of the man with limited mobility, which also helped secure the win even though Namath did put 32 points on the board.

As touched on, both teams sported identical 7–2 records going into the Heidi game. Houston, which would finish second in the East Division behind the Jets, lost their game the day of the Heidi contest, so the Jets could have wrapped up at least a tie for their division with a win against Oakland. As it turned out, even after losing to the Raiders, the Jets would waltz to the division title by four games over the Oilers. Oakland, on the other hand, was in a much tighter race in their division. Oakland wound up using the victory over the Jets to help their inertia roll on—the win was their fourth in a row, and they would win their next four to streak into postseason play.

Namath was blessed with talented receivers. George Sauer trailed only Lance Alworth for total receptions in 1968, 66 receptions to Alworth's 68. Don Maynard ended the season second in the AFL for yardage on receptions, with 1,297 (one spot ahead of Sauer's 1,141 yards), and tied for third with his 10 touchdown scores and fifth for catches, at 57. No one in the league averaged more than Maynard's 22.8 yards per reception or his 99.8 yards per game played.

He recalled, "We knew it was going to be a big game, and because of that situation we kind of didn't pay too much attention to a lot of the news media. We just knew we had to go out and play like we had to get us there in the first place." He added that, at least for the bulk of the game, "It turned out fine just by following our checkoffs and other adjustments in the game."

Of course, sometimes even the best-laid plans and adjustments don't work out, and that's often a case in high-scoring games where sometimes everyone gets the feeling that the team that has the ball last will somehow pull it out.

And make no mistake, the game was a typical AFL shootout with the two rivals duking it out, with the Raiders serving as the hostile home team in the Oakland-Alameda County Coliseum. That facility was known to baseball fans, and perhaps after the game to the Jets as well, as the Oakland Mausoleum.

The game turned out to be such a slugfest that 75 total points were scored, with nearly half of them, 34, lighting up the scoreboard like a pinball machine gone wild in the fourth quarter.

The animus between teams displayed itself from the 4:00 EST opening kickoff when a personal foul was called. It was one of 19 total penalties called. In all, 238 yards were lost due to penalties.

Maynard said more than one of his catches that day came on audibles. "At the same time, the receivers also had a signal—like I'd raise my hand if I wanted to change a play," he related. "I'd change my routes. You had to do that fast enough that there was no indecision on Joe's part."

For the most part, gimpy-legged Joe Namath was not indecisive. He was sacked six times, but overall he was undeterred, throwing 37 passes, with 19 hitting his receivers for 381 yards. It was hardly surprising because just the season before, Namath, at the age of 24, had become the first professional football player to shatter the 4,000-yard passing plateau, achieving that in just his third year in the league and just his second season as a full-time starter. He remains the only quarterback to reach that strata in a season made up of fewer than 16 games.

Namath's 4,007-yard season came in 1967. His yards passing total the next year took a nosedive to 3,147, and his touchdown throws sank from 26 to 15. He stated that until the fourth game of the 1968 season, he had yet to grasp the concept of attacking defenses with all of his team's weapons, especially Matt Snell and Emerson Boozer, two runners who were injured the year before. The most vital stat of all—one that soared meteorically—was the team's record under Namath, which improved from 8–5–1 to 11–3 thanks to his new insight in '68. What was truly surprising, however, is the fact that Namath's first touchdown toss of the

Heidi game, which didn't come until the fourth quarter, was his first scoring pass in six games.

However, Namath surely did use Don Maynard effectively in the Heidi game. His favorite target ended the day with 10 catches, a 50-yard score, and a team record 228 yards on receptions. In fact, 97 of those yards came on two straight passes to Maynard after the Jets had taken possession of the ball on their own three-yard line. On the debit side, the Jets set another team record that day, being penalized 13 times for a staggering 145 yards. Two of the penalties in this rough-and-tumble contest were slapped on Namath's roommate, Jim Hudson, for unsportsmanlike conduct, and he was ejected from the game.

The Raiders had Daryle "The Mad Bomber" Lamonica firing the ball effectively, too, spreading the wealth by hitting four different men for touchdowns. Lamonica, the AFL Player of the Year from both the year before and the season after the Heidi game, connected on 21 of 34 passes for 311 yards and those four touchdowns.

On the season, Lamonica would finish second in the league in most of the major quarterback categories, including most pass attempts and completions, most yards gained on his throws, most passing touchdowns, and quarterback rating. He also led the AFL in three lesser-quoted statistics: highest average of yards through the air per game played, at 249.6; highest average of passes completed, at 15.8; and passes thrown per game, at 32.

Namath's 1968 stats were nearly as good. He ended the season ranked third for passing yardage, completions, and pass attempts; fourth for quarterback rating; and fifth for touchdown throws.

For the record, San Diego's John Hadl was first in each of the aforementioned stats except quarterback rating, which was topped by Len Dawson of the Chiefs. On the season, Namath wound up leading the AFL in comebacks engineered by quarterbacks, with four, but in the Heidi game it was Lamonica who stole the comeback spotlight with his only comeback of the entire season.

The chronology of the scoring began with two Jim Turner field goals from 44 and 18 yards out to give the Jets the early lead. The only other first-quarter score came on a Lamonica pass of nine yards to Warren Wells, a talented receiver whose 1,137 yards in receptions put him one slot behind Sauer at year's end. Furthermore, no one pulled down a longer pass in 1968, than a 94-yard Lamonica-to-Wells reception, and no one scored more than Wells's 12 total touchdowns.

The second quarter featured Oakland extending their lead to 14–6, when Lamonica hit tight end Billy Cannon for a 48-yard TD. Namath brought the Jets back a bit, to 14–12, by halftime when he ran the ball in from one yard out, but a two-point conversion attempt that followed failed.

Both teams scored on short runs in the third quarter. New York's Bill Mathis broke the goal line first with a four-yard carry to inflate the score to 19–14, giving the lead back to the Jets. On the season, Mathis had accounted for just 208 yards rushing. When Charlie Smith ran for a three-yard touchdown and Oakland made good on a two-point conversion coming on a pass to Hewritt Dixon, they snatched back the lead, 22–19, and that's how it stood entering the final quarter. Dixon was a true threat as a runner—his 865 yards on the ground ranked number three in the league—and as a receiver—his 1,229 all-purpose yardage was the sixth-highest total in the league.

Smith, one of the heroes of the game, played the role of the goat early in the fourth quarter when he fumbled just three yards shy of the goal line, snuffing out a drive and a great scoring opportunity. That led directly to a quick New York score on a 50-yard touchdown strike to Maynard. The long pass resulted in another lead change, getting the Jets back on track once again (26–22).

A Jim Turner chip shot of a field goal followed, extending the lead to 29–22, with the Jets on top. Maynard said what happened on those two scoring drives was, "Joe went to whatever he needed to," mixing things up, calling checkoffs, and guiding a comeback.

Maynard said it wasn't exactly baffling that his Jets rebounded so often in the game, taking the lead after they trailed or were tied, and that they were able to snap back with elastic force to do that twice in the fourth quarter. "At the time, you're just playing the game the best you can, and you want to make sure you don't miss any plays," he reflected. "You just go with what you'd been working on nearly all week. You know who you're playing and what's going on, and that worked real good."

But not for long. Oakland's offensive arsenal in this violent contest featured some big names, perhaps none larger than Fred Biletnikoff, a future Hall of Famer who had caught 61 passes on the season, good for the third-highest total in the AFL. His 1,037 yards on receptions made him one of just six men to go beyond the 1,000-yard mark for catches that year (he ranked sixth).

Lamonica combined with Biletnikoff, who caught seven passes for 120 yards in the contest, on a 22-yard dart. The subsequent point-after kick by George Blanda tied the game at 29-all.

A cheap shot administered to Namath by his nemesis, Davidson, pushed the Jets into excellent field goal range. Another Turner kick, this one from 26 yards out, gave New York a 32–29 edge, but the game was far from over—and the chaos had yet to begin. To that point, no team had owned a lead larger than seven points. In addition, the lead had switched back and forth five times, with one more change to come, and a total of 20 fourth-quarter points had been scored. Miraculously, 14 more Raiders points would go on the board in the meager amount of time left.

After Turner's field goal, the ensuing kickoff was the play that opened a chapter of NFL lore. It was 7:00 p.m. EST, and NBC, which was televising the game, one that was running way long, had to decide whether they would broadcast the remaining game's final 50 seconds to its viewers to the east of Denver (including, of course, New York City) or bump football and run with the TV movie *Heidi*, which had been scheduled to air at that time.

According to Dick Cline, the man who made the decision to cut away from the contest, going into the game no one could have anticipated the possibility of a football game with a 4:00 p.m. EST start conflicting with *Heidi* because no game with that starting time had ever before gone so long as to infringe on a 7:00 broadcast of another scheduled show. Plus, he said the network had a commitment to the Timex watch company— they had bought advertising time from 7:00 to 9:00 for the *Heidi* broadcast.

Thus, after a commercial break, tons of football fans became irate when they learned the rest of the game would not be shown. Despite their phone calls of protestation, which blew out fuses on the NBC switchboard in New York City, viewers missed a fantastic finish (with the exception of West Coast viewers).

It was horribly poor timing and poor decision-making, but one imagines NBC brass may have felt the Jets would hold on to their 32–29 lead, or, more to the point, they conceded that they had to live up to their deal with Timex. In either case, Hall of Fame running back Floyd Little called that move "one of the biggest faux pas in television history." It is certainly one that has never been forgotten.

Naturally, when NBC cut away to the show *Heidi*, the players were unaware of what was transpiring. Maynard noted, "A lot of times you don't pay much attention to the media—no disrespect to them, though."

As mentioned, the Raiders had some big names on their roster; however, one of the biggest stars of the Oakland comeback was rookie running back Charlie Smith, a man who started just three games all year long. Despite that, he compiled a total of 1,169 all-purpose yards, exceeded by only seven other players. Somehow the Raiders found a way to get him the ball, as only three other AFL players had more touches than his 217. He ended the season as the league's top rusher when based on his average per carry (5.3).

The Raiders traveled 78 yards quickly to take the lead. A Lamonica pass to Smith went for 20, and 15 more yards were tacked on when Mike D'Amato was called for facemasking. D'Amato wouldn't even have been on the field if it weren't for the fact he had replaced the ejected Hudson.

Another toss to Smith, again guarded by D'Amato, turned a short pass into a 43-yard score to give the Raiders a 36–32 cushion. Forty-two seconds still showed on the clock. As a trivia footnote, Smith had only one more touchdown on a pass reception all year long.

A Mike Eischeid squib kick followed. New York's Earl Christy came up with the football initially but lost the handle close to the 15-yard line, recovered it at about the 10-yard line, and lost the ball again when a defender spun him around. The ball rolled back toward the Jets end zone before Oakland's Preston Ridlehuber picked it up and took it in, scoring on a two-yard fumble return to wrap things up at 43–32.

Ridlehuber was an unlikely player to score—in his three-year career he had just two other touchdowns to his credit. He was a reserve running back who had missed the entire 1967 season after being discarded by the Atlanta Falcons the year before, when he first broke into the league.

The barn burner over, the Raiders had pounded 14 points onto the scoreboard in a span of exactly nine seconds to put a truly crazy game away. Both teams let the football fly in that day. The Jets gained 381 yards on passes (minus 36 lost on four sacks), while the Raiders threw for 311 yards, losing 20 on two sacks.

Almost as shocking as the rapid-fire scoring binge was the fact that those 14 points, played out in front of 53,318 spectators live, were not witnessed by millions of football fans, as *Heidi* blithely continued her Swiss adventures on the TV screen.

Millions of TV viewers, those who had not already smashed their sets, were forced to stare blankly, in an apoplectic rage, at the children's show, watching the daughter of actress Julie Andrews portray a Swiss orphan. The *New York Times* had reviewed the show, calling it the best show of the day, but football fans knew the Jets–Raiders game was their only "must-see TV." They were deprived of witnessing one of the wildest conclusions of an instant classic.

Ironically, earlier in the day, NBC had interrupted their broadcast of the Buffalo Bills versus the San Diego Chargers to cut to the Jets versus the Raiders. That move was made so viewers could see the *entire* Jets game. It just wasn't meant to be.

NBC president Julian Goodman later issued an apology for yanking the game from the airwaves. He called the decision a "forgivable error committed by humans who were concerned about the children,"[2] but, of course, football fans griped, "Children be damned," and "The error is far from being a forgivable one."

Weeb Ewbank later joked that the game itself, and not just the telecast, should have been over once the Jets had taken their 32–19 fourth-quarter lead.

Interestingly, even the *New York Times* thought the events of the game were worthy of front-page coverage the following day. Also, something most people no longer remember, the day after the game, NBC *did* broadcast the game's final minute, doing so on their nightly news program. Due to the Heidi game, a new rule for televised games was drawn up guaranteeing that future contests would be shown to their conclusions.

The Raiders season roared on, and their regular-season eight-game win skein raised their record to 12–2. They then trounced Kansas City, 41–6, to break a tie atop of their West Division. That permitted them to advance to the league title game.

So, the next time the Jets and Raiders met, there was actually much more on the line than had been the case in the Heidi game. Just six weeks after the infamous Jets–Raiders game, which was a pugilistic exhibition with heavyweights going toe-to-toe, the teams played for the AFL championship.

They met in a Shea Stadium bulging with 62,627 spectators, and this time the Jets won, 27–23, despite winds that gusted as fast as 35 miles per hour. The Jets took a 10–0 lead into the second quarter, but Oakland battled back, and the Jets found themselves in a 13–13 tie in the third quarter. The Jets scored next to regain the lead at 20–13.

Like the Heidi game, this game also featured exciting scoring swings. Oakland, whose pass completions on the day were good for 401 yards (393 net yards through the air), ran off the next 10 points to go up by a score of 23–20 in the final stanza; however, Don Maynard hauled in his second touchdown catch of the day to give the Jets their final four-point cushion.

The victory earned the Jets a trip to Super Bowl III. The franchise, which began play in 1960, had not enjoyed a winning season until their eighth campaign, Ewbank's fifth season there. Now, they were headed to the ultimate game. When Ewbank had become the head coach in 1963, the year of the name change to Jets, he predicted it would take him five years to win the championship. He was off by just a year.

Of course, for most fans, the Heidi game is better remembered than the Jets' win in the AFL title game. In the Heidi game, Oakland not only resiliently stormed back, but also eventually wound up winning the game by a rather comfortable margin. A fan who simply looked at the final score might have almost thought the Raiders had coasted to the 11-point win. The next day, the *New York Daily Herald* took a dig at NBC with the headline JETS 32, OAKLAND 29, *HEIDI* 14.

Raymond Berry hauls in a pass from John Unitas. In the 1958 championship contest, known as the Greatest Game Ever Played, Berry did this 12 times for 178 yards, both establishing NFL playoff records. *Courtesy of the Indianapolis Colts*

Johnny Unitas led the Baltimore Colts to the 1958 NFL championship, winning the Greatest Game Ever Played. He poses with some of his many trophies and awards. *Courtesy of Paige Unitas*

Beaver Falls High quarterback Joe Namath, then a kid who could never imagine he'd play in the wild Heidi game many years later. He won championships in high school, college, and the NFL. *Courtesy of the Larry Bruno Foundation*

Namath returns home, a hero after winning Super Bowl III in a stunning upset over the Baltimore Colts. *Courtesy of the Larry Bruno Foundation*

Sam Havrilak of the Baltimore Colts once played in a game almost as cold as the Ice Bowl. He stated, "The traction and footing were horrible . . . and the hits, even the small ones, hurt worse than they should hurt." *Courtesy of the Mid Mon Valley All Sports Hall of Fame*

Don Shula coached many standout quarterbacks, including Johnny Unitas and Dan Marino, seen here with his Hall of Fame bust. *Courtesy of the University of Pittsburgh*

Minnesota Vikings All-Pro kicker Fred Cox, who compared his coach, Bud Grant, with Paul Brown. Cox said Grant was compassionate, not cold, as was often re-ported. *Courtesy of the Mid Mon Valley All Sports Hall of Fame*

Seattle Seahawks running back Tony Benjamin said that many years after Grant retired, his defensive concepts lived on. *Courtesy of the Mid Mon Valley All Sports Hall of Fame*

Distrustful of rookies, George Allen loved veteran players like Pro Bowl linebacker Myron Pottios. When Allen went from Los Angeles to Washington, he made it a point to acquire many of his former stars. *Courtesy of the Mid Mon Valley All Sports Hall of Fame*

Miami Dolphins lineman Doug Crusan respected his coach Don Shula but hated having to oppose Hank Stram's Chiefs, the "biggest team we played." *Courtesy of the Mid Mon Valley All Sports Hall of Fame*

4

SUPER BOWL III

"No Brag, Just Fact"

The next classic game of the golden age is Super Bowl III, which was staged on January 12, 1969, and came almost exactly two months after the Heidi game and just two weeks after the Jets exacted their revenge for the loss in the Heidi game with the previously mentioned narrow win against the Raiders in the AFL title game.

Sources vary, but the Colts were highly favored to run away with Super Bowl III—the opening line spotted the Jets an unheard-of 19 1/2 points. It is little wonder, since going into the contest the Colts' record in their previous 31 games was a lustrous 27–2–2. AFL teams were still regarded as upstarts, judged to be vastly inferior, and the results of the first two Super Bowls seemed to confirm that. Oakland and Kansas City had been shellacked by a combined score of 68–24 by the Packers, the elite of the NFL.

Just before Super Bowl III began, one NFL coach quipped, "Namath plays his first pro football game today." The game featured the continuing bragging rights of a mighty NFL representative opposing what were ostensibly empty boasts of a cocky young quarterback.

Unitas's wife Sandy said John liked Joe Namath a lot and that sometimes the two would "kid each other and carry on." That didn't stop Unitas from getting in a slight dig at Namath before Super Bowl III. When a reporter asked Unitas what he thought of Namath, Unitas dismissed the opposing quarterback, coming back with, "I never think about him."

The two quarterbacks presented a stark contrast in myriad ways, from their lifestyles to their on-field style. That even held true in the way they celebrated championship victories. Gino Marchetti revisited the ending of the 1958 title game, saying,

> If you see the film and you watch John closely, he'll hand the ball off and he'll watch Ameche go in for the score to win the game. And, as casually as he could do it, he started walking off the field. He didn't run, he didn't jump, he didn't point to God up in the sky. He didn't do any of that—just handed the ball off, and when Ameche went across, he just walked right off the field very, very slowly and casually. Another day at the office.

Joe Namath, on the other hand, would make his famous pointing gesture toward the sky after winning Super Bowl III.

Namath certainly was a free spirit, one many felt could be curbed by no coach. Marchetti disagreed, pointing out that Namath was "one of the first big-name draftees. He wore fur coats and did all that stuff. And Weeb drafted him, you gotta remember *that*. When you're winning, you can crack down. I'll tell you who would have stopped him, the guy from Alabama. Bear Bryant would've stopped him [from acting as he did]. I mean he was tough."

Weeb Ewbank, who coached both star quarterbacks, was unconcerned with any comparisons of them. Instead, he fretted about his game plan. Going into the contest, Ewbank said that because his right tackle for the Super Bowl was playing out of his normal guard spot, the Jets would run a lot of fullback slants to the left. Fullback Matt Snell, then, was to become a huge factor in Ewbank's play-calling.

Ewbank always believed that a game's ever-shifting situations, ranging from the score, the down, and yards to go for a first down and a touchdown, as well as the weather, would dictate what plays to run, but he also firmly believed his Jets could run on the Colts.

However, Ewbank advised Namath not to run sweeps against them. This was one pregame plan of his, however, that wasn't right on the button. Namath called an audible for a sweep on his second play of the game, and it worked. He then felt comfortable calling even more sweeps, mixing them in with other runs, especially by Snell. Those runs would prove to be battering rams, blasting away at the Colts defense as Snell would follow the great lead blocking of 270-pound Pro Bowl tackle Winston Hill and running back Emerson Boozer through the right side of the Colts defense again and again.

Incidentally, when Hill was in his rookie training camp, then with the Colts, right defensive end Ordell Braase had manhandled him so badly Don Shula cut him. In Super Bowl III, Hill totally outplayed Braase, who then was in his final season at the age of 36, nine years older than Hill.

Going into the game, Ewbank had apparently given too much credit to the Colts' linebacking crew, but he certainly was correct about the usual effectiveness of the Baltimore defense—their number-one-ranked team defense had allowed only 144 points all year long. The Colts also owned the league's second-best offense.

On the 1968 season, the Colts had beaten (at least once) every team they played and wound up with the third-best points differential in NFL history up to that point. After they demolished the Browns, 34–0, for their fourth shutout of the year in the playoffs to advance to the Super Bowl, they sported a 15–1 overall record, and they hadn't lost since October 20th.

The Jets weren't exactly a weak sister of a team, either, owning the second-best offense and the league's fourth-highest-ranked defense. They built their 11–3 regular-season record on the strength of two four-game winning streaks.

Coach Don Shula's plan of attack, based on his belief the Jets would rely heavily on their passing game, called for his Colts to implement a blend of zone pass coverage with a generous dose of blitzes tossed in. His Colts often charged ferociously, sending as many as eight frothing players at opposing quarterbacks; however, as the game unfolded, Namath repeatedly sensed the blitzes and stripped their effectiveness with short throws, often going to his left, connecting with George Sauer.

In fact, Ewbank had prepared his Jets so well to handle the blitz, he not only knew they were primed for it, but also actually hoped Baltimore would bring it on. He felt he could combat the blitz with short passes, hooks, and flares, a contrast to the wide-open passing game the Jets often used, with Namath heaving long throws.

Namath later confirmed that the Jets' ability to read the blitz was vital. He and Sauer had prearranged it so that when a safety came up to blitz, Sauer would break to the inside automatically—no need for an audible to be called. Then at one point, crossing up the Colts, the two men conferred and agreed that the next time a blitz came, Sauer would fake to the inside and take off on a fly pattern. Sure enough, the situation arose, and Namath hit Sauer on a deep outside route. The Jets offense, not at all one-dimensional, was so balanced it would give the Colts fits.

A simple scoring summary of the game hardly tells a dramatic tale. First quarter: scoreless. Second quarter: Matt Snell darts over the goal line on a sweep to the left side for a four-yard touchdown; 7–0 at the half. Third quarter: Jets boot two field goals to increase the lead to 13–0. Final quarter: A short field goal takes the score to 16–0, before the Colts finally get on the board with a Jerry Hill one-yard run over the left tackle with just 3:19 left to play. Final score: Jets 16, Colts 7.

Ignoring the score momentarily, the real drama and import of Super Bowl III comes from its backdrop, a dissection of some of the game's most vital moments, and a look at the aftermath of the contest.

Many people believe the Jets had one huge edge going into the Super Bowl—inside information. Baltimore's Rick Volk said Ewbank was acquainted with many of the Colts personnel, and that meant he knew their weaknesses, too. After all, he had coached Baltimore for nine seasons and was just six years removed from being privy to everything that went on with his Colts; therefore, he knew his Jets, and he knew the Colts. Don Maynard concurred, stating, "Absolutely. That would be a [plus], and it wound up being exactly that."

Baltimore Colt Sam Havrilak disagrees somewhat. He commented,

> I don't think it was as big a factor as everybody makes it out to be. I think a couple of things happened. Number one, at that time on our right defensive side, we had three players who were ready to retire. Ordell Braase, Don Shinnick, and Lenny Lyles. I think a lot of the plays went to that side because Weeb kind of figured those players were on the downsides of their careers, and they could probably exploit that side better than the other side.

Havrilak's theory aside, one thing was for certain—Ewbank believed the Colts, having gone on a season-long tear, would do nothing different from what they had done to get this far, so he was well prepped for their meeting.

Not only that, but most people feel Ewbank's inside-out knowledge of the Colts system did convince Namath they would defeat Baltimore.

That, in turn, led to his seemingly brash prediction—no, make that his bold *guarantee*—that the Jets would prevail. The details of his promise are basically as follows: Three days before kickoff, Namath made his way to the podium at the Miami Touchdown Club. Before he began to speak, one account of the tale states a heckler shouted out that the Colts were going to whip the Jets. That's when Namath said the Jets were going to win, adding, "I guarantee it."

It was as if Namath had borrowed a line from a character Walter Brennan once played in a TV Western called *The Guns of Will Sonnett*. Brennan's character had a catchphrase—after telling someone of his prowess with his six-shooter, he'd add, "No brag, just fact."

Many believed the Jets win to be an unimaginable upset. Namath and Ewbank saw it as a result of insight, preparation, and execution. In fact, other Jets had privately said what Namath had told the crowd at the club.

None of that mattered to Ewbank, who was quite upset when he discovered Namath had spouted off. Like any good coach, Ewbank didn't want his players to poke the proverbial hornet's nest, abhorring the idea that a Jet would provide fodder for the Colts' locker room bulletin board. Puzzled by his quarterback's actions, Ewbank asked him why an 18-point underdog (and at some points leading up to the game, one point spread reached 21) would want to rile up the alpha dog Colts, especially after he had warned his team not to say anything to "make them excited." Namath's rebuttal was simple. "You're the guy who told us we could do it," he said. "You got us believing it. So . . . I just told him the truth, the way I felt."[1]

Unlike many people, Volk said he wasn't bothered when he heard Namath guarantee the Jets victory, but once that quote got out, it spread like wildfire, including, of course, into the Colts locker room. While many members of the media and fans scoffed, even chuckled, at Namath's prediction, interestingly, Volk said he doesn't remember any of his teammates taking umbrage at the boast. He stated,

> I'm sure it was something that was talked about, but nothing to the point where we're so fired up and so out of control that we can't play our game. You don't like to hear somebody say something that might be detrimental to your team—and he didn't say anything like, "We're going to kill their defense," or that kind of thing, it was just, "I guarantee it." I'm sure it was something that they tried to use, and the coaches probably put it up [on the bulletin board] and made sure that we all

knew what Joe was saying. That's part of hyping the game, I guess, and he didn't have anything to lose, really, but he was able to pull it off, and that was the sad thing for us.

The game was in Miami, but both teams were staying up at Fort Lauderdale and the Jets were right next to us—we had the one hotel, and they were at the next hotel. We would go out on the beach, and here's everybody out there—not that we got down there and mingled, but you could look around and see some of those guys down there at their beach or the pool. It was just a different type of atmosphere at that point.

It was the third Super Bowl, and the Packers had won both of them before that. We felt that we could kill them too and continue the NFL over the AFL, but it just didn't work.

In a way, many Colts felt they didn't need something to get them riled up because they believed they were by far the better team.

"I've talked to Namath after that, when we retired," said Volk, continuing,

and he is a good guy, really a good guy. You know when you're in New York and [people] are making you out to be a ladies' man, and you got the pantyhose commercial and you got the raccoon coats and long hair and the white shoes—that was just the opposite of what most of the guys were doing at the time. He was just way ahead of his time. Personally, I wanted to kill him, and I didn't want to have him beat us because he was Broadway Joe, but he had a great arm and a great team around him. He was good—he was a good player and I'm sure a great teammate.

Of course, Volk realizes part of being a good teammate is coming through for one's buddies, and Namath won the "biggest game he ever played." Volk added, "And, remember, the thing that he said was I guarantee it, and it made him—that made Joe. He usually had a good game against us when we played them."

CBS, which carried the game, must have trusted the oddsmakers, not Namath. During the morning before kickoff, their technicians placed tape on the floor of Baltimore's locker room to indicate where cameras should be set up to best broadcast the Colts postgame celebration.

Maynard remembered, "Everybody, more or less, picked the Colts to win, but we had the team and the confidence with our game plan and

players, so we felt like we could go all the way." He even said the Jets'
view of the huge point spread disparity was not what many might have
expected. "We felt good about it because some players and even coaches
sometimes think, 'Hey, they're favored and we're better than them.' But
you can't read the guys' minds once the battle begins."

To Maynard, as the contest progressed and the Jets began to flex their
muscles, he wasn't really surprised the game was swinging their way. He
said, "We knew what we had to go out there and do, and we knew we
were very confident—we felt like we could play with anybody."

Another one of the game's story lines was the many Greek-like tragic
events for the Colts, who, as kings of the NFL, were about to suffer a
monumental fall. Their woes began early, foreshadowing a long, agoniz-
ing day. Their first drive lasted 12 plays and ate up 54 yards, but Baltimore's kicker, Lou Michaels, sent a 27-yard field goal attempt wide right.
Another promising first-half scoring opportunity came after the Jets fumbled on their own 12-yard line and Ron Porter pounced on the ball for the
Colts. After a run for seven by Tom Matte, hope was suffocated by an
interception. Earl Morrall threw the ball to Tom Mitchell, but it rico-
cheted off his shoulder pads in the end zone and was picked off by Randy
Beverly for a touchback, a very welcome gift, as well as a huge relief for
the Jets.

It was time to seize the day for the Jets, and they quickly seized the
lead with an 80-yard drive, capped off by the four-yard Matt Snell run,
with him slanting off wide to the left. The score, at the 9:03 mark of the
second quarter, represented the first time in the brief history of the Super
Bowl that an AFL team held a lead.

The Colts took over and ran off five plays, including a 30-yard Mor-
rall-to-Matte hookup, but couldn't score. Another Michaels kick, this one
from 46 yards out, was no good. More Tantalus-like agony and frustration came on their next possession. A brilliant 58-yard scamper around
right end by Tom Matte was wasted. After moving the ball 65 yards to the
Jets' 15-yard line, Morrall threw another pick. The pass was intended for
Willie Richardson, but Johnny Sample grabbed it just before the two-
minute warning was issued.

The second quarter ended on a trick play, which resulted in Morrall
missing a wide open Jimmy Orr in the end zone. Instead, he threw an
interception (more on this play later) and time ran out on the half, but
there was speculation about Unitas replacing Morrall. As a matter of fact,

Shula spoke with Unitas at halftime, saying he was going to give Morrall one more possession to turn things around—after all, the Colts were only down by seven points. If Morrall, still off his "A" game, didn't get the job done, Unitas was coming off the bench.

Joe Unitas, a son of Johnny U, told the tale.

> Earl deserved to get the start because of how well he had played the whole season, but Shula told my dad at halftime, "I'm going to give Earl another shot here in the third quarter on the [first] drive. If nothing happens, then you're going to go in." I think there was a really quick turnover, and Shula said, "Oh, that wasn't enough chance." Then the Jets got the ball for a while. And I think Earl went back in for maybe one more [possession], didn't get it done, then the Jets were able to burn a lot more time off the clock.

Joe's memory was correct. Here's how it played out. The Colts received the second-half opening kickoff but didn't have the ball for long. On the first play from scrimmage, Matte ran for eight but fumbled, with linebacker Ralph Baker recovering. Was it time for Unitas? It was certainly decision time for Shula. His actions, initially his *inaction*, staying with Morrall, would lead to much controversy.

Right after the fumble, the Jets reeled off eight plays, none longer than an Emerson Boozer eight-yard carry; devoured 4:17 of the quarter; and added a Jim Turner 32-yard field goal, making it 10–0. Ewbank later said he felt the fumble was a pivotal moment in the contest because his Jets transformed the turnover into the score that padded their lead.

Morrall then threw two incompletions, and the Colts went three-plays-and-punt, and the Jets turned in an encore act. This time they executed 10 plays for 45 yards in four minutes and six seconds, adding yet another field goal to their scoring column, while effectively chewing up the clock. The lead wasn't exactly large, but the way things were going, it would turn out to be insurmountable.

Finally, Shula made his move. Still dealing with an ailing arm, and having thrown only 23 passes all year long, the 35-year-old Johnny U took over. Even though Unitas had been told he'd enter the game early in the second half, he didn't get in until about 75 percent of the third quarter had expired, and not until the Jets had run the score up to 13–0.

The offense sputtered on Unitas's first possession, and Baltimore punted. That allowed New York to do it once more—they ran off a seven-play, 61-yard drive that consumed almost exactly four minutes (3:58) and put yet another three points up when Turner nudged a nine-yard kick through the uprights in the fourth stanza.

Ewbank and Namath had scored by continuing to stick to a basic short-game approach. Namath did uncork one long pass on the day, good for 39 yards, but the longest run by a Jet went for just 12 yards of the total 142 yards the Jets ground out on 43 carries.

The next time the Colts had the ball, they marched from their 27 to the 25-yard line of the Jets, but Unitas threw an interception. By the time he got the football back, only 6:34 showed on the clock, and he had to expend 3:15 of that time taking the Colts 80 yards on 14 arduous plays. The one-yard run by Jerry Hill would be their only score, a classic too little, too late scenario that closed out the scoring at 16–7.

A recovered onside kick ensued, leaving 3:14 to play, but shortly thereafter, faced with a fourth-and-five from the Jets' 19-yard line, Unitas overthrew Orr. The Jets milked all but eight seconds off the clock. Unitas threw two more times, but it was all over.

As for controversy, the decision to stick with Morrall lingers. Every contest has a postgame analysis, and this game's autopsy focused on Shula's move, one still questioned today by bitter Colts fans. After Morrall's first-half interceptions and the enormous gaffe he committed by not spotting the unguarded Orr, Shula gave him not only one chance at redemption in the second half, but also another possession, keeping Unitas on the bench too long, according to many. By the time Unitas did take over, it proved to too late.

Chad Unitas said his father didn't resent or dislike Namath, but he was confident he could have defeated Broadway Joe that day. Chad stated, "He often said that if he had gotten in the Super Bowl a lot earlier, or when Shula [originally] said he would have gotten in there, then it would have turned out a lot differently."

Matte said he can still picture Unitas pacing up and down the Colts sidelines, a lion ready to pursue and take down his prey, but one who was caged by his coach. He commented,

> He was up and down. Personally, I couldn't understand it either. I think Shula was a little worried, thinking about John's Achilles tendon. Can he get in there and do it? But he was cleared to go. I thought he should have come in a little earlier just to change the momentum

around, but that was a decision by the coach. I would imagine that a lot
of people would be second guessing Shula on that one, as I did.

Unitas had preferred playing under Ewbank and was never a big fan of
Shula, who had once been his teammate. Matte said, "When Shula came
here [to coach Baltimore], Shula and John didn't get along too well."
They clashed, and Matte remembered that at one point early on, Unitas
told his coach he should only concern himself with the team's defense,
that *he* would handle the offense. Matte said Shula's keeping Unitas
benched so long in the Super Bowl only deepened Unitas's disgruntle-
ment with his coach.

Joe Unitas said his father was positive if Shula had put him in the
game sooner the Colts would have emerged as the winner. He related a
story involving Ernie Accorsi, the Colts public relations director, who
walked with Unitas after the game, heading for the team bus. Accorsi
asked Unitas one pertinent question: "Do you think if you had started the
second half that the outcome would have been different?" Unitas reportedly looked into his eyes and replied, "Ernie, I didn't need that much
time." Johnny U believed he needed just a bit more time, and for the rest
of his days Unitas felt Shula lied to him about putting him into Super
Bowl III.

Joe added,

> So he felt they definitely could have won if he'd have gotten another
> drive or two to get what he needed done. A lot of what he did as a
> player [with his] play-calling, was he would see different things and
> kind of set the guys [on defense] up for something that he wanted to do
> down the road. He didn't have the kind of time that he needed to do
> that—it made it very difficult—you can't just walk in there and start
> throwing touchdown passes left and right.

Rick Volk said,

> I think Joe Namath always felt that when John came in the game, they
> were in trouble; and we [did get] a touchdown. You got to go along
> with the coach's decision, and John's arm had been hurt that year, and
> Earl had played real well, but Earl was not effective that much in that
> game. People have said that if Shula had put him in earlier maybe it
> would have been a different story.

Maynard, doesn't see it that way, contending that the choice of Colts quarterbacks was immaterial to the Jets. He reflected, "That call was their coaching deal—it didn't make any difference to us who was out there. When Unitas came in, we kinda' felt like, 'Well, they're really up the creek,' so to speak." It wasn't that the Jets didn't respect Unitas—certainly they knew how good he was—but with their lead and the way the game was going, their confidence wasn't about to wane.

When Unitas entered the game, it buoyed at least some of the Colts. Volk felt Baltimore really had a legitimate chance to roar back; however, he said what hurt his team was their defensive unit simply was unable to stop the Jets from picking up many a first down, meaning they were able to control the football. The Jets time of possession came in at about 36 minutes.

"We just weren't able to execute," Volk summed up. He elaborated,

> Namath sort of picked us apart, moving it down the field. It was just one of those games where I realized after that game that anything can happen in a football game. And even if you're huge favorites, in a Super Bowl game you can still get beat if somebody happens to make some key plays and eliminate mistakes. They have a better chance of winning.

Volk also felt another key was the Colts simply made too many mistakes and had failed to execute well. The largest mistake, of course, was the most infamous play of the game, alluded to earlier. It was one that should have easily resulted in a touchdown but turned into a flea-flicker fiasco.

Matte vividly remembers that key second-quarter play, which took place when the game was still tight at 7–0. A Colts score, he believes, would have changed the entire complexion of the game. He commented,

> We pulled a flea flicker on that one. I threw the ball back to Earl Morrall, and Earl isn't seeing Jimmy Orr standing in the end zone, waving his arms. I mean, he tried to throw it to the fullback who had snuck through. I had swept over to the right side with the football and I threw it back to the left, and Earl made a good catch on it.
>
> It was just before halftime, and in the back of the end zone was the Baltimore Colts Marching Band with their blue and white uniforms [getting organized, preparing to perform], and they blended right in with our uniforms, so Earl didn't even see Jimmy Orr in the end zone.

It's a play that to this day causes Colts fans to mumble, "Everyone in the Orange Bowl saw Orr frantically gesturing for the ball in the end zone but Morrall." Orr would later say, "I was open from here to Tampa." Probably all of the 75,389 spectators saw Orr. Morrall, the only one who counted, didn't.

In 2006, Bubba Smith, Baltimore's left defensive end, was *still* musing, perplexed, about how any quarterback could not spot his *primary intended receiver*.

In a 1978 interview, Shula said that in his mind's eye he still sees Orr, all alone, waving his arms futilely. He felt the Browns, a team his Colts thumped to get to the Jets game, was a better team than New York, but the loss to the Jets came mainly due to such flukes as the missed opportunity with a wide-open Orr.

Once again, Maynard didn't totally agree with what others believed. Said Maynard,

> Our free safety could get to Jimmy Orr as quick as anybody. Bill Baird was probably the second-fastest guy on the team behind myself. He knew what he was doing—he had already played seven years. He wasn't a rookie—he could get where he needed to. A lot of times you kind of bait somebody, but he was playing his position, and by the time the ball could've been thrown and got there to Orr, why, Baird could have got there just as quick, and he could have made an interception. You never know.

In any event, Morrall was unable to locate Orr, who literally was jumping up and down in the end zone in a desperate effort to get Morrall's attention. Morrall tried to hit Jerry Hill, and instead of putting six points on the scoreboard, he threw a pass that was picked off by Jim Hudson at the 12-yard line, good for the safety's sixth interception of the season.

That play killed yet another drive and any semblance of momentum the Colts had built up. On the interception return, time ran out of the first half with the Jets clinging to their 7–0 lead. Matte said there was no doubt about it—Unitas would have spotted Orr and hit him.

Many of the game's participants still reflect on other aspects of the game. Matte summed up his thoughts on one particular ramification of the stinging defeat: "It was a tough day for us, and it's been a tough day ever since then because we were expected to win. You should've heard when we played all the other NFL teams, 'You guys let us down. Let these guys beat you.' Blah, blah, blah. We had to live with that, and it wasn't any fun."

Volk remembered watching the game wind down with New York heaping first down upon first down while killing the clock. Soon the realization came—the victory for the Jets was inevitable. "It was too bad—to have all these high hopes about winning a game like that," he bemoaned.

Volk is one Colt who actually has few recollections of the game, which was not only a repercussion of the game, but also literally due to a concussion he sustained during the contest. "My whole thing in that game was I got hit early and was sort of not right," he recalled, adding,

> So I don't even recall much of that game. What I recall is watching it after the fact. Matt Snell, in I think the first series, came up the middle and I hit him low, and I ducked my head and I got kneed in the back of the head. Nothing intentional, just making the tackle, and I got knocked out.
>
> Then I went off the field and came back in and played, oh, maybe a couple of series, and played the rest of the game until I got knocked out again. That was on an onside kick with two minutes to go in the game. So I played, but I didn't play that well. I didn't play my normal game, and I don't really recall too much about that game. It's sort of vague. I know we got beat, that's all.

He snickered.

Any analysis of the game seems to come down to one thing. "Earl didn't have his best day that day, that's all," lamented Matte. "I don't know whether it was nervousness or whatever it was, but we just didn't click."

That was unfortunate for the Colts and Morrall because on the regular season, Morrall had certainly clicked like a chattering castanet, enjoying his finest season ever while taking over for Unitas, who had injured his right elbow (a muscle tear) in the final preseason contest of the year. Morrall guided the Colts to a stellar 13–1 record. On the year, he threw a league-leading 26 touchdowns, with 8.2 percent of his passes going for TDs, which also surpassed all other NFL quarterbacks. He even led the NFL with 16.0 yards gained per each of his completions. For his marvelous play, he was named the league's MVP.

All in all, the day of the Super Bowl was a horrific one for Morrall. He put the ball in the air 17 times for a paltry 71 yards and no scores. Furthermore, he completed just six passes—nine if you count the three passes he completed to the other team in the first half.

Of course, Matte was well aware that Morrall was a good quarterback and didn't blame him for the loss, relating, "Earl had had a wonderful season, let me tell you. We had a wonderful season going in there."

Havrilak noted,

> A combination of a lot of things was why the Colts lost. Morrall didn't enjoy a good game. Namath had a good game. We generally played a lot of zone defense in those days, and they exploited it pretty well. Namath, with his quick release, was able to get the ball in the dead zones pretty well.

The Jets knew the Colts' tendencies. They went to the strong side on almost every running play. They employed the safety blitz quite a bit, leaving an open area for Namath's passes, and they played a zone defense, which, again, was something Namath enjoyed facing.

Matte continued his postmortem, of the game:

> Weeb Ewbank did a very good job of coaching. I thought he did a great job [because] he took advantage of some of our weaknesses because we had a couple of injuries with, I think, Roy Hilton [a defensive lineman], Ordell Braase, and Don Shinnick [right linebacker]. They were not really healthy at that time. So Weeb took advantage of those situations and ran the ball that way.

Volk agreed and elaborated,

> I thought that maybe they felt that they could work on our right defensive side—Don Shinnick was there and Ordell Braase, Lenny Lyles, and me, and that's where they scored. They figured, I guess, they were staying away from Bubba Smith, Mike Curtis, and Billy Ray Smith over there [on the left defensive side].
>
> Snell came off our right side there, and every time I watch the highlights, I still don't tackle Snell. I had a shot at him there, but I missed him and he ran in for the score. That's where they were testing us—also just on short passes. They were just trying to hit George

Sauer on the out cut or Don Maynard also over there—nothing real long, but just moving the ball. That's how they did it.

For the record, Matte did his part and turned in a magnificent Super Bowl III performance. He busted off one run of 58 yards and, in all, rambled for 116 yards, good for 10.5 yards per carry. He also holds another record from that day, which he says no one can ever eclipse. In a 2014 interview, he stated he was the answer to a trivia question: "I was the first player in Super Bowl history to get to 100 yards. Matt Snell ended up with more yards than I did that day, but I got to the 100-yard mark before he did. The 10.5 average is still a record in Super Bowl history, most yards per carry."

Matte continued, "If we would have won the game and they said, 'Where are you going?' I would have said, 'I'm going to Disney World,' because it was one of the better games I ever had, but let me tell you, when you lose, it doesn't mean anything—when you lose a ball game like that."

Matte said it was an especially difficult loss because the Colts entered the game expecting to win. After breezing through the regular season, the Colts topped the Vikings by 10, then crushed Cleveland, 34–0, in a contest Shula still thinks may have been the best game any of the teams he coached ever played. The Colts were a torrid team, with a record of 27–2–2 from the end of 1966 through the whitewashing of the Browns.

From the Jets' point of view, Super Bowl III was a game in which 25-year-old Broadway Joe orchestrated the tempo. He had overcome a poor start to the season—12 interceptions in the season's first five contests—to pilot the Jets to their 11–3 record. After deciding he had to change his pass-happy strategy somewhat, he took Player of the Year honors.

Oftentimes, Namath's best and favorite method of attack was his salvo of long passes, although he did have some fine running backs to support his air game, as Snell proved. Now, in the Super Bowl, the riverboat gambler executed a much more cautious offense, but it was the correct way to go. Keeping the ball on the ground, while consistently chewing up yardage and racking up first down after first down, proved to be the strategy that insured the Jets their Super Bowl win.

Namath's passing game didn't exactly click—even he later conceded he hadn't thrown the ball well—but his runners got the Jets in field position to cash in on three Jim Turner field goals, which provided the nine-point differential New York needed to win.

Namath didn't really get to use his number-one receiver, Maynard, in this game. He threw his way five times, but all five were incomplete (of his 11 total incompletions), with four of the passes being overthrown. Naturally, Weeb wanted Maynard to be a big part of game plan, it just didn't pan out.

Maynard said his lack of involvement as a weapon didn't bother him, commenting,

> Not really. I knew we had an important game to play. Joe was, in a way, you might say, off target. Well, it wasn't by that much. We missed a couple by just a little bit. We might have scored another touchdown—or two.
>
> Every once in a while a pass would be in a situation that he got an extra [heavy] defensive rush on him and he had to get rid of the ball quicker, and that's a part of football. That happens a lot of times with good teams. Number one was to keep trying to win. The Colts tried to disguise coverage, but Joe could read it and get rid of the football ahead of time. So his number-one goal was to get rid of it and be ready for the next play.

Maynard also recalled there was more to his job than just snaring passes, saying, "Naturally, in the passing game, you've got your job that you've got to do—besides running your routes, you've got to entertain for the running situation also. That is, you got a job to do whether it's running or passing."

In other words, Ewbank certainly wanted him involved in the action, even if it wound up only as a blocker or perhaps on some plays as a decoy, a latent threat that, if nothing else, could not be ignored. In fact, because Maynard drew double coverage, Sauer, covered by one defender, was often open. He caught eight passes for 133 yards, both totals tops on the day for any player.

The Colts certainly had to respect Maynard—after all, as he said,

> I ran the 40 in 4.6, 4.5—that was considered fast. I always was careful running in practice because I didn't want to take a chance on pulling a muscle. I would like to say I could run with anybody in the league. Back in track you were considered fast if you could run the 100 in under 10 flat, and I could do that in college.

Namath frequently selected what play to run in the Super Bowl based on the look the Colts gave him at the line of scrimmage. He often set out simply to attack what he perceived to be the weaker spots of the Colts after he had glanced over the defense.

The game wasn't just a tale of quarterbacks, it was also a saga of two fine running backs, Matte and Snell. Because Namath was named the game's MVP, Snell's impact on the game is now glossed over somewhat. Like Matte, Snell was also out of Ohio State, and, like former NFL tight end Chuck Bryant, he was also a member of the '61 Buckeye team that ranked first at season's end in one major poll. Bryant said, "Matt Snell played a little bit of running back for us, but he mostly played 'Monster' on defense. In 1961, he was primarily back there."

In fact, that season Snell ran with the ball just 50 times and would not carry the ball again until he ran for just 491 yards in his final college season, 1963, so there was no strong indication he would churn out 948 yards as an NFL rookie. That season, he also caught 56 passes; at OSU he had a puny 13 receptions in three seasons.

Bryant said, "He was a horse in those days when running backs weren't 230 pounds. They were 175, 180 pounds, but Snell was big and he could run." In Super Bowl III, Snell enjoyed his finest day ever, toting the football 30 of the 43 times the Jets ran for his 121 yards, and the game's first touchdown, the game-winning score in that the Colts never caught up to the Jets after that.

Namath's arm didn't get a big workout on the day. He was, however, prepared to pass with his oh-so-quick release when he sensed blitzes. He didn't throw for a single touchdown (neither team did), going 17-for-28 for 206 hard-gained yards, but was said to have *controlled* the game from the start. The Jets monopolized the football and contained the Colts so well that Baltimore didn't register any third-quarter first downs, and there was no need for Namath to put up a single pass in the final quarter.

Hall of Fame tight end Mike Ditka is a Namath admirer. He believes the average fan probably has no idea how rugged Namath was. He may have had a playboy/pretty boy image, but, said Ditka, "Joe Namath was tough, man. Namath played his career on a leg that nobody else would have played on."

It seems safe to say that another factor contributing to the Colts loss to the Jets was their attitude going into the game as the 18-point favorite (the widest point spread in Super Bowl history) over an opponent from what was supposed to be an inferior league. There's a thin line between being confident and overconfident, but somehow the Colts fit both descriptions.

Volk pointed out one reason the Colts exuded confidence was they were surrounded by talent, and it started at the top. "We had Don Shula as our coach and Carroll Rosenbloom [as the team's owner]—people that you look up to. We had a real good coaching staff," he said.

However, in another way, the Colts were guilty of looking beyond the Jets, feeling too secure that they would win the game with ease. Volk gave an example of that costly approach. The Colts took their wives along for the trip to the game's venue, Miami, Florida, where they stayed an entire week. That would not be the case the next time they went to the title game, two years later. Volk stated, "We went down with a little different attitude against the Cowboys in Super Bowl V."

In short, Volk felt the team wasn't as focused on what should have been their primary—in fact, their *only*—reason for being in Miami. The Colts seemed to a bit too concerned about what they'd do as semitourists. "I think we were too confident," Volk admitted. "We were more or less worried about what we were going to do during the day and evening than we were about getting prepared to play the Jets, who had a good football team, too."

Baltimore's victory in Super Bowl V helped assuage the pain of the loss to the Jets a bit. In fact, the immediate aftermath of the loss to the Jets hurt Volk in more ways than one. He revealed,

> It wasn't a real happy evening after that game, that was for sure. I was in the hospital. I had some things that happened to me, convulsions at the hotel.
>
> The only good thing I'm thinking about is that it was the last game of the year so I didn't have to worry about playing in a week or two. I had the whole offseason to sort of get my mind and my brain right. It really took a long time.

Sam Havrilak, who played with the Colts when they won Super Bowl V, said Baltimore veterans who lost in Super Bowl III spoke of how "they were extremely humiliated and disappointed." He added,

> I got the idea that they kind of took the game for granted because of the history of the AFL, and they didn't think that Namath was all that good of a quarterback, and that the Jets personnel wasn't all that good.

> If you remember the year that the Colts had, I think they set a record
> for scoring points that year, and they had a tremendous amount of total
> offense, and Earl Morrall was having an MVP year. The players were
> just a bit overconfident, I believe.

Colts followers still believe that if the two teams had played nine re-
matches, Baltimore would've won all nine. Mike Curtis believed his
Colts were twice as good as New York. It's no consolation, but the Colts
did win the next four regular-season contests versus the Jets.

As Namath strolled off the field, a victor, he exhibited his confident,
beaming Cool Hand Luke grin and flashed his "We're number one" hand
gesture. With the win, said to be the biggest upset in pro football annals,
he had made good on his guarantee and sent the NFL representatives
whimpering back to Baltimore.

Steve Higgins, like Namath, a native of Beaver Falls, Pennsylvania,
and a man who played his college football at Alabama, said, "You take 10
experts to pick the greatest NFL games ever, and Super Bowl III is
usually number three."

Super Bowl III was not only a stunner and a classic, but also a turning
point, as the Jets had derailed the NFL and deflated the league's ego and
superiority complex. The AFL, in just its ninth year of existence, had
gained parity with the senior league. And *that* was the largest repercussion of the game.

PART II

The Greatest Coaches of the Glory Years

Through the 2017 induction ceremonies, there are 23 coaches in the Pro Football Hall of Fame. It's an impressive fact that 15 of those 23, or 65 percent of them, did at least some of their work in the 1950–1960 era. This book, then, focuses on most of them: Vince Lombardi, Don Shula, Tom Landry, Weeb Ewbank, Paul Brown, Bud Grant, George Allen, Hank Stram, and George "Papa Bear" Halas.

Some greats, such as Chuck Noll and John Madden are not included because they were head coaches in the NFL during the Golden Era for just one season, 1969. Likewise, Greasy Neale, Curly Lambeau, and Steve Owen are omitted because most of their coaching fame came prior to the 1950s, and they coached only a very short time in the 1950s and not at all in the 1960s.

For the record, the rest of the 23 Hall of Fame coaches not mentioned above are Guy Chamberlin, Jimmy Conzelman, Tony Dungy, Ray Flaherty, Joe Gibbs, Sid Gillman, Marv Levy, Bill Parcels, and Bill Walsh.

5

GEORGE HALAS

The Bear Who Never Hibernated

Place of birth: Chicago
Date of birth: February 2, 1895
Date of death: October 31, 1983
Lifetime wins, losses, and ties: 318–148–31
Career winning percentage: .682
Playoff wins and losses: 6–3
Playoff winning percentage: .667
NFL major titles won and years of championships: NFL champs 1921, 1933, 1940, 1941, 1946, 1963
Teams coached and years: Decatur Staleys 1920, 1921; Chicago Bears 1922–1929, 1933–1942, 1946–1955, 1958–1967

George "Papa Bear" Halas goes back so far in pro football, his team was a charter member of the NFL. More to the point, he (and several other men) actually *began* the NFL.

In September 1920, Halas represented his team at a meeting held at the Hupmobile showroom in Canton, Ohio. There, after two hours of labor, he would witness the birth of what is now the NFL. At the end of that meeting, which Halas later insisted ran only about 10 minutes, Jim Thorpe was named the league's president, a unified set of rules was established, and Halas's team became a charter member of the new football league called the American Professional Football Association. The cost per team to join the league? A minuscule $100. Only two of the original 11 teams from that day still live on, the Bears (Staleys) and the Cardinals (originally the Chicago Cardinals).

"George Halas is the founder of the game," began Mike Ditka. "I mean, he started the game of football in this country. He was a great man, and he had a great vision. He knew the game could be much bigger than it was. I don't think he had any concept of what it became, like it has now, but he was just great for the game."

As a quick aside, the NFL has certainly changed since that era. For one thing, in 1921, Halas's title team didn't make money—they reported a loss of $71.63 for the season. They earned his first championship with a 9–1–1 record.

Halas and the City of the Big Shoulders go back seemingly forever. One could say he *was* Chicago. He was born there on Groundhog Day in 1895, and died there on Halloween in 1983, about four months away from his 89th birthday. In between, his name was synonymous with the Bears and football in general.

He played his high school football for Crane Technical High in Chicago, and his college career was spent at the University of Illinois at Urbana–Champaign, where he lettered in football, baseball, and basketball. Even the main part of his nine-year stint in pro football from 1920 to 1928 was spent in a Chicago uniform.

In fact, Halas's professional sports roots go back to May 6, 1919, as a baseball player, not long before Chicago was the epicenter of a shock that left the baseball world reeling. That earthquake of an event was the 1919 World Series, which the "Black Sox" players and gamblers fixed. The scandal took place one year before football became the true calling for Halas.

In his major-league debut, the 24-year-old Halas pulled on Yankees pinstripes and trotted onto the field against the Philadelphia Athletics. He went 1-for-4, giving him a .250 batting average. It would never again be higher than that, and he finished his one season (12 games) in the majors with an anemic .091 batting average. Football, he now realized, was his game.

The following season, the man who joined the Yankees and became their right fielder was a guy named Babe Ruth; however, it is fallacious to say, as some sources and trivia questions state, that the man who followed Halas as *the* Yankees right fielder was the Bambino. Halas roamed Ruth's primary right-field position in just five contests, and he played in his last baseball game on July 5, long before Ruth became a Bronx Bomber. Of the 1919 Yankees outfielders, Sammy Vick played the most games in right field, at 99.

Still, it is true that Halas was a man who played two professional sports—he was once struck out by Walter Johnson, and he was once tackled by Jim Thorpe.

Halas shared many similarities with another baseball legend, Connie Mack, who enjoyed great power and job security, and went back to his sport's infancy. For example, Mack managed the Philadelphia A's for 50 consecutive years from 1901 to 1950, not at all coincidentally, the same years he was a partial or solo owner of the Philadelphia Athletics. As their manager, he lost an astronomical 100-plus games 10 times, but who was going to fire him? Of course, he also holds the record for the most managerial wins ever (and the most losses), and he took his team to nine pennants and five world championships.

Halas was a founding father of the NFL who quickly became one of the most powerful figures in the sport. He also would end up owning the team he coached. In addition, like Mack (whose team once finished last or next-to-last in 11 of 12 straight seasons), Halas went through some hard times, with a nadir of 3–8–1 in 1953, to go with several other seasons with just four or five wins. Also, if playing to a tie is like kissing one's sister, Halas must have showered his sister with passionless smooches to her cheek. Just like Mack, who managed in more tie games, 76, than any other big-league skipper, Halas's 31 career ties, accumulated when such outcomes for games were much more common than nowadays, is the most of any NFL coach. His record for ties is almost 30 percent higher than the man closest to him, Curly Lambeau.

The rule requiring that games that end in regulation play in a tie must go into overtime entered the NFL in 1974; since then, through 2015, there have been just 20 games that have gone into overtime, only to end in a tie.

Halas began his coaching career in 1920, working for entrepreneur A. E. Staley, the owner of the Decatur Staleys, who hired Halas to coach and play for the team. It was a brilliant move—through the 2015 season no other franchise owned as many victories as the Bears.

Halas goes back so far he played and/or coached against some teams in towns and/or with nicknames only historians would recognize, for example, the Racine Legion, the Frankford Yellow Jackets, the Rock

Island Independents, Milwaukee's Badgers, the Dayton Triangles, the Columbus Panhandles, and, in Duluth, a team called the Eskimos.

Furthermore, believe it or not, a town with a population of less than 1,000 named LaRue, Ohio, once hosted an NFL franchise named the Oorang Indians. The team owner also owned the Oorang Dog Kennels. The team played one home game, but because the town didn't even have a football field, the game was held in nearby Marion. Jim Thorpe, who was placed in charge of the team, which was composed of Native Americans, took them on tour to play teams in major cities.

Back then, Halas was listed as a right end and a player/head coach. During his 104-game playing career (85 as a starter), the 6-foot, 182-pound Halas scored 62 points on 10 touchdowns and two extra points made. He was named to the Pro Football Hall of Fame All-1920s Team.

The nickname "Papa Bear" is, of course, fitting (although he was said to be a rather cold, distant "father"). Halas spent 47 years with his team as an executive, and in 40 of those seasons, he was also the head coach. Incredibly, he suffered through just six losing seasons at the helm. Halas firmly ran the figurative family, and, making a patriarchal decision in 1921, he transplanted his team from Decatur to Chicago after one season.

After their successful initial season, 10–1–2 in 1920, the Staleys needed a larger venue, so the team, which would keep that nickname just one more season, moved to Cubs Park (later known as Wrigley Field). The move was a smart call, as the team went 9–1–1 and won the championship, a first for Halas.

Sharing the ballpark with the Cubs inspired the team to go with the nickname Bears in 1922—the logic being that they both dwelt in the same "den," but football players, being larger than baseball players, should go with a name that possessed a larger, more powerful connotation. That was also the year the league made a change, as the American Professional Football Association was renamed the National Football League.

It is hard to fathom, but in 1932, the Bears won the first NFL title game while playing Portsmouth on an indoor field that was just *80* yards long. It's also difficult to imagine a Bears team of that era winning it all without Halas coaching (he was the team's owner), but that year the head coach was Ralph Jones.

Officials considered the frigid weather conditions and decided Wrigley Field's frozen playing surface, which was also adorned with high snowdrifts, was not amenable to putting on a proper show or for determining the league's champion. The game was moved to the world's largest indoor sports arena, Chicago Stadium, home of the Blackhawks.

Special ground rules were put into place, one of which forbade field goals. In addition, teams were required to kick off from the 10-yard line, and another rule mandated that any time a team crossed the 50-yard line, the football was to be moved back 20 yards to make scoring on the short field more legitimate.

Another impossible-to-believe item: Portsmouth's All-Pro quarterback, Earl "Dutch" Clark, who led the league in scoring that season, couldn't play in the game because the boss of his other job as a college basketball coach wouldn't give him the day off.

The wild game featured three more interceptions than completions (five). The Bears cinched a win on a controversial touchdown and, on the very next play from scrimmage, added a safety to make it a 9–0 final outcome. The TD came when Bronko Nagurski began a run from the two-yard line; however, when he spotted no hole, he retraced his steps and fired a pass to Red Grange. The controversy stemmed from a then-existing rule that a passer had to be at least five yards behind the line to throw a legal pass.

In 1933, Halas was back to coach his Bears, who wound up going 10–2–1 and winning the championship by coming back from a 7–6 deficit at the half to win it over the Giants, 23–21. That gave Halas his second championship—his first one that was determined by a postseason game.

The Bears lumbered back to earn a rematch with the Giants in 1934, after going 13–0 on the year. In that clash, the Giants were able to outwit Halas, no small achievement. The Bears, riding high on an 18-game winning streak, held a 10–3 lead over the 8–5 Giants at the half. The scoring was held down because the Polo Grounds turf was covered by ice from a freezing rain the night before.

Reportedly, at least nine of the Giants players tossed aside their cleats in favor of sneakers with about 10 minutes left to play in the fourth quarter after head coach Steve Owen had earlier dispatched Abe Cohen, a clubhouse attendant, to Manhattan College to borrow as many sneakers, or rubber-soled basketball shoes, as he could get his hands on. When play resumed, Halas told his players to nullify any edge the Giants gained by arming themselves with the new footgear by stepping on their toes with their spiked shoes. In the end, the Giants advantage could not be overcome.

Earlier in the third quarter, the Bears had tacked on three more points while holding the Giants scoreless, taking the score to 13–3. But after a timeout for a quick equipment change, New York, now with improved footing, played well and, in the final quarter, handily outscored Chicago, 27–0, figuratively and sometimes literally skating to a 30–13 win. It was the first loss for Halas dating back to November 1933.

It probably would not have mattered, but the Bears played without their record-setting rookie, Beattie Feathers, that day. That season, he had become the first NFL runner to crash the 1,000-yard barrier when he rushed for 1,004 yards under Halas's offensive scheme. His average of 8.4 yards per carry stood until 2006, making him a rookie sensation for the ages. It's noteworthy that Feathers ran the ball 119 times in 1934; in his final six NFL seasons, he never again rushed more than 97 times in a year, averaging just 58 carries per season during that span.

Bronko Nagurski did play versus New York, and he did score the only Chicago touchdown, but, feeling as if he were merely mincing around on the field, he netted just 68 yards on 24 rushes. The Giants strategic move that led to the win caused this contest to become known as the Sneakers Game.

Remarkably, in a "fool me twice, shame on me" scenario, Halas lost the championship again 22 years later due to Giants players once more suiting up with sneakers rather than cleats. In the 1956 title game at Yankee Stadium, temperatures hovering at about 20 degrees turned the field's surface slick, with ice everywhere.

New York held a 13–0 edge as the first quarter ended, as the Yankee Stadium scoreboard lit up like the one Bill Veeck installed in Chicago's Comiskey Field: Giants 34, Bears 7. In the second half, the Bears also switched to sneakers, but it didn't help them much. New York added 13 additional "insurance" points before the clock's dwindling down to zero provided the final relief, a case of euthanasia.

Those shockers aside, Halas goes back so far, he was the most powerful man in the entire league, nearly omnipotent and comfortably unchallenged by the rest of the NFL hierarchy. For many seasons, Halas held so much sway with the league's officials, he often had the referees he favored working his games.

He and Redskins owner George Preston Marshall also rammed home a rule in 1933, changing football forever, when they permitted a forward pass to be thrown from any spot as long as it was behind the line of scrimmage, eliminating rules that had greatly curtailed an exciting aspect of the game.

The new rule soon led to the creation and importance of the T formation quarterback. The monotonous days of run, run, run, with virtually every player hunkered around the line of scrimmage ready to push, push, push, were about to end as the passing game began to open up. The so-called modern T formation was aptly named—more than 80 years later it was still a basic and viable football formation.

Credit for that formation goes to Amos Alonzo Stagg, who came up with the first incarnation of it, but the modern T was the brainchild of Halas and two other men, Clark Shaughnessy from the University of Chicago and Dr. Ralph Jones of Lake Forest College. They revised the T by employing such tactics as putting a back in motion toward the sidelines to draw an opponent away from the middle of the field, and they frequently had the quarterback pass after first faking one or two handoffs to negate a strong pass rush—basically an early play-action pass. Halas was, in fact, the first coach to use the formation in the NFL, doing so with Sid Luckman running his show.

At one point, Halas gave Luckman approximately 60 plays to run, with each one having about six possible variations. Opposing defenses often simply didn't know how to cope with Halas and his offensive plans.

By 1940, Luckman and the Bears, 8–3 on the season, had the formation and its great potential down pat. On December 8, the Bears, who were about to earn the nickname Monsters of the Midway, took on the Redskins for the NFL championship. On the game's second play, Chicago struck for a 68-yard touchdown run. Their next possession lasted 17 running plays, culminated by another TD. By the end of the first quarter, Chicago led, 21–0. The rout was on.

The Bears put 26 and then 19 points on the board during the final two quarters and won by a most improbable score of 73–0. Imagine such a horribly lopsided score in a game that supposedly matched the two best teams in the NFL. The Bears threw the ball just 10 times and, with inexorable efficiency, racked up 382 yards on the ground. That total is just 44 yards shy of the all-time regular-season record and the most ever by a team in a title game, a jaw-dropping 102 yards more than the Super Bowl record held by the Redskins versus Denver.

At one point in the 1940 slaughter, when the Redskins were only losing 7–0, Sammy Baugh's pass to Charlie Malone, standing alone in the end zone, was dropped. After the game, Baugh was asked, "Would the final score have been different if he had caught that pass?" Baugh replied sardonically, "Hell, yes, the score would have been 73–6."

A veritable Thomas Edison of the NFL coaching ranks, Halas, again with the aid of two other men, had devised the counter play a year earlier. That play is not only still a staple of football at many levels, but also Luckman said it was the one play that made other teams go to the T formation. In football, it seems as if for every move there is a counter-move, and this new play came about to attack a defense concocted by Detroit and Green Bay, the 5–4–2 set. Counter plays work when the defense is suckered into going in one direction, only to find the ball is in the hands of a runner going against traffic. Large gains often ensued using this tool.

It's difficult to pin down the date precisely, but as early as 1939, Halas was also putting men in motion, something a fan who grew up during the golden age might think began with a coach like Tom Landry. It is also something still in use and quite valuable. Moreover, Halas was the first coach to hold daily workouts and later the first to put his players through the rigors of two-a-days. He initiated the ideas of scouting and taking films, and he was the first coach to spend 12 months a year on the job.

The 1941 season was like a television rerun, with the Bears again winning it all after going 10–1 through the regular season. They needed a win in the final game to tie for first place, and they got it. Entering their locker room, everyone was jubilant—that is, until they got the news. The Japanese had bombed Pearl Harbor and a war was soon to be declared.

The season went on, however, and Chicago was tied atop their division with the Packers, the only team to defeat them that year. The two met to see who would move on to the title game. The Bears clawed Green Bay, 33–14, then methodically moved on to maul the Giants, 37–9, to finish with a 12–1 record. That contest was witnessed by 13,341 fans, far removed from the attendance figures the league would later draw. From 1940 to 1942, Halas's record was a lusty 26–4, counting postseason games, and his Bears won back-to-back championships.

Halas took the '42 team to a 5–0 record before joining the U.S. Navy. He gave up the coaching reins, handing them over to cocoaches Hunk Anderson and Luke Johnsos, who guided Chicago to an overall record of 11–0; however, the Bears fell to the Redskins in the title game. Halas was also gone the next three full seasons, which featured another NFL title for his Bears in 1943.

In 1946, Halas returned. He replaced his head coaches, who were coming off a 3–7 season, and hired who he thought was the best man to make things right—himself. Months later, he proved his decision to be a wise one when he registered a 9–2–1 record and won his fifth championship, doing so as if it were a ho-hum routine matter to be dispensed with.

Thus, from 1940 to 1946, as a coach and owner, or only as the team owner in absentia, Halas's Bears made five trips to the championship game and won four titles in a splendid span of seven years. Each of those seasons featured Luckman as the quarterback, proving how shrewd Halas was in obtaining the future Hall of Famer.

A quick aside: Halas coached the Bears on four occasions, each time for 10 years before leaving the sidelines, only to return again as the head man. It was almost as if he were an actor on hiatus.

Halas had a tough decision to make in 1948. He still had Luckman when two rookie quarterbacks, Johnny Lujack and Bobby Layne, both number-one draft picks, joined the team. Lujack started three games and Layne got one start, but Halas stuck with the man he once said he loved as a devoted friend, the 32-year-old Luckman. Overly blessed with his three "L's" quarterbacks, Halas reasoned that he could only play one quarterback at a time, so he would simply settle on one man.

Halas decided to trade Layne, who would go on to become a Hall of Famer. To be fair, Layne had hit on only 30.8 percent of his 52 passes in 1948, and posted an abysmal quarterback rating of 49.5. The trade to the New York Bulldogs gave the Bears $50,000 and New York's first-round draft pick in 1950 (one which didn't pan out), but the money was good by the standards of the day.

As for Lujack, in 1949, he took over and immediately led the league in touchdowns, yards through the air, pass attempts, and completions; however, he lasted just two more seasons in the NFL. Meanwhile, Luckman also saw his career winding down, starting only a pair of games in 1949 and 1950, his final season. Halas had to retool, and he would not win the championship again until 1963.

After sitting out the 1956 and 1957 seasons, he began his fourth stint coaching. Several seasons later, he did notch his sixth and final championship. That came when his miserly defense, ranked first in six major categories, helped the Bears go 12–1–2. Almost half of the defensive unit made First Team All-Pro: Rosey Taylor, Richie Petitbon, Joe Fortunato, Doug Atkins, and Bill George. No Bear ran for more than 446 yards, but Mike Ditka did shine on offense, with almost 800 yards on catches.

Chicago again faced the Giants for the title, and this time they earned their rings in a narrow 14–10 win to top off a great season. In that defensive struggle, the Giants scored a first-quarter touchdown before the Bears defense dug in and held them to a second-quarter field goal.

The Bears' 1965 first-round draft may well have been the most productive one ever, as Chicago picked up Dick Butkus as the third player chosen and spent their next choice to make Gale Sayers the number-four player drafted. George Allen, the team's defensive coordinator and personnel director, deserves quite a bit of credit for the draft coup. Halas gets credit, too, for opening up his change purse, albeit reluctantly, to sign the stars. The frugal Halas paid Butkus and Sayers more than he had ever forked over for any other player. Butkus inked a $200,000 deal for five years, and Sayers signed for $100,000 for four seasons.

Unfortunately for the luminaries involved, Halas and his Bears never won a championship with these stars. Even with great coaching, it often comes down to the "you gotta have the horses" (and more than just two) concept. As Ditka pointed out, "Most good coaches are made because they have good players—remember that." Sometimes not even having two of the game's greatest players ever on the same team can overcome an overall lack of horses in one's stable. Sure, give credit to Halas for obtaining Butkus and Sayers, but the best mark Chicago could muster with those two superstars under Halas was 9–5 in '65.

Sayers frequently went up against Butkus in practices and said Halas immediately advised him to beware of Butkus because he would knock his ass off.

In his own way, Halas could be as bellicose as Butkus. Sportswriter Red Smith shares an anecdote about Halas in his book *The Red Smith Reader*. During one game, Halas became contentious with referee Jim Durfee even though Durfee happened to be his friend. Smith related their encounter, which began when Durfee began stepping off a five-yard penalty. An infuriated Halas asked what the penalty had been for, and Durfee replied it was for coaching from the sideline, an infraction in the 1920s.

Halas shouted, "Well, that just proves how dumb you are. That's 15 yards, not five."

"Yeah," said Jim, "but the penalty for your kind of coaching is only five yards."

Durfee also bested Halas another time when he was marching off a 15-yard penalty against the Bears. Halas bellowed, "You stink!" At that point, writes Smith, "Jim just marched off another 15 yards, then turned and shouted, 'How do I smell from here?'"[1]

The crusty, short-tempered Halas was demanding and sometimes implacable. After a loss to an inferior team in 1961, he fumed and would not allow his team to have anything to drink when the team flew back to Chicago.

In a way, Halas was the Branch Rickey of the NFL. He was the first coach to put an African American quarterback into an NFL contest, just as Rickey desegregated Major League Baseball when he signed Jackie Robinson to a Brooklyn Dodgers contract. Halas's pioneer was a man who possessed an apt name for a quarterback, Willie Thrower. Halas signed him out of Michigan State in 1953, as a free agent.

Veteran sportswriter Chuck Finder recalled Thrower's NFL debut:

> George Halas threw him into a game after Blanda didn't do well. The Bears were losing, I think it was 21–0, at Soldier Field, and Willie led them downfield, and he got to about the 10-yard line—this is the fourth quarter, late in the game. And Halas pulled Thrower and put Blanda back in the game. It was kind of an interesting debut for an African American quarterback in the NFL. He was kind of a mop-up guy and didn't get to finish. I think that was the only NFL game he really ever played, too.

Actually, Thrower's last pass was picked off. While he never again played even a single down after he had completed three of eight throws for 27 yards, he made history that day, way back on October 18, 1953.

Halas and Lombardi had an interesting relationship. Dave Robinson, who, as a Packer, played for years in the same division as the Bears, said,

> Vince Lombardi said George Halas was the only man in the league he called Coach. He was a great coach. Vince had a great deal of respect for him, and they were very friendly.
>
> At the same time, they had this thing going on where he'd always talk about George Halas spying on us. One time there was a rumor that Halas wanted to pay $10,000 for a Green Bay Packer playbook. And Vince said, "Hell, I'll send him one. Then let him try to figure out

when we're going to run the plays." There was a great rivalry between him and George Halas, and they played off each other. They both talked about the other guy being a spy and did all this stuff.

Vince gave us all new jersey numbers in practice because he said Halas had spies coming to watch. Every time we played the Bears there was a car in our parking lot. Vince always said that was George's spy coming to watch the practice. So, to throw him off, we all wore different numbers. In practice I wore Tommy Crutcher's number, 56.

Robinson chuckled that he wasn't sure such a tactic "fooled anybody who was looking," adding, "because I was the only black linebacker any way, but that was part of the mind game to get us ready."

Robinson continued,

We played them in Wrigley Field, and Halas supposedly rented an apartment above Wrigley Field, and he'd look down into the field. We had Saturday practices there, and we always ended up those practices every year with a fake punt/pass to Willie Davis. We never used it. Vince said, "That's for George Halas's spy up there." I don't know if George had someone up there or not, but it was something to fire us up—that George was spying on us. But he and Vince were very good friends.

Halas, by the way, did not feel the same way about George Allen. When Allen was the Rams coach and was about to play the Packers in 1967, Halas sent extra reels of film of the Rams to Lombardi to help him prepare for the game. Halas hated the Rams because Allen had once been his assistant coach—that is, until Allen broke his contract to take the head job in Los Angeles. Being an enemy of the powerful Halas wasn't wise.

Being coached by Halas was quite a different matter—simply stated, Halas knew his stuff. Ditka recalled Halas saying their first objective was to "control your division if you're going to get into the playoffs and control your destiny in the playoffs. We based everything on that."

When Ditka was coming out of college, Pittsburgh, San Francisco, and Washington were interested in him, but only Halas saw him as an offensive player; the rest wanted him as a linebacker. Ditka would go on to become the first tight end inducted into the Hall of Fame.

Ditka recalled that Halas and Luke Johnsos "revolutionized the position," making him the first tight end to "ever split out to get off the line of scrimmage." He continued, "Coach Halas was the reason for all that, not me. He's the one who made it what it was."[2]

Ditka says the reason other teams didn't envision his offensive greatness was "because all of my credentials in college, really, were on defense. We didn't throw the ball at Pitt. My senior year I caught 14 passes or something." It was actually 11, giving him just 45 receptions in three seasons.

Ditka added,

> I was really a better defensive football player at end than I was an offensive football player. And that's why they thought I would be a linebacker. George Halas was the only one [who thought otherwise]. He told me for the first time when he signed me, "You're not going to play linebacker. You're going to play tight end." I said, "What?!"

After the initial astonishment dissipated, Ditka told Halas the switch was fine, adding, "Whatever you want me to play, I'll play." Ditka looked back, saying,

> I think he saw the evolution of the game. You can't just [go to] your outside relievers, you had to have a guy inside to throw the ball to— you had to have a guy inside who could block the linebackers and the defensive ends, and that's what I did. I blocked a lot, and I enjoyed blocking. It was okay, fun.
>
> And thank God that he did [switch me] because the architects of that offense at that time were Jim Dooley and George Halas. They got the tight end so involved in the offense that they were throwing me the ball all the time.

In 1964, for example, the year before Gale Sayers came along, the Bears had no running game—their top ground gainer, Jon Arnett, had a trifling 400 yards. Ditka recalled that Halas tried to boost the Bears with an air attack, commenting, "We didn't have a very good record, but I caught 75 passes and Johnny Morris caught 93 passes." They accounted for three yards short of 2,100 yards on receptions.

On May 27, 1968, after a virtual lifetime in the game, Halas announced his retirement—his fourth departure from the coaching ranks. He was 73 years old, almost 20 years older than when he had first promised his wife he would call it quits.

Halas, who as owner, or, in some years, owner and head coach, had once seen his Bears play in the title game eight times in a dozen years, winning it all five times. That stretch also included his team chalking up three titles during a four-year span. In a longer period, the Bears made it to the title game nine times in 15 years, winning six championships. That may not quite be a monopoly, but it was a Bears era of exceptional domination.

Halas also earned Coach of the Year honors in the 1963 title season and again two years later at the age of 70. That season, his Bears finished third, but he wowed voters by capturing nine of his last 11 contests.

The list of great players he coached is seemingly endless, including, to list just a handful of Hall of Famers, Red Grange, Bronko Nagurski, Bill George, Doug Atkins, Gale Sayers, Mike Ditka, Dick Butkus, and Sid Luckman, who was the first man to be acquired by using a first draft pick that had been obtained by trading away a veteran player—yet another Halas "first."

Halas passed away in 1983, about two years from the day Ditka, the man he had hired to lead the Bears in 1982, took them to another Chicago championship, their only Super Bowl victory. Halas's funeral cortege was the longest one since 1976, when Mayor Richard Daley was laid to rest.

Halas became a charter member (one of 17) of the Pro Football Hall of Fame. To review, his credentials included coaching stints that ran from 1920 to 1929, from 1933 through the early part of the 1942 season, then from 1946 to 1955 and again from 1958 through 1967. Twice after being away from the coaching ranks, his resumption of that job immediately resulted in championship seasons, as if starting anew was simply a routine matter.

Conversely, losing can be gut-wrenching, not unlike being kicked in the groin by one's sister, and Halas suffered through 148 lifetime coaching losses. Of course, that comes with the territory when coaching as long as he did. On the other hand, this legend won 318 contests, winning almost 70 percent of his regular-season and playoff contests, and six pro football championships. Through 2015, the Bears had completed 97 seasons and won 741 games. Halas was the main man with the clipboard in 43 percent of those wins.

Many players owe a debt to Halas. Ditka said,

He gave me my first job as a player—he drafted me number one—and he gave me my first job as a coach. He signed me to a head coaching job in 1982. He told me when he signed me, "I brought you here to win us a championship," so that's why I was there, and we were fortunate enough to have enough good players that we did it.

Unfortunately, added Ditka, "He passed away in '83, so he never got to see the [1985 Super Bowl] championship."

Ditka said that while Halas didn't toss his money around freely, believing a person had to earn what he got, he was, nevertheless, on the spot to help someone in need. He even helped Ditka get a good deal when he bought his first house.

Robinson said Halas "was one of the guys who put his own money on the line to get the team going. He and the Rooneys." Such a move displays gutsiness, self-confidence, and great foresight. Don Maynard called Halas a "great winner, and, just like the rest of the greats, when he got out there it was going to be a tough night."

Floyd Little said although Halas was a "little bit before my time, his name is synonymous with the Hall of Fame, and Hall of Famers, and success." He continued, "He had a great passion for the game. His name speaks loudly around the National Football League and the Hall of Fame. In fact, the Hall of Fame is on George Halas Drive." That alone says it all.

Halas has been called the most influential figure in NFL history. Author Brad Herzog wrote a book in which he selects the most important people in the overall history of American sports. He lists Halas as number 14 and states that no other sports figure has been linked to one team for more years than Halas. Herzog further notes that most of his selections were people who were known for "creation, transformation, and long-term guidance" in their field. He states that none of his 100 picks combined all three of those criteria as much as Halas did, calling him the "most important person in the history of professional football."[3] That certainly sums up this powerful, prolific man.

6

PAUL BROWN

"Act Like You've Been There Before"

Place of birth: Norwalk, Ohio
Date of birth: September 7, 1908
Date of death: August 5, 1991
Lifetime wins, losses, and ties: 213–104–9
Career winning percentage: .672
Playoff wins and losses: 9–8
Playoff winning percentage: .529
NFL major titles won and years of championships: AAFC (All-American Football Conference) champs 1946–1949; NFL champs 1950, 1954, 1955
Teams coached and years: Cleveland Browns 1946–1962; Cincinnati Bengals 1968–1975

Paul Warfield provided ample commentary on Paul Brown's career. The Hall of Fame receiver broke into the NFL with Cleveland in 1964, two years after Brown's last season there, but he said,

> Growing up in Warren, Ohio, I was an avid sports fan of all of the Cleveland teams, and, of course, the most noted sports team was the Cleveland Browns from the time they came into existence; and certainly through all of Paul Brown's coaching career in Cleveland he was known as one of the best, if not the top, football coaches in professional football.

But his legend goes beyond that to high school football in Massillon, Ohio, and then at my alma mater, Ohio State University. He
continued his legendary coaching path there before World War II.
Then afterward he joined the Browns.

Actually, Brown spent 1930 and 1931, his first two years coaching, at
Severn Prep School, where he won the Maryland state championship in
his first year on the job. Returning to his home state and the high school
he had played for, his Massillon (Washington High) Tigers lost only eight
times during his nine seasons there, going 80–8–2. In his final six seasons, his record was a gaudy 58–1–1. During that time, Massillon outscored opponents by an impossible-to-believe 2,393 to 168 margin.

In his last season, 1940, the Tigers played Kent State University in a
spring contest, and, get this, the high school team won and did so by the
lopsided score of 47–0. That season, Massillon played in front of 116,000
spectators, a total higher than that of any college in the state with the
exception of Ohio State.

High school football there dates back to 1894, and the Tigers' most
famous coach was, by far, Massillon alum Paul Brown. He didn't win the
state title in his first three seasons, but from 1935 through his final year
there, he won a phenomenal six straight championships for his old high
school—a school so rich in football excellence they have won 22 state
titles and nine national championships (from 1935 to 1961), the most
ever. Brown coached four of those nine national champs.

One year—and this is no misprint—his team went through the entire
season without punting the ball once. In his last Massillon season, his
Tigers slammed 477 points on the board, while surrendering six. His
school was harvested for 23 professional football players. It's no wonder
the Tigers now play on their field inside Paul Brown Tiger Stadium,
which sits on a street also named after him.

Moving on, Brown even took the Buckeyes to their first national title
in 1942, in just his second season as a college coach. His Ohio State
record was 18–8–1. In 1944 and 1945, he coached the Great Lakes Naval
Training Center team called the Bluejackets, who played against other
service teams and some college teams. He went 9–2–1 in 1944, and was
ranked in the AP's top 20. The next year, the most satisfying of his six
wins was a 39–7 drubbing of Notre Dame.

He later became the first, and most successful, head coach of the
Browns. The city of Cleveland has experienced world champion teams

thanks to the Cavs once, the Indians twice, and the Browns eight times—and seven of those championships were supplied by Brown.

Most experts contend Paul Brown, with an enormous assist to quarterback Otto Graham, was the first coach to mold a true pro football dynasty, figuratively owning a huge chunk of the decade of the 1940s and 1950s.

Graham had been a tailback at Northwestern when that team gave Brown's Buckeyes their only loss of 1941, throwing two touchdown passes in their 14–7 victory.

From 1946 to 1955, his Browns, with Graham at quarterback, played in 10 consecutive championship games, a feat unprecedented and still unmatched. From 1946 to 1949, his Browns went 47–4–3 in regular-season play, winning four AAFC titles in a row. A tie against Cleveland was not unfulfilling, it was more of a moral victory, and a rare victory over them was more of a miracle.

During Graham's career, his record as the starting quarterback stood at a lofty 105–17–4, which translates to an average season record better than 10–2, as he won 86 percent of his starts (ignoring ties).

After joining the NFL in 1950, the Browns won three of the six straight championship games they took part in, giving them seven titles in just 10 seasons. Graham and Brown engineered a win–loss percentage of .750 in Graham's 12 playoff games, forming an almost unbeatable combination. One could say that just as remora fish and sharks share a symbiotic association, Graham and Brown enjoyed a mutually beneficial relationship.

In 1948, Brown took his team through an undefeated season, going 14–0 in the regular season and capping things off with yet another win in the title game. Brown won the AAFC crown again the next year, refusing to slam on the brakes even though his league disbanded. His team smoothly shifted over to join the NFL, and Brown proceeded to win that league's championship three out of six seasons: 1950, 1954, and 1955.

As the upstart entry into the league in 1950, the Browns were thought to be an inferior unit (just as the AFL Jets would later be considered a team incapable of defeating the NFL's mighty Colts in Super Bowl III). Instead, the Browns proved their worth starting with a stunning win on opening day against the reigning NFL champs, the Eagles, winning in a breeze, 35–10. Cleveland would make it to the title game seven more times in the decade. Brown's Browns were far from being upstarts.

Vince Lombardi's Packers would later own the NFL's second dynasty. When Lombardi was hired by the Giants as an assistant, one of the first things he did was watch films of Giants games from the previous two seasons. Always thorough, his goal was to boost the team's offense, so he also made it a point to pay special attention to one particular coach, Paul Brown. Lombardi's scrutiny opened a new world for him and increased his respect for Brown and his genius on the offensive side of things.

Brown certainly knew how to put together a good squad, and not just on offense. Clearly a consistent winner, his only poor season occurred in 1956, when he had to replace Graham—he couldn't—and Cleveland went 5–7 using three quarterbacks as starters. Even after that losing season, Brown was resilient, taking the Browns to a 9–2–1 record and a trip to the NFL championship contest the next season.

Incidentally, that year, 1957, Brown proved himself to be resourceful. Without Graham, he turned mainly to Tommy O'Connell to fill in at the quarterback spot. O'Connell's previous play gave no indication he could help take any team to the title game. He had broken in with Chicago in 1953, but being behind George Halas's starter, George Blanda, O'Connell never once cracked the starting lineup. O'Connell didn't play in the NFL in 1954 or 1955, but the Browns were forced to give him five starts the next year, the season the Browns went 5–7. Somehow Brown coaxed some productivity out of O'Connell the subsequent season, as he went 7–1–1 as a starter.

Resorting to his old pattern, O'Connell was not on an NFL roster the next two years (Brown had settled on Milt Plum as his next quarterback), but an expansion Buffalo Bills team took him. For his two years there, his starting quarterback record was 1–5–1. Not counting the season Brown used him extensively, O'Connell's lifetime record was 4–7–1.

So, how had Brown managed to win the East Division with a journeyman quarterback? Brown, no dummy, relied heavily on a rookie fullback out of Syracuse by the name of Jim Brown. That season, for the first of five straight years, Brown topped the NFL in rushing. Along the way, he was named the league's MVP. While Brown scored 10 touchdowns, one of his lower season totals, almost all were meaningful ones. One of his touchdowns allowed the Browns to draw into a tie in a game they went on to win, and seven of his scores gave the Browns the lead, with only one coming in a contest the Browns trailed in and eventually lost. In fact, all of his touchdowns but that one came in a Cleveland victory.

Paul Brown knew how to ride a winning horse, and Jim Brown was a most durable workhorse. Cleveland sportswriter Bob August stated Brown started every Cleveland game in his entire nine seasons and missed only one entire series of plays.

Despite Paul Brown's act of legerdemain, turning a team with only one big offensive gun in 1957 into a division champion, there was only one obstacle he could not overcome—a power struggle with Art Modell, Browns owner. Modell had purchased the Browns in 1961, and by the end of the 1962 season, he had become disgruntled because Brown hadn't taken his team to the title game since 1957. Some critics felt Modell was impatient and egomaniacal, and noted that he openly second-guessed Brown. It wasn't long before the relationship between owner and coach became uncomfortably strained and eventually totally deteriorated.

It didn't matter to Modell that Brown's records in the previous two seasons before he axed Brown were 8–5–1 and 7–6–1, decent, but not great, results. What did matter, *a lot*, was the fact that Brown didn't kowtow to him. Once, when Modell dropped by the team's locker room and remained while Brown gave his pregame talk to his men, Brown asked him to never do that again, saying he didn't belong there. *That*, of course, didn't sit well with Modell. Paul Brown was a man who had to be in control at all costs, and he would soon pay the cost for that characteristic. It was a "this town ain't big enough for the both of us" scenario.

Bernie Parrish, a Cleveland defensive back, felt that toward the end of Brown's days in Cleveland, the game was passing him by and/or he was too authoritative. Many veterans, including the influential Jim Brown, usually a backer of his coach (one who later said Modell's dismissal of Brown was like firing God), felt it was time for a change.

Cleveland has always been a football town, and the real glory days there are still traced back to Brown. Even right after he was fired, the Browns outdrew the Indians. The Browns' home attendance for seven regular-season home dates, plus an exhibition contest at old, cavernous Cleveland Municipal Stadium, was 570,648, while the Indians played host to just 562,507 fans in the course of 73 more games than the Browns played at the same venue.

There were many fans who still wanted Paul Brown to guide *his* Browns to make *their* Browns a relevant team. The fans had suffered through just one losing season during Brown's 17-year tenure in Cleveland. They were cognizant of the fact that Brown had been the team's only coach since their inception in the AAFC in 1946. His firing was shocking, much like the dismissal of Tom Landry by the Dallas Cowboys. To be fair, after Brown was fired, there was roughly an equal amount of Browns fans who did feel it was time to hire a new man for the job.

After all, Brown could be rather aloof, some say even cold and cruel, and he was fired during a period in which he had gone five seasons without winning a championship. His record under Modell was a lackluster 15–11–2. Still, how many teams wouldn't drool over the prospect of winning one title (as Brown did) in a six-year span—or winning it all in virtually *any* span, for that matter.

This was a man who had taken the Browns to the championship game 10 years in a row. He won 158 games for Cleveland, good for a .767 winning percentage. Despite such credentials, in 1963, Brown was out of coaching but kept a titular front-office job for the Browns at $82,500 a year. Meanwhile, Blanton Collier, who earlier had taken over for Bear Bryant at Alabama, replaced Brown, earning $20,000 per season, half of what Jim Brown received that year. Of course, Brown ran for more yards that season than all but two of the NFL's 14 teams.

Brown rebounded from being fired by Modell in January 1963, going on to cofound the expansion Cincinnati Bengals. Granted his demand for total control of the team, he accepted the challenge of taking charge of a fledgling Bengals squad at the age of 60. Just as he had been the first coach and general manager of the Browns, now he was the first man to run the Bengals—once again as head coach and general manager.

Back in his home state and ready to operate once more, Brown took a bunch of castoffs and formed the first Cincinnati squad in 1968, and just two seasons later that team won their division, making the playoffs. Plus, he was able to mold an expansion club into one good enough to make it to postseason play in three of his eight seasons as coach of the Bengals.

His overall record with Cincinnati was 55–56–1, which, to some people's way of thinking, diminishes his accomplishments there, but that record in his eight seasons with the Bengals was a better one for any expansion team ever in its first eight years, with the exception of Miami. By the way, most of the Miami success back then came under another coach of the golden era, Don Shula. His Dolphins won 46 of the franchise's 61 wins in the team's initial eight seasons.

Brown retired at the age of 67, going out on top in 1975, with an 11–3 record, after coaching 45 years. During that time frame, Brown had gained renown for his ability to produce winning teams. Even into the 1980s, he won as the Bengals owner and general manager. It was Brown who selected the coaches and, to a large degree, the Cincinnati players who would go to the Super Bowl twice before he departed from the game.

An examination of just how he became such a consistent winner—his inventive ways, his methods, and his organizational skills—is in order.

Brown is said to be the second most prolific innovator in football history, behind only the "Father of American Football," Walter Camp of Yale fame. Brown is also said to be the first coach to scout other teams using game film (he even filmed some practices dating back to his days at Massillon), the first to use game film to grade his players, and the first to put together playbooks. During meetings, he made players take notes, jotting them down in notebooks as if they were back in a college class-room. The collegial parallel was extended when he also required his players to take tests to show whether they had mastered his playbook.

Brown also is credited with devising the taxi squad, concocting the draw play, and inventing the modern version of the facemask. When opponents began to grab the Browns by those masks, Brown had the masks wrapped with tape, under which were tacks pointing outward. The wholesale grabbing ceased.

The list goes on. He was even the first coach to have his team spend the night in a hotel before a home game. He initiated the practice, still in use, of timing players in the 40-yard dash. He knew the average punt traveled that distance, so he wanted to know how fast his men would be if placed on the coverage squad. In addition, it was Brown who came up with the idea of having his offensive linemen form a protective pocket around his passer, and he is also said to be the first coach to send plays in from the sidelines.

Then, there was his early use of the two-minute drill. Raymond Berry remembers how efficiently his Colts practiced and then executed the two-minute drill, especially, and most memorably, in the 1958 title game; however, he believes his coach, Weeb Ewbank, learned that tactic when he was Paul Brown's offensive line coach.

Paul Warfield said,

History shows clearly that he was a coach who was ahead of his time, particularly in the National Football League, with his concepts, ideas, innovations, and organization—all of the things that are very much a part of the NFL today.

If, as the legend goes, and I could be slightly inaccurate here, but if you take one idea, such as communication, he was a forerunner in terms of communication between him and his players, mainly the quarterback, while a game was in progress. This concept of his started with his calling the plays for his quarterback, and at a time when all the second-guessers or the sportswriters felt like quarterbacks being on the field, being aware of what's happening and going on during the course of the game, should call their plays. But Paul Brown called the plays for his quarterbacks with the Browns.

Initially, his method of doing that was the exchange of one player position on every play, and that was the messenger guard system, in which two players would play, let's say for example, the left guard position. Both had starting team abilities, but he would rotate them every play, and legendary coach Chuck Noll was one of his messenger guards. So he would rotate with another guard, taking the play in on every down.

Noll, of course, was destined to become a Hall of Fame coach himself. Warfield continued,

Brown wanted to improve on that system, as the legend goes, and he wanted to have the capacity *not* to rotate guards—he wanted his very best guard to play every play instead of being rotated with another guard who may have slightly lesser ability. He then went over to Case Western University to consult with their engineering department to come up with a device that would enable him on the sidelines, through essentially a walkie talkie, to give the quarterback his command or the play selection on every play.

Apparently, what occurred was they worked on the project, came up with a device, much as the system is today, which, if you trace its history, really wasn't fully implemented until after my time playing in pro football, which ended in the mid-1970s. Certainly by the '90s, devices were placed in all quarterbacks' helmets throughout the league.

But Paul Brown's early experiment did not work. It worked when they tried it out, practicing it, but when they tried to implement it, for some reason, the technology was not as advanced, not perfected enough, and there were other radio signals in the area—so during the course of the ballgame when they tried to implement the direct contact, the device was picking up another signal of a radio station in the area. So, of course, they junked it, but here he was back in the '50s with his innovation that wouldn't become a part of NFL until [38 years later in 1994]. That's how far ahead he was.

Two opposing assistant Giants coaches, Lombardi and Landry, tried to combat the radio transmissions. They had benchwarmer Bob Topp in charge of a radio receiver that could pick up Brown's signals.

Topp would then tell teammate Gene Filipski, who had spent time on the Browns squad, to translate Cleveland's terminology. Filipski would tell Landry what play had been called, and Landry would signal what defense to go with. Brown had come up with a good scheme in theory, but it didn't last long versus the Giants because Cleveland's quarterback, George Ratterman, finally told his coach that he was unable to hear the transmission above the din of the crowd. That and a subsequent ruling from the commissioner, Bert Bell, ended the experiment and the espionage.

When Brown's plan to become a sort of disc jockey broadcasting to an audience of one, his quarterback, was scrapped, he went back to his guards shuttling plays to the quarterback. While that was not the most practical method of communication, it was one that was later borrowed by another Hall of Fame coach, Tom Landry.

One problem with the guards acting as ferry boats traveling to and from quarterback Otto Graham was it sometimes resulted in a play being called that Graham believed wouldn't work after he had surveyed the defense. He said he sometimes vetoed Brown's calls, but he was wise enough to do this rarely, unwilling to rile his boss. Graham believed that Brown's play-calling sometimes became predictable and that his strong reluctance for his quarterbacks to call "automatics," or audibles, because he felt that often led to mistakes, could border on the ludicrous.

In the Graham era, Brown was pretty much the exception to rule that coaches permitted their quarterbacks to call their plays, although Graham has stated he did call plays in his first five seasons, and the Browns won championships yearly during that time period. Graham felt as if Brown handcuffed him. To Graham, it was almost as if Brown was being draconian in his treatment of his quarterback because he felt that to deny a veteran quarterback the right to exercise his experience and his brain for play-calling led to atrophy. When a quarterback sees no need to think for himself but merely carries out the plays that have been called for him, great opportunities to exploit a defense often go by the board.

In any case, that philosophical difference aside, Brown truly was a visionary. Warfield, a college running back and defensive back who Brown converted to a wide receiver, said Brown was far ahead of the other teams organizationally. He related,

> When he started out most of the teams did not have his kind of organization with playbooks and that sort of thing. They did not do intelligence testing. Football was a barbaric game in which you lined up guys on one side, and they were the guys who were the toughest, the strongest, the meanest, with less thought about strategies and so forth. Mainly the team that was the most physical would win the game. He brought an entire [new] element into pro football.
>
> And then organization in terms of practice sessions—highly structured to the moment in terms of what they were going to do, and practices were very efficient. They were designed to emphasize from a mental aspect what his team would be doing and how precise they would be doing those things, and how structured it was. Those were just some of the innovations that I was aware of, and there were a number of others, so, yes, he was a very innovative person.

Brown felt practices should be short and stress repetition through drills, and also not be so rough his players would have nothing left for Sundays.

Mike Ditka had a concise take on Brown, stating, "I played against Cleveland when he was coaching. He had good football teams. They were always very well prepared." Tom Landry agreed, saying the Browns were physical under Brown, but they also won by using precision.

Like any complex man, Brown had a multidimensional personality. He has been described as autocratic, dedicated, almost obsessive, a taskmaster, a stern disciplinarian with rigid rules, and a powerful owner and league pioneer hell-bent on getting his way. Regardless, players wanted to play for him.

He demanded his players wear jackets and ties when they hit the road, and they were never to swear, drink, or smoke around him. On nights before games, players were to be in bed by 10:00 p.m., and bed checks were routinely conducted.

Former Brown Paul Wiggin recalled Brown giving an annual speech to his troops saying he had never once had to fine a player for rules violations. When Wiggin was a rookie, he asked veteran Lou Groza how that could possibly be true—was Brown that lenient? Groza replied, no, that certainly wasn't the case; the explanation was simply that no one ever broke Brown's rules. Now that's respect and/or fear.

Warfield said although he didn't play for Brown, he heard from other players who had, and he came away with some impressions. He said,

> I wouldn't call him authoritarian, I would say that certainly he was demanding. I think that aspect was very much a part of Paul Brown, who was demanding for preciseness, for people understanding—a real teacher's approach was Brown's, which I think is somewhat missing today as I look around, certainly in pro football.
>
> Many people who are a part of the coaching fraternity have kind of lost this aspect of teaching and developing players—even though players should be fully developed by the time they come to the National Football League. Certainly, other aspects of teaching should come into play. I think that computers are wonderful today, and you get great information, but hands-on emphasis on some of the requirements from yesterday, I think, are missing.

For the record, Warfield said one NFL organization, not coincidentally the most successful one, is not lacking in such elements—the Patriots, a team he called a "throwback to what we're talking about."

Speaking of throwbacks, long ago players made it a point not to show others up. One famous story that demonstrates NFL social mores dates back to Brown, a man who, in some ways, was the opposite of Vince Lombardi. Brown didn't yell at his players, and he seldom scolded them, especially to the press or in public (but when he did, he could make a player cringe); however, he did have his limits. When one of his players scored a touchdown and then went into a "look at me" flashy, grandstanding celebration in the end zone, Brown called the player aside, gave him a withering look, and simply said, "Act like you've been there before."

First of all, as Brown knew, it's a team sport, and the player didn't score on his own—he had solid blocking and perhaps a perfect pass thrown his way as well. Secondly, it wasn't as if his touchdown had won the NFL championship, so calm down—and don't antagonize the opponents. The attitude of placing the team before the individual was what most people believed in back then—certainly Brown did—as was the belief that one should display some class and not disrespect opponents.

Brown himself was so respected, even revered by many, that the Bengals' home venue was named Paul Brown Stadium. Furthermore, and even more impressive, is the fact that his first NFL team was named after him, surely a first and a last in the NFL. Don Shula is the winningest coach ever, but he didn't lead the Miami Shulas. Many legendary coaches have a field or basketball court named after them, but, again, you'll never hear of a team like the Duke Krzyzewskis or the New York Stengels.

Actually, the origin of the nickname for Cleveland's NFL franchise is not totally clear. Some say it was named after heavyweight boxing champ Joe Louis, nicknamed the "Brown Bomber," but that seems doubtful. A more likely story has it that in 1945, team owner Arthur McBride held a contest to determine the nickname. The most popular submission from fans was "Browns," as a tribute to the coach; however, Brown initially turned down the honor, saying he preferred the name Panthers, but when a Cleveland businessman let it be known that he owned the rights to the name "Cleveland Panthers" and wouldn't give it up unless he were paid, that choice of nickname was vetoed by McBride. Brown soon relented, allowing the team to take his surname for its moniker.

Praise for Brown comes from many sources. Mel Renfro played for him in Pro Bowl games. Remembered Renfro,

> He was a very nice man. You'd almost think he wasn't a coach because he was so nice and calm and easy spoken. He really treated all of us that way in the Pro Bowl. I got along with him really well. He was an excellent coach because that was in the Jim Brown era, and they were winning a lot.

Jim Brown respected his color-blind coach for breaking down barriers, helping to integrate the NFL by signing black players. Paul Brown's first pro team featured two black rookies, bruising runner Marion Motley (from Massillon's rival school, Canton McKinley) and middle guard Bill Willis, two future Hall of Famers.

"What a great guy he has been to the game of football," said Floyd Little. "His name is synonymous with the game of football and the success of the game. And what he did for football is remarkable. He's a guy that we all know who he is and what he's done. Kudos to him for all he's done."

While many have praised Brown's offensive bent, Little noted, "He was an unbelievable defensive kind of coach. He brought a diehard, hard-nosed philosophy to the game. I think he was a defensive genius."

Raymond Berry agreed with Little, relating,

> He was a genius of a coach. He was a very small man physically, he always wore a suit, tie, and hat the day of the game, and he was cerebral. He mastered something that I learned from studying him and Ewbank—that it takes a genius to keep things simple. Weeb experienced up close one of Brown's stupendous strengths—Brown had very, very few plays.
>
> He was one of the most brilliant coaches that's ever been in the football business, and he only used about six or eight running plays, and, I don't know, eight, 10 pass plays. Simplicity and soundness. Weeb either had that same philosophy himself when he first coached there or he learned them from Brown, and he never varied from it.
>
> The significance of that is when a player is absolutely, no doubt, sure of what he's doing when the ball is snapped, his physical and mental abilities flow at full speed. When the opposite is true, the player leaves the line of scrimmage and he's padding around here and there because he's not really sure what he's doing.

Even a legend can misjudge talent, however. Chuck Finder, who covered sports for the *Pittsburgh Post-Gazette* for many years, shared a seldom-told story about Brown. In the 1957 draft, Pittsburgh had the fifth overall pick, and Cleveland was to draft next. Stated Finder, "The Steelers drafted Len Dawson and passed on Jimmy Brown. The story was that Paul Brown was furious when that happened. He smashed his hand on a table because he wanted Dawson." It's a laughable tale now, given what Cleveland's alternate choice, Brown, wound up achieving.

In the meantime, as they did with John Unitas, the Steelers let Dawson go, and in 1960, Brown got his wish and acquired Dawson. Once again, his judgment was lacking, as Brown let Dawson go after he had thrown just 28 passes in two years with Cleveland. Of course, later, with the Chiefs, Dawson put up Hall of Fame numbers.

Of course, on the other hand, Brown frequently was right on the button in judging talent. When Brown was the team's vice president, no longer coaching, using his Ohio State connections, he was the first person in the organization to recommend the acquisition of Buckeyes star Warfield. Additionally, two years after Blanton Collier replaced him, he used

Brown's system and, for the most part, Brown's players. Twenty-five of the 42 men who were on the 1964 championship team were Brown's acquisitions, and only six regulars hadn't played under Brown.

Regardless of occasional slips, Brown is, of course, an all-time great. If anyone needed evidence, all they'd have to do is sample just a few of his accomplishments. Take, for example, a quick review of Brown's first 10 seasons, which reveals an astonishing run of success. From 1946, his initial season, through 1948, the Browns went 38–3–1, winning more than 90 percent of their games, and they won the championship each year. From 1949 to 1951, he "slipped" to a record of 30–4–2, and they "only" won two out of three titles, giving them a string of five consecutive championships.

Then he really faltered in 1952—that is, if winning 67 percent of his games is faltering (8–4). During the next three seasons, he was victorious 29 times, lost six times, and was held to a tie once. He also tacked on two more NFL titles during that stretch (in 1954 and 1955). That's sheer domination. In fact, in 1948, the Browns *never* lost. Counting their 49–7 demolition of the old Buffalo Bills in the championship contest, Brown went 15–0 in AAFC competition that season.

No, it's clear Brown's name and legacy will live on forever, long after he passed away in 1991, at the age of 82. The three-time (in three different decades) NFL Coach of the Year spent 45 years on various sidelines, where, armed with his wits and clipboard, he amassed a total of 338 wins. He won a marvelous total of seven pro championships and 15 total championships counting the ones he earned at amateur levels. To this day, Brown remains the only coach ever to win championships at the high school, college, and pro levels.

7

WEEB EWBANK

The Short Coach Who Stood Tall

Place of birth: Richmond, Indiana
Date of birth: May 6, 1907
Date of death: November 17, 1998
Lifetime wins, losses, and ties: 130–129–7
Career winning percentage: .502
Playoff wins and losses: 4–1
Playoff winning percentage: .800
NFL major titles won and years of championships: NFL champs 1958, 1959; Super Bowl champs 1968
Teams coached and years: Baltimore Colts 1954–1962; New York Jets 1963–1973

There was no hint that Wilbur Charles, better known as "Weeb" Ewbank, would become an NFL Hall of Fame coach until he was deep into his coaching career and over the age of 50. In fact, his early days in coaching also gave no clue he would become more than, say, a successful high school coach—one of hundreds and hundreds of good, but anonymous, men, known only in his local area.

The image most people have of Ewbank is that of a roly-poly, squat man (about 5-foot-7), holding court on the sidelines. His body type belied the fact that the Indiana native was an excellent multisport athlete in his youth. He graduated in 1924, from Richmond's Morton High School (the same school that later produced NFL star Lamar Lundy), and attended Miami (of Ohio) University, where he played basketball as a forward, served as captain of the baseball team, and starred in football as quarterback and was a teammate of Paul Brown.

When Ewbank went on to become a famous football coach, he added his name to a long list of alumni whose excellence contributed to his college becoming known as the "Cradle of Coaches." The list of notable coaches out of Miami of Ohio is almost interminable. It includes Brown, Woody Hayes, Sid Gillman, John Harbaugh, Ara Parseghian, Bill Arnsparger, Jim Tressel, Bo Schembechler, and more than a dozen others.

After graduation, Ewbank coached at several high schools in Ohio from 1928 to 1944. He helped his teams win various titles, one of which was an Ohio state championship in 1937. In 1944, he joined the U.S. Navy, and one of his duties was to assist Paul Brown's football team, made up of servicemen at the Naval Station Great Lakes near Chicago. After being discharged, he spent 1946 coaching at Brown University, where he was the backfield coach for Charles "Rip" Engle. Ewbank then moved on to become head coach at Washington University at St. Louis the next two years, building a fine resume with a 14–4 cumulative record.

Ewbank finally moved up to the big time, becoming Paul Brown's assistant with the Cleveland Browns, who were then playing in the AAFC. Ewbank spent five years under the tutelage of Brown and saw firsthand what it was like to win a championship during his first two seasons there, 1949 and 1950.

Brown had lured Ewbank away from Washington University to coach his tackles. Ewbank pointed out he had been a quarterback in college and had otherwise always coached backs as an assistant. Brown said that didn't matter, and Ewbank later said how happy he was that he went along with Brown and accepted the Cleveland job, as it helped him enormously when he became a head coach.

Then came the really big break. Ewbank was hired to coach the Colts in January 1954, at the age of 46. When he took the helm for the Colts, the team was in just its second NFL season. Nevertheless, Ewbank promised he would develop them into a championship team within five years—his prophecy was perfect, as he had made good on his promise by December 28, 1958.

Years later, he said he felt no other NFL coach had ever inherited two teams worse than he did when he took on the duties of running the Colts and later the Jets. He felt his challenge with the Jets was even larger than the one he faced in Baltimore, but neither turnabout was an easy one.

Start in Baltimore, where he transformed a Colts team that had gone 3–9 in 1953, to a winning team by 1957—the Colts' first winning season ever. When he got the job, he made immediate, sweeping changes. In 1953, a total of 39 men had appeared on the Colts roster. Only 19 of them returned to play the next season.

In 1955, he drafted 12 players who all made the team, including seven who became starters, with Raymond Berry and Alan Ameche among that group. Lenny Moore and John Unitas would join the team a year later as bargain-basement acquisitions. Ewbank's two-year shopping spree remains one of the greatest displays of coaching/front-office evaluation and acquisition periods ever.

As recounted in chapter 1, Ewbank's Colts, packed with talent, won the NFL title with their dramatic win against the Giants in the Greatest Game Ever Played. What many people don't seem to recall is that Ewbank and his Colts repeated the following season—no small feat.

Gino Marchetti said that after he and his teammates retired,

> A lot of us have gone back to Baltimore for celebrity events, and the thing that really amazes me, probably more than anything, is they never talk about the 1959 championship. That's almost a forgotten part of our career. Everything with the fans was the 1958 championship game, which, as has been told many times, *made* professional football.

Fans may have been shortsighted, but experts give credit to the mighty two-year run of the Colts of Ewbank. Sadly, however, due to many factors, the Ewbank years in Baltimore did not produce any more champs. From 1960 to 1962, his composite win–loss record was 21–19, not enough to keep Ewbank employed by the Colts.

Still, as is said about Willie Loman in Arthur Miller's *Death of a Salesman*, attention must be paid. In Baltimore and elsewhere, Ewbank always had the ability to ferret out talent, often hitting the jackpot and saving the careers of men who, instead of never making even a minor impression in the NFL, went on to become giants of the game.

Raymond Berry stated,

> Weeb Ewbank is the key to the career of one Baltimore Colt after another. Number one on his list is John Unitas. Number two on his list

is Raymond Berry. If it hadn't been for Weeb Ewbank, neither one of us would even have had a pro career. John and I would have been gone. Perhaps the single most important thing that happened to both of us was going to the Colts under team owner Carroll Rosenbloom and head coach Weeb Ewbank.

In Unitas's case, the Pittsburgh Steelers had him in their training camp, never gave him a shot at playing, and rejected him. He bounced over to a semipro team in an area of Pittsburgh known as Bloomfield, seemingly doomed to obscurity.

However, legend has it that an 80-cent phone call made by Colts general manager Don Kellett to Unitas was all it took to obtain the great quarterback. Another bit of Unitas lore has it that Ewbank first received a letter from a fan informing him of a kid named Unitas, too talented to have his career become enervated by playing for a bottom rung of a football team, the Bloomfield Rams. That letter, and Ewbank's willingness to look into Unitas by checking him out with the quarterback's old college coach at Louisville, gave impetus to the acquisition of Johnny U.

Berry once stated he had the feeling that Ewbank was about the only one around who knew much about the young quarterback, and what he knew and believed about Unitas was more important to him than the fact that Unitas was a young man whom such schools as Notre Dame had turned down, positive that he was too small to play big-time college football.

Ego in check, Ewbank once said that early in Unitas's career, he was able to teach his young quarterback a considerable amount about the game, and he willingly admitted that after a while, it was Unitas who began to teach him.

Floyd Little, a college All-American, said there was a time Ewbank had wanted to make him a key member of his Jets. He revealed,

> The biggest thing with Weeb and Sonny Werblin [team owner] is they had the 12th pick when my time came up to be drafted. Weeb and Sonny did everything he could to raise his draft pick because they had watched me, they went to some of my Syracuse games, and they thought I was the best college player that they had seen. But the Broncos had the sixth pick, in front of the Jets. Weeb and Sonny were pissed off, but I would have been a Jet and I would have been in a Super Bowl with Joe Namath.

Weeb was a great judge of talent, no question. He was a great coach for years and years and years. And he had a great relationship with his players. You know, coaches like Don Shula, had great relationships like that.

I got to know Weeb and hang out with him at a couple of golf tournaments, and what a great person he was. Not only was he a great coach and a great judge of character, but he was just the kind of a coach that you would love to play for.

Along with recognizing and obtaining talented players, another approach Ewbank took to improve his team was moving players from one position to another. For example, he converted Gino Marchetti from left offensive tackle in 1953, into the best defensive end in pro football. He also moved Joe Campanella from his right offensive tackle position to a linebacker slot.

Star running back/flanker Lenny Moore, like Berry, a Hall of Famer, was yet another player helped by Ewbank, who was wise enough to use Moore frequently as a runner and receiver. Ewbank was also persuasive enough to change Moore's way of thinking. At Penn State, Moore had made it clear he wasn't crazy about being used as a flanker. In 1958, Moore's 938 yards on catches placed him second in the league, while his 7.3 yards per rush led the league and is still the sixth-best average in NFL history. His tools were used effectively by Ewbank.

Marchetti, one of Moore's teammates, said, "During our day Lenny Moore was the number-one back. He was one of the few backs who played the out position, a flanker, that Weeb made famous."

Moore appreciatively said,

Coach Weeb Ewbank richly deserved praise. He was knowledge personified. To listen to him and take notes, we understood the game as a whole; Weeb Ewbank was tops. He knew the game inside and out, and he taught it to us in all the aspects of the game from the standpoint of not just knocking the hell out of other people, but *how* to do it in the right way.

And how to increase and build your own stamina—guys get tired, but you still have to know how to do things even though you're tired as hell and worn out. Weeb would give you that mental capacity to try to think and do that what your body is capable of doing to the nth degree even though your body is tired.

And he would teach all of us that, but the main thing was to know your initiative, your basic initiative is how to do it, when to do it, why do you do it, and where you do it. All of that, with all the answers to those questions, too.

Plus, Moore pointed out, Weeb would teach his troops how to do blocking, tackling, and so on "without getting called for a foul."

In Baltimore, it was soon evident that Ewbank had learned much as an assistant to Paul Brown. The autocratic Brown usually insisted on calling plays from the sidelines. Ewbank, an apt pupil, would probably have permanently emulated that strategy as the Colts head coach, but he was able to change his ways when it benefited his team. After he observed Unitas in his first Colts training camp, he soon gave him virtual carte blanche to call his own plays.

Basically, said Unitas, Ewbank simply handed over the game plans and, in effect, said, "Go get 'em." Quickly realizing his quarterback had not only an arm and a brain, but also a competitive nature and many other intangible attributes, he took the manacles off Unitas.

Raymond Berry stated, "Things changed. Ewbank instinctively knew that this guy had what it took to do that. That was the key to it—Weeb understanding that Unitas was a natural play-caller and leader." Ewbank's decision paid off again and again for his Unitas-led Colts.

Later, coaching Joe Namath and the Jets, Ewbank again showed his willingness to delegate authority, permitting Broadway Joe and his go-to receiver, Don Maynard, to work out a set of hand signals that enabled them to switch the pattern that would be run after they had already broken their huddle.

Ewbank followed Brown's thinking when it came to keeping his playbook short, yet effective. Berry said the Colts' usual playbook contained about 10 runs and a dozen pass plays, and each receiver had about four routes he would run. He felt his players could not possibly carry out an inflated playbook with a high degree of success.

Berry elaborated,

He believed execution would fall off, and that even players' physical abilities wouldn't operate at full speed because there's hesitation, doubt, and indecision when there are so many plays, resulting in a lack of rehearsal. You can call plays in a game that you may not have worked on for three weeks under a complicated system, and that goes along with having a massive game plan. The quarterback would have to carry a huge load that way, and that's not good.

Berry called Ewbank's offensive philosophy and offensive system "utter simplicity."

He further described Ewbank's basic tenet:

> Don't do very many things, but do them well, and your players just instinctively know what to do. And they'll adjust to anything the defense does. You don't have a whole bunch of adjustments for a whole bunch of plays, you've just got one play and you know how to make it work, no matter what they do.

Berry also said that according to Ewbank's plan, the timing between Unitas and his receivers became "automatic," and that the Colts practiced and ran their basic plays so often (not unlike Green Bay's executing of their power sweep), that the team "under Ewbank really knew how to run our stuff—we knew how to shoot our weapons. It didn't make a difference what the enemy was doing, we knew how to shoot 'em."

Actually, at first the conservative Ewbank shackled Unitas and the offense a bit. He simply did not like for his quarterbacks to throw the bomb, preferring crisp, short passes. Berry related,

> So he discouraged us from working on the deep ball. But I discovered very early that Weeb was wrong about that, and I talked to him about that. I told him, "You can throw this ball short all you want to and they're going to start reading your mail, and what you're doing is making it easy on these guys on defense. They know you're not going to go deep. You've got to let us go deep when it's there." He reluctantly said okay. We started hitting the long ball big time and showed him real quick.

Ewbank became a believer in the power of the bomb, trusting the arm of Johnny U.

Another example of Ewbank's faith in his stars comes from Berry, who said, "I remember a situation when Weeb sent in a play and John didn't run it. Later, Weeb questioned why John didn't call the play, and I simply told him, 'John didn't think the play would work,' and Weeb just said, 'Oh. That's okay.'"

Ewbank knew how important having players with versatility can be, so he drafted and helped mold a young Tom Matte into a valuable NFL player. Matte recalled his college days at Ohio State, stating,

> I was averaging good yards per carry and all that kind of stuff, but I also played defensive back, I was the punter, I was the kickoff return, I was punt return. I was going 60 minutes.
>
> I think that's why the Colts drafted me, because I was good at everything, not great, by no means, but I was good at everything I did. And I could play all these different positions, so they said, "Hey, we need a versatile player," and that's when Paul Hornung was around—he had been the quarterback at Notre Dame. He went to Green Bay, they put him at halfback, where he could throw the ball and run the sweep and that kind of stuff. So that's what Weeb Ewbank thought about when he drafted me; he wanted me to be a Paul Hornung.

Ewbank was also unafraid to use his version of Hornung on defense. "I was playing defense, playing safety back there," said Matte, "and I could read the plays pretty well. So Weeb used me back there and Don Shula did [too] in an emergency situation if anybody got hurt."

Coaching in the glory years was much different from what goes on today. Marchetti pointed out,

> It's not like now, they have coordinators and everything that call the plays. When John [Unitas] was the quarterback in those days, they had to know the offensive plans, they had to know what you do on third-and-two, third-and-three, and that type of thing. They had to study. During the season I don't think they had as much fun because they had to work too hard to study the plays and call their own plays. Weeb might have called five or six plays a game or whatever, but nowadays I don't know how many they call.

Moore said Ewbank would

> write up the game plan and then John executes whatever the game plan is—whenever he wants to call it, and *how* he wants to call it. John calls the plays—whatever he thinks the linemen can handle and whatever. I just went along with what Weeb and the other coaches worked out on the board—these are our plays that we're going to run, what we think we can do.

When Marchetti was with the Colts and Joe Kuharich, who had coached Marchetti at the University of San Francisco, was coaching the Redskins, he wanted to acquire Marchetti. Said Marchetti,

> And I used to go to bed praying that Joe wouldn't get me. I had found out how easy it was to play under Weeb Ewbank—it was a piece of cake compared to Kuharich. He made you run your butt off. It was like a boot camp.
>
> Weeb was the guy that got me playing defense, which I'm totally grateful for. He was a nice guy, and I told him this after a season or after a beer party or whatever, "You know, Weeb, your problem with this team is you're too nice, too nice with guys that don't want to play by the rules. You gotta get tough, otherwise you're going to lose the team." And he said, "Gino, I got a lot of people I have to make happy."

He particularly meant the front office.

Ewbank admitted he was unlike the hard-line, old-timer type coaches who ranted, cussed, and raged at their players for the sake of intimidation. He basically stated he abided by the Golden Rule when it came to his coaching style. Because of that, he was mindful of putting together teams with solid citizens rather than creating a roster of wild men.

Ewbank even believed his teams should have a player like the humorous Art Donovan to keep the rest of his squad loose and relaxed with his funny antics and clever comments.

Marchetti believes Ewbank felt the way to wind up on the winning side of things was to be a "nice guy." And, it turned out, it seems to have worked. Marchetti added,

> It has. He won because he knew the offenses and the defenses. He was a great coach, but after five or six years, if you look at his record, he loses control. He lost it with Baltimore, then he lost it with the Jets in about the same amount of time, four years or whatever. I'm convinced that tough coaches make good coaches.

When Ewbank coached Namath, he was dealing with a free spirit, and many observers felt no coach could entirely curb him. Marchetti believed Ewbank was not the kind of coach who could rein in Namath, pointing out that Namath was "one of the first big-name draftees. He wore fur coats and did all that stuff, but Weeb drafted him, you gotta remember *that*."

At times, Ewbank could fit the bill of a tough coach. For example, after the Colts won the 1958 championship, he refused to allow beer into the locker room. He was not averse to fining those who broke his rules, either, and Donovan, who felt Ewbank saved his career, said his coach could be a real son of a bitch at times.

Maynard knew both the soft and the tough side of Ewbank. He played under Ewbank from 1963 until Maynard's retirement in 1972, and that included every season Ewbank was with the Jets, except 1973. The bottom line for the Hall of Fame receiver is he had a deep appreciation of Ewbank, calling him a "fine coach who treated players—each player— real fair." Maynard continued, "He'd been down the winners' road some. It worked out real good for me."

Overall, Ewbank may have been relatively easy on his men, but it all worked out "real good" for him, just as it had for Maynard. After all, Ewbank did win it all with the Colts in 1958 and 1959, and again with the New York Jets in Super Bowl III.

Ewbank drilled his team so hard and so effectively, they executed a savage defense and well-run offense. Berry spoke of one of the most noteworthy examples of the Colts' ability to execute their famous drive in the 1958 title game against the Giants, which resulted in a tie to shove the game into overtime. The drive succeeded, said Berry, because Ewbank had trained them to go rapid-fire, catch-and-run, then catch-and-run some more. Berry elaborated, "Ewbank had trained us in the no-huddle offense, so I don't think we were ever in the huddle but one time on this drive. Weeb taught John and all of us to operate with two plays called in the huddle." Furthermore, they had worked on their two-minute drill throughout the year, something relatively new back then.

Maynard recalled how one key to the Jets' success was Ewbank's stressing repetition. He also felt it was important that Ewbank chose "good assistants," saying, "That made the difference. He had the knowledge and the skill of football, and it just made it easy to play for him."

Donovan said Ewbank also made it easy on his defensive linemen when he taught them to read keys of offensive players as tip-offs as to which direction ensuing plays would be run. The line knew to follow the flow of the blocking, understanding that where there was an attack of blockers, runners would surely follow. Donovan added that their defensive scheme was so simple the Colts lined up exactly the same way, over and over again, for eight seasons.

Ewbank's success at his next stop, with the Jets, was tied to his permitting his quarterback, Namath, to be unorthodox. Maynard stated,

> I was always interested in knowing what opponents were going to do on third down. Joe was real good about some of his play-calling. Most teams kind of run on first and second downs, and throw on third. But, we just threw the ball on first down. As a result, if you complete it, you move it on down the field. If you didn't, why, you were still going to have two more tries at it.

At times, those two more tries would both be passes, as Ewbank, for the most part, allowed Namath, who wasn't gun-shy when it came to putting the ball in the air, to call his own plays.

"Yeah," continued Maynard with a chuckle, "but I remember every once in a while Weeb would send in a play, or a third-down substitute for Emerson Boozer or Bill Mathis, because it was a passing situation, and then we'd really go against the grain."

In those cases, Namath would obey Ewbank's instructions to cross up opponents (unlike Unitas, who was known to ignore plays Ewbank sent in rather often). "He did [obey]," Maynard said,

> but when it came right down to it, Joe would be setting up some ideas and he'd turn to wide receiver George Sauer or to me and say, "Hey, what looks good over there? Let's make sure we're going to get this first down." Well, I'd tell him, and we'd do that sometimes, deciding before we got ready to go from the huddle.

Like many coaches, Ewbank could be flexible, especially when his quarterback's overriding of his plays worked.

For critics who might downplay Ewbank's role with Namath, it's not as if Ewbank had nothing substantial to offer his quarterback. Ewbank did with Namath what he had done with Unitas—he taught him some valuable lessons and fundamentals early on. For instance, Ewbank made one significant change to Namath's passing style. At Alabama, Namath used a five-yard drop back and tried to have the football off his fingertips in just fewer than 1.5 seconds. Ewbank instructed Namath to fade back eight yards, which he believed would allow Namath to wait as long as 3.2 seconds before getting the ball off. The change helped greatly, especially on Namath's many bombs.

Maynard, on the receiving end of many of those long heaves, said that winning the Super Bowl was, of course, the "ultimate for every player and every team, and, as far as that goes, every coach—to get to the top of the game. It's the ultimate game to play in, and if you win it, why, golly, you wind up getting the ring and you've played at the top."

Ewbank not only won more than his fair share of rings, but also was, in large part, responsible for his players earning the right to wear championship rings. Donovan and Berry both make mention of Ewbank in the dedications to their autobiographies, and Donovan went on to say Ewbank made him the Hall of Famer that he was. Moreover, Berry has avowed that without Ewbank, he would not have had a pro career.

Aside from the obvious example of winning the Super Bowl with the Jets, Ewbank enjoyed one other big season in New York. The year following Super Bowl III, the Jets again made it to postseason competition, easily capturing the East Division crown over the Houston Oilers by a convincing four games in the standings. After going 10–4, just one win less than they had posted on their way to the Super Bowl, the 1969 Jets hosted the Kansas City Chiefs at Shea Stadium in the first round of the playoffs.

The entire game was a basically battle of two men booting the ball. Jim Turner kicked a field goal to give the Jets the game's first lead before Jan Stenerud retaliated with two field goals. Turner came back with a short kick in the fourth quarter to tie the game at six-all. Unfortunately for Ewbank, Len Dawson sent the Jets home a loser when he connected with Gloster Richardson on a 19-yard strike to push the final score to 13–6.

Although Ewbank gave Namath a free hand (or arm) to put the ball in the air 40 times, the Kansas City defense proved to be too good. The longest pass Namath hit on went for a mere 18 yards, and he misfired 26 times. The ground game netted 87 yards, with Matt Snell accounting for 61 of them on 12 carries. The Jets did move the ball enough to rack up 19 first downs, aided by the Chiefs' five penalties for 63 yards, but by and large the offense was rather stagnant. It would prove to be Ewbank's final trip to the playoffs.

The 1970 season was miserable—a precipitous drop from a 10–4 record to a 4–10 mark was, however, not inexplicable, nor was it Ewbank's fault. Namath started just five times, winning just one of those games, and Snell started only three contests, producing a puny 281 yards.

Ewbank's final three seasons as a head coach resulted in records of 6–8, 7–7, and 4–10. It had taken him four seasons on the job in New York before he had a campaign with a better than break-even record, and it took four subpar seasons before the Jets could no longer let the 66-year-old coach continue.

Ewbank lived to be 91, and throughout his long life he experienced much to savor. True, he only made the playoffs four times in his 20 years as an NFL head coach, but he won the league championship three of those four times, chalking up a .800 winning percentage in postseason play and becoming the only coach to win it all in both the old AFL and the NFL. His regular-season winning percentage may be the lowest of the men featured in this book, at .502, but Ewbank was an acknowledged winner. For instance, when the Colts fired him, the Jets quickly gobbled him up, signing him to be their head coach for the next season.

Surprisingly, Ewbank won only one game more than he lost during his career (130–129), but voters knew his many wins and his place in history made him a legitimate Hall of Famer. No, the name Weeb Ewbank will never be forgotten.

8

VINCE LOMBARDI

Dynasty Builder

Place of birth: Brooklyn, New York
Date of birth: June 11, 1913
Date of death: September 3, 1970
Lifetime wins, losses, and ties: 96–34–6
Career winning percentage: .738
Playoff wins and losses: 9–1
Playoff winning percentage: .900
NFL major titles won and years of championships: NFL champs 1961, 1962, 1965; Super Bowl champs 1966, 1967
Teams coached and years: Green Bay Packers 1959–1967; Washington Redskins 1969

Vince Lombardi's roots go all the way back to high school coaching, a far-fetched dream away from the NFL. He was on the job at St. Cecilia High in Englewood, New Jersey, as an assistant coach in 1939, and got paid $20 a week early on.

When he became the team's head coach in 1942, he immediately installed a modified T formation into the offense. The next year, the team went undefeated, including eight shutouts. They won the state championship and gave up a measly three touchdowns all year long, outscoring opponents by an outlandish margin of 267 to 19. In fact, his teams enjoyed four unbeaten seasons, and they once won 25 games in a row, while going 32 consecutive games without a loss—during the streak they played to three ties. Lombardi even coached the school's basketball team to a state title.

In 1947, he was the freshman coach at his alma mater, Fordham University. Employing the T formation with his freshmen, his squad outperformed the varsity several times during their scrimmages. The next year, he advanced to take an assistant coaching position at Fordham.

He also coached at West Point as the team's offensive line coach—becoming an assistant at West Point from 1949 to 1953. Having paid his dues in college, he finally made it to the NFL as offensive coordinator for the New York Giants from 1954 to 1958, coaching his first season under rookie head coach Jim Lee Howell.

It's difficult to believe now, but things didn't exactly go swimmingly for the all-time great at first. Lombardi had little or no credibility with the pro players, who saw him as an NFL nobody, a college-caliber coach not worthy of working with the big boys. They also found him to be abrasive, too loud and self-important, but he eventually won over the players. He learned he had to gain their trust and began by cozying up to veterans, modestly asking players for their help, and confessing he had a lot to learn. It was as if he was conceding, "I'm the new guy here and I can learn some things from you, so let's work together for a common goal." It worked.

Another lesson he learned early on came during a game when the Giants had built up a 17–0 lead over the Bears early in the third quarter. Lombardi had his offense play it cautiously, mainly keeping the ball on the ground. Eventually, the Bears knotted things up, and the Giants offense was unable to suddenly turn it on and score again. The game ended in a tie. Lombardi said from then on he always coached games, regardless of the score, as if the scoreboard read 0–0.

Given a chance to take over as head coach, Lombardi grabbed a job offer from the Packers. A quick overview of what Lombardi accomplished with Green Bay right out of the gate reveals he took a team that had finished dead last in 1958, in sixth place in the West Division, at 1–10–1 (a woeful .091 winning percentage), and, with the aim of an ancient alchemist, soon turned their record into gold. The Packers were coming off the worst record in franchise annals, dating all the way back to 1921, and they hadn't managed to put together a season above .500 in their previous 11 seasons. But in his first season at the helm, Lombardi

piloted the Packers to a 7–5 record, leaping up three rungs in the standings. For this, he was selected as the 1959 Coach of the Year.

His Packers then won their division in 1960, before conquering the
NFL with consecutive championships the next two seasons. After a two-
year hiatus from postseason play, coming off an 11–2–1 record in 1963
(the Bears beat out the Packers for the West Division title with a record of
11–1–2), and an 8–5–1 1964 season, Lombardi methodically added three
straight titles to his resume. During that three-year span, his Packers went
38–9–2. Forget alchemy, this man was King Midas personified.

Paul Hornung recalled Green Bay's pathetic pre-Lombardi days. "It
was the Siberia of pro football," he began. "Any player who did something wrong was threatened to be sent to Green Bay."[1]

He also admitted that, above all, he wanted to get away from the
Packers. Obviously, Lombardi changed all of that. Not long after he got
the job with the Packers, he contacted, among other players, Hornung,
and, paying strict attention to details, told his running back he expected
him to report to camp in shape, to prepare assiduously for his new regime,
instructing him on how many hours he was expected to spend daily on his
workouts. He even went so far as to tell Hornung to report at 207
pounds—not 205, not 210, but *207*.

Another one of Lombardi's earliest moves was to inform Hornung that
his days of being used as a fullback, halfback, *and* quarterback by the
Packers were over. He assured him he was now his halfback. The move
proved to be a turning point in Hornung's career. Inspired, in 1959, he ran
for more yards than in his first two seasons as a pro combined. Lombardi
was Green Bay's (and Hornung's) third head coach in three years, and he
had already proved to be the best of the lot. In their previous six seasons,
the Packers averaged 3.3 wins per season. Lombardi more than doubled
that total in his first season.

When Lombardi addressed his first team meeting at Green Bay, after
he had signed a contract calling for a salary of $36,000 per year for five
seasons, he had a terse message. He coldly informed his players, "Gentlemen, I have never been associated with a losing team, and I don't intend
to start now."[2]

He never was, not once throughout his 10 seasons as an NFL head
coach. He did lose the 1960 NFL title game, his first postseason game,
but would never again lose in the playoffs, racking up a 9–0 record from
that point onward, while winning it all five times. That translates to him

winning the championship in half of the seasons he coached. By bringing five of their record 13 championships to Green Bay, he was instrumental in having the city become known as Titletown. The closest team to the Packers in terms of titles won is Chicago, with nine.

Lombardi wisely began his first season's early practices, promptly teaching his offense their first play, his power sweep (49-Sweep), saying if they could execute it, they would be able to run the ball. That, in turn, would help create win after win after win. The play, one the team always ran with confidence as the staple of their playbook, became known simply as the Lombardi Sweep, or the Green Bay Sweep.

The sweep actually began when the Rams employed it. Lombardi first studied film of the play in 1956, when he was still with the Giants, and he fell in love with it. It was one he would later unleash on the NFL in full force with the Packers. It was as if Lombardi, borrowing from Shakespeare, told his team to "Cry Havoc, and let slip the dogs of war." The sweep would indeed create mayhem among opponents.

Lombardi paid such close attention to everything, he wound up improving the sweep by directing his offensive linemen to stop lining up 36 inches apart, convinced that a gap of just four more inches would make a significant difference. He also positioned a key man on the sweep, the tight end, nine feet away from the tackle, wider than had been the case before.

Two other men were essential on the sweep, the guards—perhaps not coincidentally the same position Lombardi played when he was a member of Fordham's famous offensive line known as the Seven Blocks of Granite. Jerry Kramer and Fuzzy Thurston became a terrifying two-man green and gold wave that bolted out of the starting block by using the crossover step Lombardi had learned from Frank Leahy. The guards, coupled with, say, Jim Taylor and a tight end also blocking on the sweep, became a terrible tsunami that obliterated defenders, freeing Hornung to romp for significant yardage over and over again.

Raymond Berry saw that play many times when his Colts faced the Packers. He said even when teams were pretty sure a convoy of blockers was about to begin yet another sweep, the play still worked. It was a case of, "Just try and stop it." The key to this, and other Green Bay plays, for that matter, was repetition. Lombardi had his troops run plays ad nauseam, drilling his men to the point of tedium and utter fatigue, but once game time arrived, they ran the plays with pure precision.

Lombardi believed in the idea of running to daylight, and he instructed his blockers to create enough daylight to figuratively blind his ballcarriers. Lombardi told his blockers gaping holes would be created for runners simply by moving a would-be tackler the way he wants to go. That is to say, if a defender wanted, for instance, to make a move inside, the blocker was to drive him far inside, which permitted the runner to then scoot outside. Lombardi believed a runner was better off running to daylight than being mandated to run through a specified hole. Using this style, the Packers began to grind out yards, control the football, and wear down opponents to the point of submission.

Lombardi was a complex and often contradictory person. He would attend Mass faithfully, then cuss up a storm hours later on the field. Kramer called his coach a "cruel, kind, tough, gentle, miserable, wonderful man whom I often hate and often love and always respect."[3] Kramer also concluded, "If I live to be a million, I won't be able to figure Lombardi out."[4]

In short, Lombardi was indeed a paradoxical man. In fact, as tough as he could be, he unabashedly allowed his tears to flow at emotional moments, for instance, when he won his third NFL title in a row. And once, after Ray Nitschke had played a great game, Lombardi walked up to him in the locker room and planted a kiss on his linebacker's cheek.

Packers great Dave Robinson observed,

> What made Lombardi great was he was, in hindsight, a typical Italian father, and to an Italian father, nothing is bigger than his family. He took the Green Bay Packers as being his second family. His son used to quip, "Sometimes I think my father loves you more than he does me," but you know it's not true—an Italian loves his sons more than anything else. But Vince treated us like that, like we were his sons. He was always jovial, always happy. Nothing but the best. No second class—we weren't second-class citizens, always the best, always first class.

Jerry Kramer agreed that Lombardi saw himself as a patriarch who loved his players, his surrogate children, but he demanded a great deal from them, especially the talented ones. In fact, never wanting to look bad, he expected perfection from everyone from the top, himself, down to his water boys. Like a master child psychiatrist, Lombardi knew just how to handle his Packers family and how to get the most out of them. He could use an ominous stick or a tantalizing carrot to motivate.

As Packers general manager, Lombardi was usually stingy when it came to negotiating players' contracts. Yet, he was generous on other occasions. After the 1967 season, when the Packers were divvying up their championship bonus money, their voting to determine how much money should be awarded to nonplayers like the groundskeeper proved to be quite chintzy. When Lombardi saw how selfish his team was, he exploded, saying he was ashamed of them and that as far as he was concerned they could take his cut of the money and split it up, he wanted no part of it. Later, still livid, he demanded they take a new vote, to make things right.

On the other hand, there were times when he wasn't so benevolent. There are several versions of why Lombardi traded away 11-year Packers veteran, team captain, and future Hall of Famer Jim Ringo in 1964, but the most commonly told one states that when Ringo reported to Lombardi's office to negotiate his contract, he brought along an agent, a virtually unheard-of move back then, and Lombardi excused himself from the meeting. Shortly thereafter, he returned and told the agent he should be negotiating not with Green Bay, but with the Philadelphia Eagles—that he had just made a phone call to, and a deal for Ringo with, that team.

Lombardi definitely had his own set of values and rigid beliefs. One of his most famous quotes was, "Practice does not make perfect. Only perfect practice makes perfect." Robinson recalled another version of that, commenting, "As Vince used to say, 'Practice makes perfect if you do it right every time. If you do it wrong, the more you practice, the worse you get.'"

Lombardi was often candid about himself and his personality. Probably more than any other NFL coach of his era, he was recognized as the maestro, and he knew it. He noted, "As a person, I am not well enough adjusted to accept defeat. The trouble with me is that my ego just cannot accept a loss."[5]

Vikings kicker Fred Cox once said players like quarterbacks and placekickers *must* have strong egos, otherwise they would dwell way too much on their failures and lack the confidence necessary to succeed. The same theory can be applied to coaches, and Lombardi certainly did have a healthy ego. He may not have been an egomaniac, but he once stated, "This is a game for madmen. In football we're all mad."[6]

One of Lombardi's most salient traits was his pride. Being a proud man, he insisted his players also take pride in their work and never let down. He contended games' outcomes often hinged on a few vital plays and that it was sometimes impossible to know when such plays might arise; therefore, it was imperative never to relax.

While pride and loyalty were important to the Packers of the time, things have changed, and one wonders if Lombardi could still have enjoyed his same great success if he were coaching today. Robinson stated, "I know right now, with the team we had, Vince couldn't have kept them together because he would have had to have paid some of our second-stringers first-string money. And with free agency, they'd have jumped ship in a minute."

Who knows what would transpire. Perhaps Lombardi was so skilled he may still have won, say, three titles in a row, as the odds are he would have adapted to his situation, and that was something he was quite used to doing, even from one play to the next. One thing is for sure, betting against the demanding, rugged Lombardi was never the way to get rich.

It's possible that because Lombardi played through pain himself, something he felt winners did, he expected, sometimes demanded, his players to do the same. One of his players suffered a broken leg, and Lombardi felt he should be up and running after just three weeks, about four days after his cast had been removed.

The coach, who once required 30 stitches to seal off a wicked cut in his mouth when he played for Fordham University, believed pain could be overcome by sheer willpower. His father had told him that "hurt is in the mind," so looking back on the time he was blasted in his mouth, he quipped, "I certainly was hurting in my mind."[7]

Lombardi displayed his pragmatism when he asked a great rhetorical question, one that destroyed the ancient concept of "all that matters is how you play the game" in sports. He realized, of course, that such bromides were nonsense at the professional level. With that in mind, employing the deadpan brand of humor of comedian Steve Wright, he pondered, "If it doesn't matter who wins or loses, then why do they keep score?"

Then there's yet another famous quote attributed to Lombardi, even though John Wayne, playing a coach in a movie, and not Lombardi, was the first to utter the words: "Winning isn't everything; it's the only thing." Some argue that what Lombardi really was saying was winning is the only thing to *strive* for, that the effort to win is vital. Others, of course, interpreted the line to show a monomaniacal, perhaps unhealthy, attitude toward sports and, by extension, life itself.

When Herb Adderley came to the Cowboys from Green Bay in 1970, he had played his entire career under one coach, Lombardi. In 1972, the future Hall of Famer retired (after also playing for Landry). In Dallas, Adderley roomed with Mel Renfro, who said,

> He talked a lot about Vince Lombardi and his strong, tough attitude. Vince wouldn't put up with anything.
>
> He and Landry were a lot different. I remember one week after a loss, all our guys are sitting around moping with their heads down, and Herb just stood up and said, "You guys act like a miserable bunch of losers."
>
> It got our attention because Landry would never say anything like that—we didn't have that type of atmosphere where someone got tough and really put their foot up our butt. But Herb had that tough attitude, and he got that from Vince and the Packers. We realized why the Packers were consistent winners, [even] when they weren't always the best team—because of Lombardi's mystique and that toughness that he portrayed; and Herb brought that to our team.

Adderley played in 15 postseason games, winning 14 of those contests. He played in seven title games and lost only once. He appeared in four of the first six Super Bowls, winning three times. The Adderley-combined-with-Lombardi-and-Landry concoction was just about indomitable.

One thing Lombardi could not abide by was prejudice, and he loathed racial slurs. Dave Robinson remembered, "There was no difference between the whites, the blacks, the yellows, the browns, the purples—everybody was the same. He was very strict about that. He said many times that the only colors we have here are green and gold, that's it, and that's how it was. That's how he coached."

Another Packer, center Bob Hyland, concurred, declaring, "One thing I really liked about the Packers was there was no color discrimination whatsoever. Blacks and whites, we all spent a lot of time together."

Robinson noted that when "Lombardi went to the little town of Green Bay and saw a lot of racial disparity there, he handled it, and we had no problems. Anything like [racial intolerance], Vince put a stop to it."

It's been said Lombardi told his players if any one of them, no matter how valuable he might be on the field, ever muttered a single racial epithet or made any negative racial comment, he was gone. Hyland said, "I believe that. I never heard of any incident occurring there—it just didn't happen."

Now, throughout the years, there had to be at least one Packer who, for instance, grew up hating blacks, but Lombardi demanded that his men obey him and either change their ways or, at the very least, keep their vitriol hidden. "It's amazing how you change when you put that green and gold on," concluded Hyland.

Lombardi doted on his wife Marie, who occasionally joked about his strict football ways. At Super Bowl XV, Marie, by then a widow, performed the ceremonial coin toss. Asked what her husband would have thought about this, she replied, "He'd probably wonder what the hell a woman was doing on the football field."[8]

The portrayal of Lombardi as a martinet with his players and a marionette with his wife is only partially correct. It's true that he did defer to his wife frequently, but it's difficult to picture him as a stammering, henpecked husband.

It's certainly true that he was tough and demanding with his players. Using that booming voice of his, he even threatened such veteran stars as Fuzzy Thurston to play harder and better, or expect to be shipped out of town. He often upped the threat by saying he would trade a player to a losing team.

Nevertheless, he was far from being heartless, and his men respected him. One reason is because when it came to hard work, Lombardi was never guilty of having double standards. On Christmas Eve 1967, for example, he and his staff reported to work early in the morning, and during the entire season the group toiled for as many as 16 hours a day. Furthermore, after each season, the coaches didn't get a vacation until as late as June. Jerry Kramer heard that when the salary of those men was broken down into an hourly rate, a Packers coach made less money than a garbage man in Green Bay.

Former NFL running back/receiver John Isenbarger said the team that impressed him the most as he grew up watching TV was the mechanically effective Green Bay Packers. After reading *When Pride Still Mattered: A Life of Vince Lombardi*, Isenbarger commented,

I just think I'd have liked to have played for that kind of coach. Things have changed so much—let's say I just signed my new contract for $125 million a year for four years with $75 million guaranteed. You're the coach and you tell me to do something—today's players, not *all of them*, might say, "Hey, look, you can't do this without me. I don't want to do that." Everything's questioned. Not all the time, but you wouldn't do that with Vince Lombardi. He'd tell you to, "Go hit the showers, punk. I'll find somebody else to do it."

Clearly, Lombardi was not to be questioned.

Lombardi subscribed to the coaching idea of running grueling training and practice programs to find out who would quit on him. He would rather find out someone was a quitter in practice than during games. His players knew he had a bit of the taskmaster in him. Henry Jordan put it this way, "Lombardi treats us all the same—like dogs."[9]

Lombardi appreciated some of his players more than others, but he played no favorites. As a strong disciplinarian, he freely dished out stiff fines when necessary. He once hit Max McGee with a then-stinging fine of $250 for breaking curfew. The next time he caught McGee breaking his curfew rule, he upped the punishment to $500 and admonished him, saying the next time would be $1,000. He added that if McGee found anything worth $1,000, he would go with him.

On the other hand, he was wise enough to know when to look the other way. Robinson said of Lombardi,

> The thing is, like the typical Italian father, he was a real strong discipli-narian. As long as everything was going right, you couldn't ask for a nicer guy. He'd do anything for you, anything he could. But when you got out of line, he could bring you back into the fold. He knew how to do it. He had real strict rules.

One such rule dealt with promptness. Robinson continued,

> I guess what was strange was that he had "Vince Lombardi time." The clock in Green Bay was set 15 minutes fast—that was Lombardi time. If he called a meeting for 1:00, he'd start that meeting at 12:45. If you came in at 12:50, you were five minutes late. But you really were 10 minutes early from the time the meeting was supposed to start; there-fore, he didn't have to *fine you* for being late—you were early, but you were really late.

And he would stare you down and address you in such a way you felt like two inches tall. A grown man, and he made you feel like you were a little six-year-old kid talking to his daddy. You'd apologize and then have a good reason for being late. He'd say something like, "You mean you keep all these fine young people waiting for you. Everybody's waiting for you." Consequently, because of rules like that, Vince Lombardi fined fewer people less money than any coach I ever had.

Lombardi may have been exaggerating somewhat when he told Otto Graham that to be successful, you had to be always be a S.O.B. So, yes, Lombardi was tough on his men, but he also knew that discretion can sometimes be the wiser part of coaching. Robinson spoke of a time reporters questioned Lombardi about Hornung and his sometimes free-spirited ways:

Vince said, "If I ever catch Paul in a bar, he's through here." And Marie said real quietly, "Oh, Vinnie will never catch him," and he wouldn't. Even in the offseason we were not allowed to sit around at a bar. If I was in a bar and got in trouble, or even if he just saw me, it was an automatic fine. You could go to a restaurant, sit down at a table, and drink with your meal, but you *could not* sit at a bar.

One time Hornung or Nitschke—I remember it as being Hornung—had a glass of ginger ale at the bar. And he sent a drink to Vince's table. Vince told him, "Get out of here. Go back to the hotel." The bartender said, "He's just drinking ginger ale." Vince picked up the drink, smelled it, and put it back down, but he kicked him off the team and told the whole team he had violated the rules. Then he said, "It's up to you guys if you want him back on the team or not, but as far as I'm concerned, he's no longer a Green Bay Packer."

Then Vince left the room, and our captains ran the meeting and we talked about it. We had a vote, which was a sham. We weren't going to kick him off the team, but that was Vince's way of making sure we followed the rules. Hornung apologized, and he got back on the team. But that says something about Vince—that was his rule.

Now, if you are in a bar in Green Bay and someone saw you there and called Vince and told him, that didn't mean anything. *He* had to see you himself—him or one of his assistants, and everybody knew that. Green Bay had only 60,000 people when I got there and about three or four bars in town where everybody went, and coaches knew where they were. If you caused no trouble, Vince did not go to the bars looking for Packers. He did not want to find us. *He did not want to .*

One time after a game we won, Elijah Pitts, Bob Jeter, and I went to one of the better restaurants in town. We got done eating, we were sitting at a table, and Vince came in with about five or six people—he had parties after every game. We didn't know what to do, so we did the same thing they did—we were at a table so we were legal. We had told the waitress we would like to buy drinks for that group over there. Vince looked at us and waved at us. Then I said, "Let's get the hell out of here," but the waitress said, "Don't worry about it, Vince Lombardi picked up the check."

The next day Vince came up to me and said, "Dave, you didn't have to leave. You could have stayed there." I said, "Coach, we were done eating, and to be honest with you, we were a little uneasy sitting there with you and Marie and your guests there." He just laughed and patted me on the back. He let me know he appreciated us getting up and leaving because he didn't want us to see him drinking, and he didn't want to see us drinking, either. He appreciated his private time with his little group. That was the way it was.

People wonder, would a sometimes almost unbending disciplinarian like Lombardi be able to be so strict with today's players? The answer is a somewhat guarded yes. Hall of Fame defensive back Mel Renfro opined,

The one guy that's close to Vince is the Patriots coach [Bill Belichick]. There are a couple of others that are tough, but, no, it's hard nowadays because of the players. I mean, they're different. They're rich, they're spoiled. It's all about me, me, me. It's tough. I think there are some coaches that are able to get through to their players, where they instill that sense of team and loyalty—wanting to do it for the team and not so much for themselves. There are not many coaches like Vince around anymore.

Despite (or perhaps due to) Lombardi's toughness, he was admired and deeply respected by his men. As a matter of fact, Willie Davis respected Lombardi so much that when he heard his former coach was gravely ill in the Georgetown University Hospital in Washington DC, he hopped a plane in Los Angeles, flew out, visited Lombardi for just a few minutes, and promptly took a return flight to the West Coast, respects willingly and duly paid.

Still, no one, no matter how stellar his resume, is loved by *everyone*. Were there former players who disliked him? Former Green Bay running back Chuck Mercein fielded that question:

> There were just a couple of guys I know, and I wouldn't want to mention them; I don't want to speak ill of anybody. Most everybody respected him.
>
> And most everybody especially appreciated the fact that he made them a better player. And we all had aspirations to be better. You don't get to be where you are in that league, and get to be a pro, without wanting always to improve. So you get under his tutelage and all of a sudden your intensity picked up a lot, your concentration picked up a lot, and you started playing harder. He just expected more out of you. One hundred and ten percent was no lie as far as he wanted your effort [to be].
>
> And as far as errors go, no errors—not mentally or anything like that. He could make anybody better. He could make Bart Starr better. He made Chuck Mercein better. So I was very happy to have the chance to have him coach me and very happy to play for him.

Playing for Lombardi paid off in many ways. Bob Hyland stated, "The most enjoyable thing was winning the Super Bowl with Coach Lombardi and a great bunch of players in my first season. That was a tough act to follow. There was no other season that came close to that initial one."

Some sources state that Lombardi's players all addressed him as "sir" at all times, but Robinson said that wasn't true. Stated Robinson,

> We had to call him Coach. You didn't call him Vinnie—but we did among ourselves. We sometimes called him V. L. Macnish, because he was a Scotch drinker and that was a [brand] they made in the 1960s. We joked about that, but that was in private. And we called him the Old Man, but we never said that to his face, either. But all that was in the locker room—that was *real* locker room talk, not what Donald Trump said about locker room talk.

Many people basically saw just one aspect of Lombardi, the volatile shouting coach image. Robinson saw much more. He added,

> The "What's going on out there," was a real small part of his persona. Vince provided a good sound bite, that's what you hear on TV. The other 99 percent of the time he was [different]. I have a very inquiring

mind, and he fulfilled all my questions—he always answered them for me. He was so aware of everything.

Lombardi was, in fact, often aware of things other coaches didn't realize or concern themselves with. Robinson said Lombardi had the ability to look more deeply into situations most people only dealt with superficially.

There were times when the Packers were to play the Rams in Los Angeles, and Lombardi, fearing someone from the Rams organization would try to spy on Green Bay's practices, held his workouts on the University of California, Santa Barbara field. He gave the college $3,000 and instructed them to put a large canvas screen around the entire field to ensure privacy.

Another example of Lombardi's attention to details, even minor ones, is this: Robinson contends most coaches and players see the home-field advantage as simply a case of having the crowd on your side, or the players having the comfort of carrying out their routine home life—relaxing, eating, and sleeping habits, and so on—for an entire week prior to a game.

Lombardi, said Robinson, went deeper and even tried to nullify a bit of opponents' home-team advantage. According to Robinson,

> Everybody has big ballplayers, smart guys, fast, who can run, jump, and everything else, but a team is mental—you have to be in the right mental frame of mind. And that frame of mind starts when you walk in that locker room. When we were at home, we went in the locker room, and we'd tell [the clubhouse attendant what we wanted] and he'd bring it to you. Jerry Kramer had a thing—he used the same roll of tape [until it was used up] and broke his leg, so he never did that again. At the end of a season, he'd have maybe 30, 40 rolls of tape in his locker that he'd used just one time.
>
> When you go on the road—let's say you go to Chicago—the Bears [attendant] couldn't compete with the man in the Packers locker room.

Robinson said that oftentimes attendants who took care of the Packers on the road had a "relationship to somebody in their organization, like a secretary's son." He continued,

Almost 99.9 percent of the time they are avid hometown fans who *do not* want to see the Green Bay Packers win. They treat you like crap, and they get you off your game mentally.

Kramer wanted some tape; they wouldn't give him the tape. Now he's worried about breaking a leg the whole game and not concentrating on blocking Bill George. So what Vince did was take a collection—we had a pot of maybe two, three, four thousand dollars, whatever it was. Every time we went into a locker room, if we got good treatment, the same as we did when we were at home, he left a tip for the locker boys—maybe four or five hundred dollars. If the service was not up to Vince Lombardi standards, *nothing*. It wasn't like you'd get $100, no. It's all or nothing. And the word passed around the league like wildfire. I'll tell you, when we went on the road, we got the same service we got at home. In other words, anything to ease our minds.

That's the kind of little things Vince Lombardi did. He was that type of coach. Two last examples. First is we played in New York, and he knew that when the fullback came to try to block me—I was playing left linebacker, a natural left-hander—I used my left forearm to come across his face to take him out and then fill the hole with my body when he tried to drive me outside. What they did was they came at me and the fullback came up and he looked like he was going to try to block me out, and the halfback would get the ball and wouldn't even try to hit that hole—he'd run outside. I'd close that hole, so he'd veer outside, and they had Homer Jones, a wide receiver, take off on a fly pattern, run downfield to take Herb Adderley out of the picture. The first time they ran that, they got six, seven yards on it. Then they ran it to the other side on Lee Roy Caffey.

Then Lee Roy and I talked, which is what the better defenses do, and we decided we would stay on the outside. So the next time they ran the play, the fullback came at me, and I took my *right* forearm and jammed his body into the hole. That left me free, and when the halfback veered, I released and made the tackle, and that was it.

That week in New York I was the AP Defensive Player of the Week with two interceptions and a sack on Fran Tarkenton, and a partially blocked punt. I had a great game. Now, because of that play, because they ran that play on me successfully one time, two at the most, Vince Lombardi had me, not scared, but uneasy about going into the Tuesday meeting because I knew he was going to point out that play to me, and sure enough he did.

And he told me, "We're going to run it every day. The film is going out, and everybody in the league is going to see the film of that play, so we have to be ready for it next week." And, sure enough, next week the team we played ran the play. See, in the NFL, at that time, you sent film of your last two games to your next opponent. For the next two weeks I saw [our opponents run] that play early in the game, and I stopped it and they never went back to it, so everything went along fine.

Then, about four or five weeks down the road, Vince came to me one day and said, "Dave, you remember that play that New York ran on us? I'm going to have Phil [Bengston] run that on you about 10 or 12 times this week. I want you to get used to it. I think you might see it again this week. Look for the play." I said okay but didn't know why he said that.

Robinson explained Lombardi's thinking process, which he later became privy to. The canny Lombardi knew the team (Robinson said it may have been the Cardinals), which had played the Giants the week after they had run the play on Robinson, had studied the film of that contest. Call it a hunch, an educated guess, coaches' intuition, or whatever, but when St. Louis opened their game against the Packers, they did, in fact, run the play in question right out of the gate. Forewarned, Robinson sniffed it out and said he never saw it run on him again, all thanks to Lombardi, who believed the Cardinals had to be thinking, "Let's try this play out to see if you've solved your problem with it."

"That's the thing. I never had a coach like that, so well prepared." Robinson continued. He then cited his final example of Lombardi's shrewd ways.

We were playing the Rams in Los Angeles, and before the game I pulled a groin muscle, bad. I limped off the field and went into the locker room. They taped my groin up, and they shot it up with novocaine so I could go, but they knew I couldn't go long. Vince said, "Dave, we can let you go in there or put somebody else in there and they'll go at him, and run at him and run at him, and sooner or later they'll break down anybody."

Now, while I was getting my groin taped, Bill Austin, who had been our coach in Green Bay, was coaching with the Rams. He came into the locker room on a pretense to say hello to our trainer, and he saw me getting taped. The trainer told Vince, and he said something I won't repeat now. Then he called me over and told me, "They know you've got a bad groin. The first three plays they're going to take you deep. If you run with them and handle it okay, they'll leave you alone and go back to whatever game plan they had. But if you can't, they're going to run at you and run at you and run at you." And, again, if you run that long at anybody, you can break down anybody.

First play of the game, Dick Bass, their running back, came up, one-on-one on me, and ran me on a deep fly pattern, about 30 yards deep. And I ran with him—if my leg didn't hurt so much, I would have intercepted that ball, but I knocked it down and jogged back to the huddle. My leg started hurting, all that novocaine wore off. It hurt so bad, if they would have run me the next play, they would have beat me, but they didn't. And you know what, they didn't come after me anymore the rest of the day.

Robinson said Lombardi believed that if his Packers could shut down a given play in, say, the first set of plays of the game, they might abandon that play for the entire game, as was the case with Robinson covering Bass. Opponents would probe the Packers defense, only to discover quite often there simply was no weak spot.

Lombardi stacked a ton of talent on the right side of the field on defense, nearly taking away half the field from opponents who were, quite naturally, reluctant to run plays that way. Robinson recalled,

They ran enough plays on our side to keep us from falling asleep—you keep your head in the game, but teams did not pick on our side of the field. Look, we had Willie Davis, Herb Adderley, and myself in a row.

And the inside support came from Ray Nitschke. And, at times, if they went strong to the left, Vince put Willie Wood as our safety over there. What that meant was if you looked to your left, then looked back to your right, on our side of the field, the five defensive men there are now in the Hall of Fame. So why would people want to pick on us? That's how it was. Vince knew that.

Don Maynard looked back on Lombardi's attention to details when the two of them were with the Giants. Maynard focused on Lombardi's approach in third and long situations, relating, "In the passing attack, if you needed 10 yards, he set up the scheme of the play so he was always going to make enough yardage. You could bet that he was going to put the ball down there 12, 15 yards—he wasn't going to be close when it came down to the nitty gritty."

Before Lombardi became the Green Bay coach, the quarterback's job was very demanding, as he had to call the play, the offensive formation, and the blocking scheme in the huddle. Lombardi changed that so his quarterback simply had to call out the play.

Raymond Berry pointed out that Lombardi's playbook was slim, and game plans built on their existing plays were "easily constructed." Lombardi's primary quarterback, Bart Starr, once said the Packers usually would run fewer than 20 plays per game, using as few as six to eight run plays and sometimes even fewer pass plays. Jerry Kramer remembered it as Lombardi and his staff selecting about 25 to 30 plays for each game from their repertoire of 120 to 150 total plays. Furthermore, in the 1966 title game victory versus the Cowboys, Lombardi's game plan included just eight run and six pass plays. Starr made four pass plays go for scores, riddling Dallas for 304 yards. Sheer simplicity augmented by execution. Sheer Lombardi.

When Green Bay manhandled the Chiefs in Super Bowl I, Lombardi did so again using basic plays, causing Kansas City coach Hank Stram to observe, "They were pure vanilla. No nuts, no chocolate, just pure vanilla." He said all of Lombardi's teams had that in common, "like a sledgehammer. Nothing fancy. No frills. No gadgets, just a straight-ahead attack designed to run over you or through you."[10]

Lombardi, of course, realized pro football is a business, played by grown men and not, for example, pimply faced high school teenagers. It was not a hobby or a mere pastime, it was serious business, and it provided the livelihood for him and his players. He knew, then, that there was no "rah-rah" speech, no sophomoric pep talk, not even a "Win one for the Gipper"–type oration he could utter that would magically motivate his men to play harder; however, he also knew that football is an emotional game and that a well-thought-out fiery talk could prod his players to excel. Moreover, he knew his own fiery nature could motivate his men.

Lombardi also stressed the positive quite a bit. In his mind, the Packers never lost a single game. He insisted that was true, while reluctantly conceding that there were a few times when the scoreboard clock *did* run out when his opponent had more points scored than his Packers. Now *that* is the power of positive thinking personified.

David Robinson mentioned another way Lombardi employed psychology:

> Lombardi was very careful. In those days, the Pittsburgh Steelers, a good team now, were crap. The Steelers and San Francisco were two of the worst teams in the league, and Vince would get you up for the game, but he only tried to get you so high so you wouldn't be burned out.
>
> Then, the next week, you go against Baltimore, our archrival in the Western Division, and we're getting ready for Johnny Unitas. Vince would do everything in his power to get you as high as he could get you. When you walked out of that locker room to play the Baltimore Colts, you were ready to play. But he knew that you couldn't keep a team at that high of a pitch 16 weeks in a row. He'd only get you high enough that you were up enough for the game that you were going to win.
>
> And he never wanted to beat a team real bad. I'll never forget when we beat Cleveland, 55–7, one time. Vince came in and read the riot act to us. He said, "They got beat bad like that, so now they have something to put on their bulletin board."
>
> We won the division one year, we beat Chicago in Milwaukee. We had them, 20–0, with two minutes to go in the game, so we decided we were going to play it easy, right? They went down the field, they went down, down, and finally kicked a field goal. We won the game, 28–3, and we're in the locker celebrating now as the division champs, right? We didn't have any alcohol or anything, but the guys are patting each other on the back.
>
> All of a sudden, *boom*, Vince came in and kicked the trash can clean across the locker room to the other side. He said, "The defense quit on me, huh? I never had a defense quit on me before and never will again. If you guys do that one more time, I will have a whole new defense here next week." We looked at each other, but that's how it was.

Robinson said that after the Packers enjoyed a key victory, Lombardi would not let complacency creep in. He invariably found fault, perhaps concentrating on some minute point to force his players to focus on the future and ways to continue winning rather than revel in the win at hand.

Robinson cited a prime example.

Like that big game in New York in 1967, when the Giants were the number-one offensive team in the league and we were the number-one defensive team in the league. Number one versus number one. It was built up as Lombardi's return to New York City to play at Yankee Stadium, a big game, the game of the week, everything. And we won.

The point is, after that big win, and I knew he was going to do it, he chewed me out for one play, one play all game, even though I got Defensive Player of the Week, but he was going to get on me because he didn't want me to go around strutting, "I'm the Defensive Player of the Week." He'd bring you back to reality.

Since then I've noticed, and I don't know how many times I've seen it, teams that weren't supposed to win, have a big, big upset win over an archrival. Something like that would happen this week, and the next week they'd lay an egg. They go back home and their family tells them they're the greatest thing since bubble gum. Their fans and their coaches all tell them how great they are, and they're on every TV show, getting pats on the back. And the next week and you think, "We're great," and they lay an egg.

You never saw Lombardi teams do that. If you get high, he'd bring you back. He'd find *something* in that game to get on you about, to bring you back to reality, to let you know you're not as big as you think you are.

Football psychology at its best.

Robinson also observed, "There was [another] thing Vince Lombardi knew: When a team is down and they got beat, he always did his best to find something to pick us up."

Lombardi took nothing for granted, and he made sure his players never did, either. Coming off winning the NFL championship in 1960, he decided to address his team on day one of his next training camp by going back to basics, even to the point he began his talk by holding up a football to his assembled group, saying, "Gentlemen, this is a football." Max McGee shouted out, "Uh, Coach, could you slow down a little? You're going too fast for us." Lombardi laughed, but he continued to go over the most basic of fundamentals of tackling, blocking, and so on, early each season. [11]

Lombardi kept players from becoming too comfortable another way, by making them unable to anticipate what might come next from their coach. Players feared his wrath and loved it when he lavished praise on them, but Lombardi was often inscrutable, unpredictable. Just when a player thought a tongue lashing was about to be administered, Lombardi offered praise or simply ignored a bad play that usually would have merited a reprimand. Conversely, as Dave Robinson recounted, when a player thought Lombardi absolutely had to be delighted with his showing in a game, he'd rip him for some real or semi-imagined fault.

Lombardi, who had quit law school to coach, would use the power of suggestion on his troops, too. Even though everyone in Green Bay knew how cold games could get there, Lombardi tried to convince his players conditions were just fine and dandy. Former Packer Fuzzy Thurston remembered that vividly. Said Thurston, "With Vince Lombardi, it was never cold here. Before games he'd just say something like, 'Men, it's a little blustery out there today.' Blustery, see? Then he'd say, 'It's our kind of day! Now get your asses out there and strut around like it's the Fourth of July.'"[12]

Yet another ploy Lombardi used was instilling a sense of peer policing. It may not have been as severe as a military "blanket party," but it was effective because money talks—quite loudly and eloquently. For example, if a player was dogging it in practice, Lombardi might point out that such behavior could lead to losses, which, in turn, could lead to the Packers not winning it all—and *that* would lead to everyone losing out on playoff money.

Robinson said that when Lombardi left the Packers to become coach and general manager of the Redskins, the first thing he did was take safety Tom Brown along with him, giving him a sort of ally, a man he was comfortable with. Later, he did basically the same thing with receiver Bob Long. "Then he had a man in the locker room," explained Robinson, adding,

> Bob Long is the only man who played [regularly] for Lombardi in both places. Brown was there [in Washington] but didn't play [he appeared in just one game].
>
> See, the thing with Tom Brown in Washington was he was the guy in the locker that teammates could ask, "What's this guy Lombardi like?" And he told them, "Be at meetings 15 minutes early. Be there or you're late." So there were no surprises. When Vince called his first meeting at Washington for 1:00, everybody was there at 12:45.

Lombardi had even used that plan when he had left the coaching ranks at New York to become the head man in Green Bay. Robinson said in that case, Lombardi brought along veteran defensive back and future Hall of Famer Emlen Tunnell. Robinson related,

> That did two things. Tunnell told teammates what kind of guy Lombardi was in New York, and he also was the African American representative on the Green Bay Packer team which Lombardi [brought to] an all-white town. Lombardi foresaw there might be some problems, and he nipped them in the bud—as Barney Fife would say, "Nip it in the bud." There weren't any problems, and that's how Vince Lombardi was. We were the first team to stay at the Waldorf Astoria. There were so many facets to the man.

Early on, Lombardi also once disciplined Tunnell in front of the entire team. Tunnell could laugh it off, as he knew what Lombardi was doing. By making an example of an established star, the message was sent: "Nobody is above the wrath of Lombardi."

Lombardi had strong opinions on how to handle *his* team. For instance, prior to Super Bowl I, league officials told him he was to bring the Packers to the game's venue, Los Angeles, about a week before kickoff. That was *not* Lombardi's way of doing things. He wanted to prepare at home and wait until a day or two before the game to fly out of Green Bay. He wanted to keep the team's normal routine going.

He also was uncharacteristically less than his usual unflappable self at that time, feeling pressure from peers to prove the NFL was the stronger league. Some players and coaches felt the Super Bowl was more or less the game that had to be played after the *real* title game, the NFL championship contest, which led up to the Super Bowl.

At any rate, flexing his muscles, while compromising a bit, he agreed to take his team West but refused to have them stay in bustling Los Angeles. The Packers, he said, would stay at Palo Alto, about 400 miles out. Then, realizing the NFL was demanding better media access, he relented (but not exactly benevolently) and headquartered the Pack in Santa Barbara, 80 miles away from the midst of the hurricane. Lombardi never had total faith or trust in the media to begin with. By the way, while there was somewhat of a media crush for Super Bowl I, although nothing like nowadays, fans were hardly in a frenzy—there would be 31,000 unoccupied seats in the Coliseum for the contest.

All distractions aside, the Packers pulled away from the Chiefs after being tied, 7–7, and won convincingly, 35–10. After the game, Lombardi, pressed by the media, finally said that, yes, the NFL was the better league.

Green Bay proved that once again in Super Bowl II, cruising by the Raiders, 33–14. On January 7, 1968, his team had flown to balmy Miami, where the temperature was 75, some 82 degrees higher than what they had left behind. Actually, Lombardi had his team stay about 20 miles away from Miami, in Fort Lauderdale, and he held mandatory meetings just about every afternoon and evening to remind the Packers they were in Florida to win a football game, not sightsee. In fact, he hadn't even taken his players down South until a week before kickoff. Needless to say, his players weren't too happy about holding Wisconsin workouts shortly after winning the Ice Bowl in Green Bay, no, not during the start of January, with temperatures some days continuing to dip below zero.

Lombardi made it a point to warn his team that a loss in the Super Bowl would hurt the prestige of the established NFL. "You damn well better not let that Mickey Mouse league beat you. It'd be a disgrace, a complete utter disgrace," he said. [13]

With the addition of a semifinal round of playoffs to the schedule, the 1967 season was the first one in which a team had to win three rounds of playoffs to claim the championship. Counting the exhibition season, the win against Oakland was the 23rd game Lombardi coached that season. It was also to be the last game Lombardi ever coached his Packers.

Lombardi's methods could sometimes be termed unusual, but there was a reason behind every move he made. Robinson remembered a unique situation.

> We had a playoff game in 1967, when we ended up in a tie with the Rams, and we ended up playing them in Milwaukee instead of Green Bay. I don't know why Vince did that. He probably had enough power to change [the venue] if he wanted to. But I'll tell you one thing, though, all week long it was like 10 below in Green Bay, and we went down to Milwaukee and it was 23 degrees. We felt like we had gone to Florida—the warmth! The guys [who] came in from LA froze to death at 23 degrees. So we had a distinct advantage.

Then take the case of Travis Williams, a return artist with spectacular speed, which gave him the ability to break off long returns seemingly at will. Teammate Bob Hyland said, "He was a rookie when I was a rookie [in 1967], and we became pretty good friends. We lived in the same apartment complex. He was a really good guy. I still have good memories of Travis."

Well, at first Williams had bad memories due to his having a hard time holding on to the football. Coach Lombardi quickly devised a learning technique. Hyland said,

> He made him carry the ball everywhere. Into the chow hall, getting out of his car, and walking into the locker room. He had to have that football in his hand. Going to the meeting, Travis had to have that ball. He wanted it to become second nature to him.
>
> You talk about a guy who had a load of talent. He returned four touchdowns his rookie year. He was just a bullet.

Williams's four kickoff returns for scores still stand as the most ever in a season (since tied by Cecil Turner). His average of 41.1 yards per kickoff return and his longest kick return of 104 yards both led the NFL in 1967. In 1969, he was still running wild—his 1,517 all-purpose yards trailed no one. In 1971, he returned a kickoff 105 yards, and he again led the league with the highest average of yards per return (29.7).

Hyland concluded, "I thought so much more was going to happen with his career, but things changed when Coach Lombardi left."

Myron Pottios, who went to the Pro Bowl three times, made a good point about how much talent the Packers, under Lombardi, had. Pottios played with Robinson in Washington, and while Robinson did get recognition and went on to become a Hall of Famer, in some respects he got lost in the shuffle a bit on the Packers. "Here's the thing about Dave in Green Bay," began Pottios.

> They had so many players in the Hall of Fame, but the publicity can only go so far. You can only give certain guys most of the publicity. So you had a situation there where, boy, on that defense you had Ray Nitschke, you had Willie Wood, Herb Adderley, Willie Davis, and Henry Jordan. You had five other guys [aside from Robinson] that made the Hall of Fame.
>
> So you've got all these guys, and it's tough no matter how good you are to stand out, to be head and shoulders above these guys, and that's what you have to do to get in the Hall of Fame. And publicity has a lot to do with it.

Fortunately, Robinson did make it to Canton, but Pottios was correct—Robinson did not get inducted into the Hall until almost exactly 40 years had passed since his retirement. Imagine, however, that this was a team with more than half of their starting defensive unit bound for the Hall of Fame.

Perhaps one reason there were so many Hall of Famers on the Packers is rudimentary. Lombardi preached a strong lesson about teamwork to his players, and that paid off in championships that earned a river of media ink for the Packers. Lombardi argued that even if an opposing player was smarter than a given Packer, or even if that opponent was, in fact, a better football player, that did not tell the entire story of what it takes to win in the NFL (and subsequently gain glory). Robinson said Lombardi told his players, "You have that one certain quality we saw and we nurtured and developed. And because you have that quality, you have become a Green Bay Packer. Now, *you* may get beat, but nobody, *nobody*, can beat the Green Bay Packers *as a team*." Robinson said, "That was his credo. That's what he told us all the time."

Raymond Berry, a former Southern Methodist University teammate and close friend of Forrest Gregg, said he and Gregg discussed Lombardi, and they concurred that both the legendary Packers coach and Berry's Baltimore head coach, Weeb Ewbank, not only shared a simple approach to play-calling, but also, said Berry, possessed an uncanny ability to "spot talent in unknown players."

Lombardi, as Pottios noted, was blessed with an overabundance of talent on the Packers, but obviously he still deserves credit for acquiring great players, helping to mold them, and putting them in situations where they could succeed. Take the case of Bart Starr, for one example.

From 1960, the first season in which Starr played in more than five games and didn't have a sub-.500 record as the starting quarterback (he was 4–4 in 1960), to 1967, Lombardi's dynastic Packers put up a fantastic winning percentage (disregarding ties) of .774, going 82–24–4, with 73 of those wins coming with Starr as the starting QB. They went to the title game six times in those eight seasons and won it all five times, once with a 37–0 rout of the mighty New York Giants. In 1963, as touched on earlier, Starr's Packers dazzled at 11–2–1. Yet, they did not make the playoffs in this talent-packed period—the Bears squeaked by to win the division title at 11–1–2.

Another salient example of Lombardi's sagacity: Green Bay hit it big in the 1958 draft, when he selected bruising fullback Taylor in the second round and then acquired ferocious linebacker Ray Nitschke one round later. Those future Hall of Famers were crucial cogs in the Packer machinery that rolled like a juggernaut over most of their opponents.

Hyland said there was one time Lombardi's usually unfailing judgment went south—but it did not relate to him as a coach. Hyland revealed,

> When he decided to leave his coaching capacity at Green Bay and just be the general manager, I think he made a mistake in Phil [Bengston] being named the head coach. He was a great defensive coach, but he just really wasn't cut out to be the head coach, and I think the record proves that afterwards. Phil was a gentleman who knew the defense and so forth, but he had a tough act to follow in Coach Lombardi.

For the record, in Green Bay's first season sans Lombardi, the Packers finished third, with a 6–7–1 record. The last time they had recorded a losing record was the season before Lombardi came to town. Furthermore, the Pack's next trip to a Super Bowl came many years later, in 1997.

Dave Robinson spoke of one aspect of Lombardi's coaching ability that wasn't as strong as most facets, stating,

> I think Vince didn't really understand how the defenses worked sometimes, but he did know offenses. We were having a drill, a seven-on-seven out there on the field, and a guy breaks open into the clear—Vince knew that somebody had blown their assignment. He wasn't sure who it was, but he knew somebody must have because the offensive guy shouldn't been that wide open.
>
> Phil Bengston, our defensive coordinator, would be right beside Vince. They stood side by side at all the scrimmages, at all the meetings, and whatnot. You'd see Vince would turn to Phil and say something, probably, "Who's man was that?" Phil would say, "Well, that's Robinson's," and then Vince would holler, "Robinson. What the hell you doing out here?"

Lombardi had stock phrases he loved to repeat, for instance, "Fatigue makes cowards of us all." He often vowed to his men that he would make them the best football players he possibly could, something Chuck Mercein still attests to.

Naturally, Lombardi grew close to such players as Starr and Gregg, perhaps his favorite player ever (some argue that would have been Hornung). Raymond Berry stated Lombardi preferred the kind of player Gregg was, one who, "when that whistle blew, went 100 percent on every play, every time. He had the heart of a lion with a great competitive spirit."

Praise for Lombardi comes from many sources. Hyland played one season under him. While he appreciated the ability of excellent assistants like Bengston, he observed, "Nobody had any questions about who the head coach was, that was Coach Lombardi. In my opinion, the best ever."

When Charley Taylor, Hall of Fame receiver/running back, was asked for his take on Lombardi, he replied,

> What a man. You hear the stories about Lombardi in Green Bay, and you feel like, "Everybody wants to play for him." I was with him for one season, and he just turned my whole theory around about coaches and players—what's expected of you, what you have to do to maintain a position, and just how you play the game, period.

Taylor said being able to play for Lombardi was one of the biggest highlights of his career.

When asked for his thoughts on Lombardi, Mike Ditka immediately shot back,

> The best. Coach Lombardi was special. I mean, he took the Packers from a bunch of guys to probably one of the best teams in the history of the game, and you gotta love that. You gotta appreciate that. When he first went there, he didn't mess around very much. He did it pretty quick, you know.

Andy Nelson, an All-Pro defensive back for the Baltimore Colts, marveled at Lombardi's accomplishment of leading his Packers to an unprecedented three consecutive NFL titles. He noted, "Mr. Lombardi was a disciplinarian and a fundamentalist." It hardly surprised Nelson that Lombardi was sometimes called "Invincible Vince" and "St. Vincent."

When Jackie Smith retired after the 1978 season, he had caught 480 passes for 7,918 yards, the most ever by a tight end. He became the third tight end inducted into the Hall of Fame. Smith said he would have loved to have known and played for Lombardi, adding that while he never met him, there was a time before a Cardinals versus Packers game "when he got my attention and just winked at me and gave me the high sign. I thought that was one of the biggest things that happened to me in a long time."

Smith continued,

> He was an unusual guy that a lot of players would have liked to play for. And what's interesting about so many of the players that do play for coaches like him is that they have a special thing [with their coach] and they've learned a lot with someone like him who they came to revere—those real good coaches. They had a real positive effect on players on and off the field.

Some casual fans might be surprised to learn Lombardi only coached 10 seasons and only won 96 games, but his regular-season winning percentage of .738—the third highest in NFL history, behind only fellow Hall of Famers Guy Chamberlin, who coached just six years in the early years of the league, and John Madden—comes as no surprise. Plus, Lombardi only lost 34 regular-season contests.

Furthermore, his 9–1 record in the playoffs is no surprise to anyone who follows football. That record works out to a scintillating .900 winning percentage, the best of all time. Not only that, but his only postseason loss came in the first playoff game he coached, the 1960 title contest versus the Philadelphia Eagles. Lombardi had taken his team to that encounter in just his second season as a head coach.

He learned a few lessons from the defeat, grew as a coach, and never again lost in postseason play. Reportedly, after the loss, he told his players, nine of whom would become Hall of Famers, that they would never again lose a postseason game—and they didn't.

Another legendary Green Bay coach, Curly Lambeau, laid the foundation, and Lombardi built from there, making the Packers one of the winningest franchises in NFL history. In fact, entering the 2016 season, the only team with more total wins in their history was the Chicago Bears, and their lead over Green Bay may soon disappear. Counting postseason games, only the Bears, Packers, and Giants had won more than 700 games through 2016.

Lombardi died of cancer in September 1970, and within months, prior to the next Super Bowl, the award given yearly to that game's winner was renamed the Vince Lombardi Trophy.

Perhaps Robinson summed up Lombardi's excellence most simply: "The fact that Lombardi was a pro coach, better than the coaches I had until then, was a given, but you never knew how great Vince Lombardi was unless you left and went somewhere else."

9

TOM LANDRY

The Man in the Funny Hat

Place of birth: Mission, Texas
Date of birth: September 11, 1924
Date of death: February 12, 2000
Lifetime wins, losses, and ties: 250–162–6
Career winning percentage: .607
Playoff wins and losses: 20–16
Playoff winning percentage: .556
NFL major titles won and years of championships: NFL champs 1970, 1975, 1978; Super Bowl champs 1971, 1977
Teams coached and years: Dallas Cowboys 1960–1988

Tom Landry filled many roles in his life, from being the warm, loving patriarch of his family to being a star football player to being a combat pilot and, later, a coaching great.

Many players from the early glory years were World War II veterans, and when asked about how fearful they were when playing in the violent world of the NFL, they scoffed. Nothing, they said, could ever be frightening after witnessing and experiencing the perils and terrors of combat. An NFL opponent might gouge, head slap, or even cheap-shot you, but that was a mere distraction compared to, for instance, seeing a Panzer tank bearing down and taking dead aim at you; and a real blitzkrieg made a wave of blitzing linebackers seem like a gentle ripple in a kiddie pool. Landry would prove to be fearless as a player and coach.

By the time he had proved his mettle as a coach, it was safe to say that Landry was to the Lone Star State what Winston Churchill was to England. A Texan through and through, Landry and football go back to his days as a high school quarterback who steered his Mission, Texas, team to an undefeated, 12–0, championship season. As a senior, Landry helped his team pile up 322 points, while the defense gave up *zero points* all year long.

Scholarship in hand, he moved on to the University of Texas, but Landry took a break from football and college after one semester to fight for his country as a U.S. Army Air Corps bomber pilot in World War II.

He flew 30 missions over territory controlled by German troops before being honorably discharged in 1945 (when he'd return to the college campus). The courageous Landry had even volunteered to fly extra missions in his B-17 airplane. He also survived a crash landing in Belgium, coming down between two trees, which ripped his plane's wings off. Only the fact that the B-17 had run out of fuel prevented a catastrophic fire. As mentioned, after such experiences, there was absolutely nothing about the world of football that could intimidate him.

Back at the University of Texas, Landry mainly played defensive back and fullback, although at one point he was a backup quarterback for future Hall of Famer Bobby Layne. Landry gained All-Southwest Conference status as a junior. That season, Texas went 10–1 and ranked number five in the nation in the final AP poll. Landry was also named team cocaptain in his senior season. In both his junior and senior seasons, the Longhorns went to and won bowl games—the Sugar Bowl in January 1948, and the Orange Bowl the following year.

Landry's pro career began in 1949, as a member of the New York Yankees, and not the Major League Baseball team—these were the Yankees of the short-lived (1946–1949) AAFC, the All-American Football Conference. There, already knowing football inside out, he did everything but serve meals and shine spikes as a rookie—he was a back on defense and offense, punted, returned kickoffs and punts, and even filled in for the starting quarterback.

He ran, or, more accurately, he *lumbered* through the 100-yard "dash" at about 10.5 seconds. In one game as a cornerback, he was burned by Otto Graham's pinpoint passing to (the *very* speedy) Mac Speedie. Landry was exploited for a league-record 11 receptions and 228 yards during a 31–0 annihilation. It was much like the time Don Shula was schooled by Raymond Berry (more on this later).

Instead of sulking, Landry took this as a learning experience and set out to study teams' tendencies so he could anticipate, and not merely react, to opponents' moves. That awakening helped him survive in pro football as a player, and last forever as a coach. He taught his defenses to read keys and understand teams' tendencies. Like a guess hitter in baseball, being able to anticipate what was coming often led to big payoffs.

With the death of the AAFC, Landry moved to the NFL and played for the New York Giants from 1950 to 1955, exhibiting a physical style of play as the team's left cornerback.

He began his coaching days as the New York Giants' defensive coordinator in 1954, while still an active player—the same year he was an All-Pro. He remained on the job through 1959, before moving on to Dallas. When it came to covering his personal expenses, his coaching salary was fig-leaf small, but his future earning power would soon flourish.

So would his reputation as a shrewd coach. ENIAC, the world's first electronic general-purpose computer, came along in 1946. Landry's computer-like brain preceded ENIAC by perhaps as many as 16 years. Owning an engineering degree from the University of Texas, he was analytical, and it's been said he was probably dissecting defenses and studying offensive schemes since he first touched a football, say at about age six, in 1930.

Mike Ditka said Landry was very defensive minded, "so everything he did with offense was to figure out a way to beat a defense. He would defense his offense, then figure out a way to beat it—that's the way he coached."

When Landry signed a five-year contract for $34,500 per season to become the first head coach in Cowboys history, the task he faced was almost insurmountable. One thing he had going for him was total autonomy with his on-the-field running of the team.

Raymond Berry recalled that while the NFL did grant Dallas a franchise, the other teams' owners were not exactly charitable with the new team. "They gave them absolutely nothing," said Berry. "So when Landry started in 1960, he basically had no talent whatsoever." Dallas came into the NFL too late for the 1959 draft, and missing out on that opportunity to snatch up some real talent hurt sorely.

Naturally, the Cowboys couldn't compete against the established teams, and that is exactly what those teams' owners wanted. Instead of stocking Dallas with several decent players off their rosters or giving them, say, an extra high draft pick or two, Berry said the Cowboys were given the "bottom three players off the rosters of all 12 teams. The teams didn't want anybody to compete with them, but they wanted the money they'd get for the new franchise. They took the money and gave them nothing." Plus, Landry was given just 24 hours to make his selections.

Perhaps the league figuratively put a cumbersome ball and chain on Landry, arming him with 36 discards, but he was such a gifted coach it only took him until his third season with the Cowboys (1962) before his offense came in second in the NFL for total yards. Sure, they would need more than that to become a winner—their first season with more wins than losses didn't come until 1966 (10–3–1), but after that Landry would be, for the most part, off and running. No more threadbare or retread players for him.

Landry proved he could overcome adversity, patiently going through the lean years and the drafts that followed each sad season before finally putting together a team that could compete.

How bad were the early years? Well, the Cowboys didn't win many games at all. Their record for the first five years of their existence revealed they were still struggling to get the personnel they would need to win. In their first season, they went winless, at 0–11–1, and scored a total of six touchdowns and six field goals. Furthermore, they never topped five wins until 1965.

Once Landry overcame inertia, he rolled on, engineering good to great seasons almost yearly. He took Dallas to postseason play every year from 1966 to 1973; missed out in 1974, when he posted a record of 8–4; and made the playoffs again annually from 1975 to 1983. In other words, in an 18-year span, Landry's Cowboys took part in postseason play every year but one. In five of those seasons, Dallas advanced all the way to the Super Bowl, winning it all in 1971 and 1977.

Despite such success, early on picky critics weren't on board. Mel Renfro, an All-Pro in 10 of his 14 seasons, played his entire career (1964–1977) under one coach, Landry. He recalled that after Dallas began to make postseason appearances yearly, but without winning it all, the Cowboys "had all those next-year's champion labels in the 1960s—in 1966, '67, '68, and '69—of not being able to win the big ones." He added, "But we were right there, knocking on the door. For a long time we had a great football team, we just couldn't break that barrier until 1970."

Even in 1970, they won many big games *until* the Super Bowl. It wasn't until their 24–3 win the next season versus Miami in Super Bowl VI that the label was shredded.

Just how was Landry able to take a team from a junkyard and mold them into an undeniable winner? For one thing, he knew the game inside out, capable of improving every facet of a team. Unlike Weeb Ewbank, Vince Lombardi, and Paul Brown, to name three, Landry mainly focused on the defensive side of the game.

However, he was also quite clever, willing to explore and implement innovative offensive schemes. Coaching the Cowboys, Landry installed the most complicated offense in the league, tricking defenders with plays and a vast array of formations. Dallas sometimes had about eight to 10 formations from which Landry could call 50 plays, giving opponents, in effect, as many as 500 different plays to fret about.

Perhaps it's more accurate to say his offense was *ostensibly* the most complicated in the NFL, but it was paradoxically, said Berry, not complex at all—not if one looked beneath the surface.

Berry declared,

> Landry had one of the most simple offenses you could ever imagine. That's one of the reasons he was so potent. The main impression that you had when you played the Dallas Cowboys was that they used multiple formations, something Landry had learned as a defensive coach with the New York Giants. There, one of the things he had discovered and dealt with was that what gave him problems were formation changes—like an opposing team would line up in the I formation, then shift to spread backs, or they'd motion the flanker, and the defensive guys had to discern what was going on, and that interfered with their concentration on where the point of attack was going to be.
>
> What Landry explained to me was the Cowboys were very basic in plays, very fundamental, but they might run their off-tackle play off of six different looks. The Cowboys would shift the split backs, motion a guy, use "trips" and double wings, but he only had a very few plays.

This was designed. Doing this stopped the enemy from marshaling their forces at the right point. If they wanted to hit the right tackle area, Landry didn't want six guys being there because defensively that's what he did—he studied other teams' offenses and he knew from their formations what teams liked to do from given formations. So he taught his players, "When they get in this formation, these are the two plays they like to run." He was ahead of his time and ahead of other teams using computers to learn such things. He'd have people at the right spot to stop those plays. And that's what he neutralized against other teams with his own offense.

Landry often stressed the importance of recognizing and anticipating the point of attack, contending that if a defense could predict the point of the offense's attack, it was relatively easy to then muster enough defensive forces to stifle the attack. Failure to recognize the point of attack meant the defense had to spread itself all over the field to cover a multitude of possible attack points.

Conversely, when Landry's offense was on the field, his aim was to disguise his point of attack, preventing the other team from anticipating where the ball would go.

Berry went on to say Landry "became one of the greatest offensive coaches of all time because he understood what screwed up his defense. The offense he put in at Dallas was what he knew bothered him, what was difficult to defend against, and that's what he was going to use against opponents." For instance, Landry loved using an occasional gimmick play, and he constantly was putting men in motion, anything to create even a moment of confusion or doubt for the defense. He may also have been unparalleled when it came to making situational substitutions.

An innovator, he saw a need to give his quarterbacks time to throw. Thus, he went to the gun rack, took the old shotgun formation out, cleaned the weapon, made a few alterations, and brought it back into the game (in 1975).

As a side note, at the end of the 1975 season, when Paul Brown retired, Landry, who at 35 had been the youngest head coach when he was hired, was now, at 52 and in his 17th season, the dean of all coaches.

Landry also deserves credit for embracing his organization's pioneering use of computers. That helped Dallas unearth talent in small colleges, often black ones, which turned out such men as Jethro Pugh.

Dallas also discovered and signed free agents the likes of five-time Pro Bowl defensive back Cornell Green out of Utah State. Green was an All-American, but in basketball, not football. Renfro said of Green,

> He was [player personnel vice president] Gil Brandt's prize pick. Cornell never played a down of football in high school or college, but he was a great basketball player who had great instincts, great feet, and good speed. That was Gil's pick, but Landry developed him into a star at cornerback.

The Cowboys were unafraid to use a draft pick on a college player who wouldn't be available to join the team for at least a year. A classic example of this is Roger Staubach, who won the Heisman Trophy in 1963, while at Navy, but had a four-year commitment to serve in the U.S. Navy. In 1969, he was a 27-year-old rookie, but one headed for the Hall of Fame.

Landry was great at quickly spotting talent. For example, the Cowboys scouts knew what Renfro could do long before he joined the team, but said Renfro, "During the offseason I went to Dallas and worked out for Landry. He took about five minutes watching me, and said, 'This kid can play,' and he walked away."

Speaking of walking away, Landry even found talented players who had ostensibly done just that, walked away from the game, finished with their football days. Consider Jackie Smith, who played for Landry in 1978, coming out of retirement to do so. Smith reflected,

> He called me after the fourth game of the season. I was at my restaurant, and he said, "Hey, Jackie, this is Coach Landry." I said, "Right," and I hung up because I felt somebody was jacking with me. He called me back, quick, laughing. I was concerned about being able to play because I had been out for a few months. My legs felt pretty good because I had just got back from hiking four weeks out in Colorado. I expressed to him some hesitation about it, but he said, "Well, you get on down here and we'll be the judge of that." I said, "Thank you, sir," and I hung up and went there. And there was never a question about it in his mind—at least nobody mentioned it at all.

There's a chance that, had Landry not recognized Smith's talent and talked him out of retirement, the Cowboys would have been eliminated from postseason play in their first game. In the third quarter, Dallas needed two scores to defeat the Atlanta Falcons, and a Danny-White-to-Smith strike provided them with the first of their pair of touchdowns, leading to their 27–20 comeback win. Smith said players typically respect the legendary coaches and "would like to get to know them a lot better, and I was glad I got to know Coach Landry a lot better."

Berry believes Landry's military training carried over into his football strategies. One prominent point that was the residue of that background was that if a coach wants to attack his opponent, he should try to use a sleight-of-hand-like distraction or misdirection technique, anything to disguise his true point of attack.

In short, Landry studied everything, and his diligence frequently led to his teams' involvement in big games. Starting with his role as a Giants assistant coach, consider some of Landry's most defining moments and accomplishments.

Win or lose, Landry always did his job, preparing for any eventuality. For instance, in the 1958 playoff contest to determine who would advance to the championship game, Landry's defense rendered the mighty Browns offense impotent. It turned out they absolutely had to stop them cold, as the Giants offense sputtered, feebly managing just one field goal and one touchdown in their shutout win.

Incredibly, Landry's troops smothered Jim Brown, who did break off a 20-yard run but, tackled for repeated losses, wound up with eight net yards on seven carries; it was his worst NFL game ever. The great Jim Brown held to an average of 1.14 yards per rush? Impossible!

Later, Cleveland's Lou Groza told the media, "Only one man could have done this to us." He paused, before providing the answer: "Tom Landry."[1] Once, a Ewbank-led Colts team held Brown to 14 yards in 11 carries, his worst regular-season output.

One of the biggest reasons the Giants defense shined under Landry was something he did starting with Sam Huff and then continued for decades—he centered his defenses around his middle linebackers, using the 4–3 defensive setup.

While he did not invent the 4–3 defense—Steve Owen gets credit for coming up with that in 1950, for his Giants—Landry perfected it. In fact, by the time he was through tinkering with it, his brainchild was so effective it didn't take long for other coaches to realize Landry had come up with a good thing. By 1960, virtually every one of the league's 13 teams was using Landry's three-linebacker look.

The fact his defense is still a standard more than 60 years after he polished it is tremendous testimony to his brilliance. Think about it, how many coaches have actually been credited with discovering or perfecting something totally new in football? Not many, and only the great ones. Plus, Landry came up with numerous other elaborate, creative concepts, from the flex defense to his multiple formation offense.

Like any coach, however, Landry's career demonstrated that you win some and you lose some. Unfortunately for him and the Giants, in 1958 and 1959, they did win a ton of games building up to the title games, but they were defeated by the Colts both years.

As a former defensive back, Landry decided to have his cornerbacks work man-to-man in the 1958 title game. His purpose was to give the rest of the team more support to hold the Baltimore running game at bay. He often had his linebackers, defensive front four, *and* his two safeties up tight to the line to force the Colts to pass. It didn't work, as Unitas and Berry, in particular, foiled the strategy—even when Berry was double-teamed. Furthermore, when the Giants overloaded their defense on Berry, Lenny Moore would find himself covered by just one man, making him yet another dangerous offensive weapon.

The following year, Landry knew he had to make some adjustments. Berry believes the Giants were convinced that, given the success the Colts had in the '58 title game, with Unitas and Berry teaming up to hurt New York repeatedly, Landry's defense was determined to stop the passing duo; however, to concentrate on Berry was to somewhat neglect Moore, trying to handle him with one-on-one coverage. "And you don't forget Lenny Moore," said Berry. Unitas threw Moore's way three times for 126 yards, including a 60-yarder to open the game's scoring.

Landry later said his original plan was to stop the Colts running game and double-team both Berry and receiver Jim Mutscheller. Berry knew Landry's job was thankless because the Colts simply had too many weapons for the Giants to cope with, but Landry was hoping New York would somehow manage to overcome whatever damage Moore might do.

Despite the early Moore touchdown, the plan worked for some quite some time. The Giants even clung to a 9–7 lead at the end of three quarters. That was before Baltimore exploded for 24 unanswered points to put the game out of reach.

To be fair, the Colts were so talented all around, it would have been next to impossible to shut down either their running or passing game—

there was no way Landry could win, no matter what he zeroed in on or how long and hard he planned.

When Dallas made the playoffs for the first time in 1966, they went 10–3–1, marking the first double-digit win total for Landry. In all, he won 10 or more games on 16 occasions, and that included a run of six seasons and another of seven seasons with 10-plus victories. But in the 1966 postseason it was one-and-done. The Cowboys had a shot at winning the NFL championship but lost a heartbreaker, 34–27, to Green Bay.

They lost the title again to the Packers the next season on another demoralizing defeat in the Ice Bowl. At least they had been able to come up with the franchise's first-ever postseason win a week earlier, dismantling the Browns, 52–14.

The next bulleted item from Landry's resume came in 1970, when Dallas won the NFL championship. After going 10–4 in the regular season, they earned a trip to their first Super Bowl by dispatching the Detroit Lions by the unusual score of 5–0, and by squeaking by the San Francisco 49ers, 17–10. A late 32-yard field goal by Jim O'Brien of the Colts ended the Dallas reverie, 16–13, in Super Bowl V.

In that game, Landry again showed he had the uncanny ability to detect what opponents were about to run. "That year," attested former Colt Sam Havrilak,

> we ran a gimmick play or two every game, and I was involved in most of them. So every time I came into the game, Dallas coach Tom Landry [would warn his defense] to watch out for something screwy. When we ran a flea-flicker, he had it figured out, and I went to throw the ball back to Earl Morrall, but he was covered, so I look downfield and threw a pass to Eddie Hinton.

For the record, Hinton fumbled the ball out of the end zone.

The Detroit Tigers once had a player named Charlie Gehringer, who earned the nickname "Mechanical Man" for his productive, dependable ways. The joke was one could wind him up on Opening Day and just let him go and he'd do the rest. Well, Landry won games with mechanical regularity, once reeling off 20 straight seasons (1966–1985) with a winning record. That helped him reach 250 lifetime wins (#3 all-time). In the 2017 season, Bill Belichick tied Landry's win total. Landry's 20 postseason wins stood at the zenith of coaches for decades, from 1982 to 2014, before Belichick eased beyond that number. Moreover, in 18 of Landry's

29 seasons, the Cowboys played in at least one postseason game. He made it to the playoffs eight years in a row, missed one, and made it back to postseason play for nine more years running. Consistency.

It's no wonder that by 1978, Dallas had become known as "America's Team"—even though Landry, at first, wasn't fond of that nickname, fearing every team in the league would try to tear them down. It didn't matter, Landry won regardless of the odds or his enemies' determination.

Even in 1975, when a dozen rookies made the team, an otherwise aging, supposedly rebuilding squad made it to the Super Bowl (even though they'd lose there to Pittsburgh in a close-but-no-stogie contest). That was the year Dallas, a team famous for its unfathomable comebacks, executed a play that even now symbolizes miraculous finishes, the Hail Mary pass.

In the first round of playoff action, Dallas traveled north to face the Vikings. Down 14–10, with 24 seconds to go, Dallas, having earlier converted an improbable fourth-and-16 situation into a 25-yard gain on this desperation drive, heaved a pass. Staubach, out of the shotgun, pump-faked to his left and then hurled the football deep to Drew Pearson. Pearson and defender Neil Wright made contact at about the five-yard line, but Pearson somehow still caught the ball and walked in for a 50-yard game-winner.

Landry, who won his second Super Bowl just two years later, was a devoted veteran of 40 years of NFL action as a player, a player/coach, and coach for a fantastic unbroken string of seasons from 1949 to 1988, bridging almost six decades.

The 1988 season was Landry's final one. It was also the year he put up his worst record since his first year with Dallas. When Dallas lost its seventh in a row in the middle of a 10-game losing streak, George Bush had just won the presidential election. Landry points out in his autobiography that the last time he had dropped seven straight games, Dwight Eisenhower resided in the White House. Landry's Cowboys had certainly fallen on hard times, with a dismal record of 3–13; however, to most folks, he *was* the Dallas Cowboys.

His luminescent reputation and superlative record didn't matter one iota when Jerry Jones bought the team. Jones ignominiously fired the legendary Landry after he had guided them to five championship games and a slew of divisional titles. Despite all of that, he was dismissed by Jones, thrown away as if he were a wrapper from a candy bar. Less than two months later, Dallas celebrated Tom Landry Day, proving that, unlike Jones, the city appreciated this legendary coach.

With football having been such an enormous part of Landry's life, he naturally was crushed. He rarely made a public display of his emotions, but this was an exception. There may be no crying in baseball, as the movie *A League of Their Own* contends, but upon being fired, tears were permitted to flow unabated.

Landry's personality, especially his stoicism, has been a widely discussed and analyzed topic throughout the years. He was constantly portrayed as being coldly analytical, and many members of the organization, mainly players, felt his major flaw was that he was too unemotional.

One season, near the end of the days of training camp, team owner Clint Murchison reported to the media that there had been just one significant injury that had taken place. "Tom Landry smiled and pulled a muscle,"[2] he quipped.

An often-repeated joke about the soft-spoken Landry's serious ways came from Walt Garrison. When his career with the Cowboys came to an end, Garrison was asked if he had ever seen Landry smile. He grinned and replied, "I don't know. I only played there for nine years."

Too many people went for the quick, easy, rather cheap laugh. Landry *chose* not to be too demonstrative as a coach; he most certainly did have feelings, but he controlled them. He didn't want to get too close with his players, fearing it might impair his judgment regarding his men and the decisions he had to make pertaining to them. He also believed players need to have rules and he had to enforce them. Furthermore, he tended to get tough on his men when things were going well to prevent complacency. Still, he refused to use fear as a motivational tool, and when off duty, he was a warm person and a family man. He simply felt a leader had to get the best out of his followers, and sometimes that meant not winning any Mr. Congeniality contests.

Plus, Landry's stoic facade wasn't perpetually in place. Once, after a loss to Pittsburgh, he called a team meeting in which he praised his players' effort, then, in a rare moment, expressed doubts about his own ability to improve the team with his offensive and defensive plans. At that point, he broke down in tears for several minutes. Dallas star Bob Lilly said after that meeting, the team, now seeing him as a person with emotions and realizing Landry's devotion, became more serious. They went on to rattle off six wins in the next seven contests.

Mike Ditka said those who portrayed Landry to be cold and distant didn't know the man. "He was the most caring, thoughtful man I've ever been around," Ditka declared. "And emotion? Yeah, he had emotion, but he didn't show it in public, but I've seen him show it in private when he had to cut players and things like that—it hurt." Pointing to Landry's military record, Ditka added that, beyond football, Landry was a true American hero. "Pretty special guy,"[3] he concluded.

Despite Landry's reputation for being humorless, almost robotic, he came up with a pretty good line on occasion. Take the time he and his Cowboys made the trek to St. Louis to play the Cardinals in Busch Memorial Stadium. The facility was new back then, and the turf that had been used to cover the infield portion of the field used by the baseball Cardinals was not in good shape. As his squad practiced on the field, Landry walked by his lineman, whose cleats caused clumps of grass to fly up at him. He bent over, inspected some of the sod, and dryly said, "This is really Busch,"[4] an obvious play on words referring to something "bush," or not up to big-league quality.

Another time, when Landry was asked to evaluate a poor showing by his defense on a one-to-10 basis, the coach replied, "Do we have to start at one?"

Landry was also a man of morality and strong religious conviction. Renfro said,

> A lot of his players became strong Christians after their playing career because of his influence. Reflecting back on how hard it was for Landry, being a strong Christian, to deal with some things: He realized the way that certain things were in the South and in Texas [specifically] that some of the black players were going through. And some of the racism that was in the White Citizens' Council—he struggled with making decisions sometimes, but he always did the right thing in professing his Christian belief, rather than go the other way.

Renfro said he remembered "one episode at a practice when we were in the Cotton Bowl and Landry was demonstrating a linebacker drop because they couldn't seem to do it the way he wanted it, so he thought he'd get out there and physically turn and run like he wanted them to." Renfro added,

And he tripped and fell flat on his face. Everybody laughed, but not out loud, they kinda' snickered under their breath. And he got up and said, "Gosh darn." That was probably the strongest use of language that we ever heard him use. Anybody else would've said something a lot stronger. Never, ever, did we hear him say one curse word. He was aware of [what happens] in the heat of the battle, and he heard some strong language, but we never heard him use any.

Throughout his days in Dallas, Landry was always a picture of sartorial perfection, topped off with his famous fedora, which led to his being sometimes called the "Man in the Funny Hat." From the early years, when he had little talent to work with, throughout his winning seasons and to the very end, he also remained a man with quiet, but unquestioned, class and dignity. In fact, he said he set out to dress in a businesslike manner beginning with his days coaching in New York, when he thought he'd wind up going into business.

Landry was always seeking to improve himself and others. After the 1966 season, he took a course in psychology, figuring it would help him as a coach and, in turn, that could help his players.

Don Meredith, a star quarterback under Landry, called his coach a perfectionist, stating, "If he was married to Raquel Welch, he'd expect her to cook."[5]

Well, Landry was, in fact, a perfectionist, and, despite Meredith's joke, being a perfectionist shouldn't be a rap against a great football head coach. NFL legend Tony Dorsett said Landry could not tolerate players who made the same foolish mistake over and over, never learning from a physical or mental lapse. Dorsett said such players would not be on the field for Landry. Stated the famous running back, "He'd be sitting on the bench or unemployed."[6]

Renfro further reflected on Landry, relating,

I think the number-one thing was his consistency, and he was a very intelligent coach. He left no stone unturned. I remember in the film room he would grade every player, every play. The coaches would grade their position players and give Landry the report, and when we went through the game films he would study them, then go over every play that you were involved in where you were at the point of attack, and he'd grade you. If you made nine great plays and one bad play, he'd focus on the bad play.

Sometimes you'd sit there, hoping that he would miss something, but he never did—he'd catch every single thing you did on every play that, like I said, you were at the point of attack.

He really expected you to do your job, and he wasn't the rah-rah type, and he wasn't going to joke with you. He was going to get right to the point and let you know how he felt.

But the one thing is he was hard to like the first two, three years, but when we became winners, it became a whole lot easier to get along with him. I think once we got past a certain point in winning and performing, he eased up a little bit, and it was a pleasure to be coached by him.

Landry didn't buy into the philosophy "If it ain't broke, don't fix it." His theme was, "If it ain't broke, but it isn't perfect, improve it." In other words, Landry was constantly seeking to improve his schemes, even when they were already good, and he had faith in himself and his ideas when he concocted something new.

That was true even when one of his ideas was widely criticized. When he had two valuable quarterbacks, veteran Eddie LeBaron and a young Don Meredith, he decided at one point to shuttle them into the game on alternate plays. He did the same later with Craig Morton and Roger Staubach, although he came to find that an untenable situation. He even briefly tried starting Morton one week and Staubach the next. In both instances, he was ripped for being indecisive, but he did what he felt was right, and when he did feel the time was right, he wisely went with Meredith over LeBaron and Staubach over Morton. Such moves paid off. Meredith was the first standout quarterback for Dallas, and Staubach played in five Super Bowls, started four of them, and won two. In two of the losses, Dallas had a shot at winning as time was expiring—both times Staubach's last action was throwing a pass into the end zone on a hope and a prayer, both unanswered. He steered the Cowboys back from trailing to winning 23 games, and in 14 of those contests he did so in the final two minutes of play.

Berry, who coached under Landry, shared a revelatory story along those lines:

> Coach Landry once told me about what happened when he introduced a new defensive system to his Cowboys. It was a sound one, better than what they had been using. He said he wanted to get to "level 10,"

moving up from what was in place, which was only working at about a level five. When Tom installed the new system, they went through a period at level two.

Berry said Landry was unperturbed by the initial setback because he believed in himself and what he was doing. Soon, due to his dogged determination and faith, his defense was playing at his level-10 goal. Berry noted, "He stuck to it and hung in there. He never gave up, and he maintained a belief in what he was doing."

Landry's engineering background was evident every time he drew up a play. Former Cowboys still recall how intricate and well-thought-out his plays were. In addition, unlike a vast majority of coaches, Landry prepared every game's offensive *and* defensive game plans.

Jackie Smith said,

> He was a guy who, before I went down there, you knew about him, but you really didn't know him. I was delighted to play for him. My biggest highlight by going to the Cowboys for a little while, was to be able to watch him and to observe him. He was an absolute genius at offense *and* defense. He got a lot covered in a hurry.
>
> One of the things that always fascinated me and made me scratch my head was when we were with the Cardinals, the defensive coaches did all their work and it was handed out [to players], and the offensive guys were handed out [information], but Coach Landry did *everything*. He did short yardage plays, invented plays, he did all of that as far as the offense was concerned. And I'm sure he did the same thing on the defense. He was quite a guy.
>
> I remember I was sitting in there on a Tuesday morning, and all the coaches were there along with us waiting for Coach Landry to come in with a game plan. It's hard to give him enough accolades as far as how he had such a tremendous depth of confidence—that he was going to do the right thing and call the right play.
>
> I think that everybody noticed and observed his real stoic character. He was that a lot of times—most of the time, but he would really come up with the right play at the right time. It was quite remarkable that he could sort of predict what players were going to be doing, and he would [put] the plays together to take advantage of the weakness in individual players.
>
> That sounds kind of crazy, but he did that. I first noticed that when I was in the Pro Bowl and he was our coach. He would design a play

and explain while he was going through it, that we were going to run this play for this guy because when he sees this action on offense, then he'll step here first, or he'll have a certain action first, so we're going to run it for him. So he would go through a game plan for us, even though you don't have a lot of time—but he'd go through it in about 30 minutes. We'd have a game plan based upon really sound logic as far as what the players on defense would do when they'd see a particular action or movement on offense.

He was an unusual character—I've never seen him be wrong on stuff [such as that]. We had a game where he called a play that most coaches wouldn't call. For example, Don Coryell [Cardinals head coach] would usually go back to a play that he was really confident in and that had worked before. Coach Landry was good at calling a play that he had put together and that he had seen on film that something might work. He'd have enough courage to call it in situations where you really needed it. I saw him do that in one of the last games I played there. He had called a play that, if it was going to work, and it had to work to win the game, meant that a free safety would have to go to a certain area and the strong safety would have to do a certain thing.

And he called the play anyway because he had observed it so much that he felt sure, or confident, anyway, that the players on defense would go run a particular type of play in that down and distance. And be damned if it didn't work! I just sat there, jumping up and down. I couldn't believe it. I walked off the field with him, saying, "Coach, that was amazing," because I had never seen a coach do something like that. The play that he had designed [played out for] the very situation that occurred.

I thought it was interesting that he could do things like that. And I think the players on the Cowboys never did exhibit a lot of enthusiasm, jumping up and down and hollering—I could see why. Because all of their confidence came from the fact that they knew that the chances are he was going to call the right play at the right time, and all they have to do is just execute it. And that's really how I felt about it—that he's going to call all the plays, and they're going to be the right ones at the right time and *for the right reasons*. I think the players finally understood that, and they were willing to play the game like they did without, seemingly, a lot of enthusiasm. But, I guess, internally, obviously they had it going.

One innovation Landry firmly believed in was his flex defense, a concept he introduced in 1964, then toyed with to refine it. It became an awesome weapon. By about 1966, the Cowboys had it down pat. Havrilak described the defensive scheme as follows:

> They played that Doomsday Defense, with a kind of staggered defense line—that was Tom Landry's brainchild. One guy would be on the line of scrimmage, and the other linemen next to him would be back about a yard or two. It made it very difficult to block, especially if they had any games going up front, like a tackle–end game or an end–tackle game.

When the flex clicked, it halted first-down running plays, giving other teams no daylight to run to, often forcing opponents into passing situations, sometimes as early as on second down. Having a staggered line helped defenders plug the gap opposite themselves to deter the running game.

From 1965 to 1974, this defense allowed only 3.2 yards per rush, which meant, in theory, a team that kept the ball on the ground three straight times would never get a first down versus Dallas. In reality, it did indeed force teams into many an unfavorable passing situation, allowing the talented front four to tee off on the offensive linemen, unleashing a wicked pass rush.

However, some say the flex defense was a style of play that was fine for its time, but not for today. Bob Hyland elaborated,

> Depending upon your formation, they would either have the defensive tackle up or back. The defensive end would counterbalance that. I could never really understand what their philosophy was there, but it was very helpful to linemen when Bob Lilly was a yard off the ball instead of right on your nose. You have a guy like that, you want to try to have some space between yourself and him, and the flex defense did that for you.
>
> Another thing about the flex defense is you knew they were very rehearsed, where their first step was going to be, they had to take an inside gap, or whatever, and that helped the offensive linemen anticipate some of the things they were going to do. It was very predictable.
>
> Landry knew exactly what he wanted. Your first two steps are going to be here, basically covering every offensive hole. After that is taken care of, then, of course, you react as a football player, and you get to the ballcarrier or the quarterback. Especially on the early downs, he wanted to stop that run. That's what the flex defense was pretty

much built for. Generally speaking, they were very successful. In that era it was a very credible way of defending.

Nowadays, I don't know if you could do it because the players have changed so much. Back then, the discipline the Cowboys had, which emanated from Tom Landry, made it a pretty good formula for them. Now, the players are probably a little bit more athletic than they were in the old days—bigger, stronger, faster. They really like to be able to let go a little bit more. They like to be able to sack the quarterback. They like to be able to not have the restriction that a flex defense puts on players.

It's probably not coincidental that right about the time the flex was beginning to come around, Landry was awarded a 10-year extension on his contract, which meant he was given an 11-year commitment to stay on the job. No coach, regardless of his sport, had ever been given a commitment for so long. The year before he accepted the new contract, 1963, Dallas had gone 4–10, but the front office, with great faith and foresight, wasn't about to lose this guy—and that was despite his overall record to date (13–38–3), with four consecutive losing seasons.

Landry was always prepared, and he wanted his players to follow his suit. Once, when the Cowboys were training under the unforgiving California sun, they asked Landry if they could conclude their last set of wind sprints with their helmets off. Landry calmly vetoed the idea, saying, "Do they let you take off your helmets in the last two minutes of the game?"[7]

Landry clearly possessed a firm philosophy of coaching, which included his belief he should draft the best man available. In 1970, for example, his Dallas Cowboys roster already included fullback Walt Garrison, who had ground out 818 yards, along with the reigning Rookie of the Year in running back Calvin Hill. Yet, Landry drafted another runner, acquiring Duane Thomas.

In acquiring the recalcitrant, enigmatic Thomas, a fullback, Landry also showed he believed he could deal with any type of personality, and he routinely did that very well. For the record, this time Landry was not correct in his assumption. Thomas, defiant and reticent, did give Landry some impressive stats for his two seasons as a Cowboy—he led the league with an average of 5.3 yards per carry as a rookie and in touchdowns the subsequent season—but he also gave Landry pounding headaches before he dumped him.

Mel Renfro pointed out Thomas didn't take issue with Landry alone. Remembered Renfro,

> One thing about Duane, he had a problem with almost everybody, even some of the players. As time passed and Duane kind of relaxed and probably cleaned up his life, because he had some substance abuse problems, he came around and really became a great person to be around. As I think back, he really became kind of a Chatty Cathy after his career was over—sometimes it's hard to get him to shut up.

Renfro said another man who gave Landry cause to reach for aspirin was Thomas "Hollywood" Henderson, but, like Duane Thomas, he later changed.

> Yes, Hollywood was also like that. There were certain players that didn't really appreciate Landry and the way that he was and the things that he did until after they retired and reflected back on the influence he had on their lives. They'd say, "Well, Coach Landry wasn't so bad after all. Maybe it was me and not him."

Off the field, Landry was quite conservative, but going against that grain, on the field at times, he could be daring in his play-calling, a bold tactician. Former Cowboys running back Dan Reeves said Landry didn't label his special plays with the usual terms, for instance, trick, gimmick, or gadget plays; he preferred to call them exotic plays. Reeves knew about such plays firsthand, as he was one of the best at throwing the halfback option pass, a play Landry had used earlier in New York, with Frank Gifford handling those passing chores.

Reeves said Landry always had a couple of exotic plays on hand, ready to pull out of a hat with a tah-dah, magician-like flourish, and usually with crowd-pleasing results. He even had the gall to call trick plays in the Super Bowl. In 1978, with 7:04 to play against an unsuspecting Denver squad in Super Bowl XII, Landry had fullback Robert Newhouse throw the option pass, his first throw since 1975, to Golden Richards, going for a 29-yard score and icing the game's outcome, 27–10, to cap a 15–2 season.

Landry didn't always save his surprising plays for late in the game. He opened Super Bowl X against the Steelers with a reverse, and he did it with a linebacker, not a speedy running back or wide receiver, handling the ball. Unafraid of trying the new or the daring, Landry had instructed his kickoff return man, Preston Pearson, to begin running to his right with the ball but then hand it off to Thomas "Hollywood" Henderson, who would reverse his position from the right side of the field to head back toward the goal line to take the ball and then run down the left side of the field. The trickery worked, and Henderson scampered for 53 yards to put Dallas in great field position in Steelers territory for their first possession, which was Landry's intention from the moment he conceived of the play.

Yet another exotic play took place when quarterback Roger Staubach pitched the football to Tony Dorsett, who then handed it off to wide receiver Drew Pearson as if Dallas was running an end around. Instead, Pearson got the ball back to Staubach, who then hit Tony Hill for a touchdown.

Trick plays were not, however, a real staple of the Landry playbook. "I don't recall many," reflected Renfro,

> because in that area he was very conservative. He went by the book. He went by the Xs and Os. Occasionally, he'd have the reverse, the wide receiver pass, and maybe a reverse on a kickoff or a punt, but usually that was the idea or the advice of the special teams coach or a particular position coach.
>
> No, for so many years we controlled the game and the line of scrimmage, especially defensively with Doomsday I and Doomsday II, so he really didn't have to do anything that was kind of out of the ordinary—a lot of the things that you see these days.

Former linebacker Nick Buoniconti saw many similarities between his coach, Don Shula, and Landry, a coach he got to observe up close during the Cowboys win against the Dolphins in Super Bowl VI. Both men were well-respected winners—that was a given—but Buoniconti gave a specific example to show the degree of respect Landry had throughout the league.

Prior to a practice session for a Pro Bowl game, the collected group of AFC players was behaving boisterously when the NFC coach, Landry, entered their locker room. "I mean, it was almost like the Pope [had walked in]," said Buoniconti. "Everybody just hushed." He added that it wasn't a case of Landry demanding their respect; rather, "his persona demanded respect. And Shula was the same way." Dorsett agreed, saying Landry was, again, like Shula, an "icon" who had "this aura about him."[8]

Dorsett also praised Landry for touching the lives of many and teaching his players that having a goal was fine, but it was ultimately meaningless "without a method on how to accomplish the goals." He continued, "He worked the heck out of us, but he made us better football players."[9]

Landry not only deserved respect, but also he was worthy of every ounce of praise he received. He was the first and, until 1988, the only head coach in the annals of the Dallas Cowboys. He ruled there for 29 seasons, bringing fame to the team he helped make known as "America's Team."

Everyone, even opponents, praised Landry, a man of conviction. He was atypical of the stereotypical ranting, loud, profane coach. As Floyd Little said,

> Tom was very quiet. He didn't say a lot, but he had great players—his Cowboys were always a competitive team. Tom is synonymous with the success of the Cowboys. He's been gone many, many years, but his name still means a lot to the Dallas Cowboys and the fans. Tom Landry was an excellent coach and certainly deserving of being a Hall of Famer.

Less than a year after Landry, a man who had tied the record for coaching the same pro football team for the longest consecutive streak, was fired, he was inducted into the Hall in his first year of eligibility.

While Dallas and Washington always had an acrimonious relationship, Charley Taylor of the Redskins stated,

> Tom Landry was one of my best friends. Being from Grand Prairie, Texas, I was across the street from the Cowboys, and every time I was down that way, I'd make it my business to visit and see Tom. We'd have lunch together and just talk about football. He did a good job with those Cowboys. He was fair with his players. He put an elite team on the field. He was dedicated and it showed; those guys hung in there.

Asked to sum up what made Landry great, Renfro stated,

> His intelligence of understanding the game. If a pass was completed in an area, or if a running back broke through the line, or if a play broke down, he knew what the problem was. He knew his system so well, that he didn't have to look at what just happened, he'd go on to the next play because he knew what happened.

Also, Landry was great at making in-game adjustments. "Absolutely," Renfro continued. "If someone would come to the sidelines [with this new information], he would say something to the position coach and let him take care of it. Then he'd go on with calling the plays because that was what he did."

Like a quarterback who is said to excel at being able to see the entire field, Landry did that, but from the sidelines. Renfro concurred,

> No question about it. He didn't wear the earphones, and he wasn't getting messages from the press box. He just knew. He knew so well what was going on with formations and plays and assistants. Linebacker play, secondary, offensive line. He knew so well what everybody was doing that, according to the result of the play, he knew what to do next.

Ditka played for Landry from 1969 to 1972. Landry then immediately signed him on as an assistant coach. "He was a wonderful, wonderful man and a wonderful coach. He was the greatest man I've ever met," Ditka praised, continuing,

> I played against Coach Lombardi's teams, and I had a great, profound respect for the Packers and for Coach Lombardi because, to me, I thought they were the best organization I've ever seen in pro football. And then I got to go to Dallas when my career was really on the brink of being finished, and I got resurrected because of Coach Landry, who made me understand my part in this whole, big puzzle was to be a team player.
>
> His influence on me . . . was immeasurable. . . . He made me go the right way. He influenced me, and he showed me that there was a path to doing things right, doing them the right way and being part of a team instead of worrying about being an individual.

Shortly after Landry acquired Ditka from Philadelphia, where his career had languished for two years, he candidly told Ditka he couldn't promise him he'd make the team or that he'd play a lot, but he stated he was willing to take a chance on Ditka if he, in turn, was willing to take that same chance on himself. Ditka appreciated Landry's honesty and said the Dallas coach was never duplicitous. "You got no curveballs—they were all high, hard ones," the former tight end commented. "You couldn't handle it? Get out of the batter's box."[10]

Statistics don't always tell the entire tale, but Landry did put up sterling numbers, for example, his 270 wins, counting postseason play. His regular-season winning percentage was .607, even though his early teams' many failures yanked that percentage down. For instance, the Cowboys' records in their first five years were 0–11–1 in 1960, 4–9–1 in 1961, 5–8–1 in 1962, 4–10 in 1963, and 5–8–1 in 1964. It wasn't until his sixth season that he had a team play break-even football, at 7–7. The next year, 1966, he won the Eastern Division crown and earned his first Coach of the Year award.

In fact, Landry's lifetime record didn't reach the .500 point until November 16, 1969, when he won a 41–28 contest against the Cowboys' rivals, Washington. Several weeks later, on December 7, he hoisted his career record above .500, and it never again dipped below that plateau. By the time he left pro football, his coaching log stood at 88 wins above .500, and he even registered 22 straight winning seasons at one point.

Berry once commented, "I believe there is no way to succeed without persistence and perseverance, and Landry is a perfect example of this." He is also a perfect example of a winner—in more ways than one.

10

HANK STRAM

Dapper Mentor

Place of birth: Chicago
Date of birth: January 3, 1924
Date of death: July 4, 2005
Lifetime wins, losses, and ties: 131–97–10
Career winning percentage: .574
Playoff wins and losses: 5–3
Playoff winning percentage: .625
NFL major titles won and years of championships: AFL champs 1962, 1966; Super Bowl champs 1969
Teams coached and years: Dallas Texans (AFL) 1960–1962; Kansas City Chiefs 1963–1974; New Orleans Saints 1976–1977

Hank Stram was a colorful coach with a background to match. His father, also named Hank, was a wrestler who appeared with the Barnum and Bailey Circus, one who took on all comers from the audience. He was also a tailor, which gave birth to his less-than-creative nickname, the "Wrestling Tailor." Hank's father gave his son his athletic genes and taught him to strive for a fine sartorial sense of style.

Mel Renfro found Stram to be a "happy guy, a good and very success-ful coach who always encouraged his players." Added Renfro, "He was like a little cheerleader out there. I liked him, his attitude, and the way he did things. In my opinion, he was one of the best coaches in the league."

Floyd Little remembered, "He was a guy who always had a suit and tie on. He always had a conversation with [opposing] players. I liked Hank." Stram, then, was as convivial as he was dapper. On game days, he was outfitted with a sports jacket and red vest, and he insisted that when his Chiefs went on road trips they, too, would don blazers and look natty. Before Super Bowl IV, he booked the entire top floor of his hotel and used one bedroom just to house his clothes.

In his youth, his mother initially forbade the 5-foot-8 Stram from going out for football at Lew Wallace High School in Gary, Indiana, but he did so anyway, unbeknownst to her. When she eventually learned the truth, spotting his picture in a newspaper's sports section, she did an instant turnabout and ardently followed his games. She was soon rewarded, seeing him go on to become an All-State running back and a four-sport star. After graduation, Stram stayed in-state, enrolling at Purdue. It was there that he earned four letters in baseball and three more in football.

Descriptions of Stram almost exhaust a dictionary's supply of adjectives. He's been called dictatorial (even by himself), imaginative, vain, caring, cocky, glib, animated, creative, and flashy—with phrases calling him a man on a mission and a man who never shunned the limelight thrown in as well.

Stram was not unlike UCLA's John Wooden, who clutched each game's program as he sat on his bench. In Stram's case, he had his play sheet rolled up in his fist as he paced in front of his players.

"I think Stram was an excitable guy," said Jackie Smith, continuing,

> He was absolutely animated. He was always going up and down the sidelines, and inserting himself in what's going on. He was always observing—he wasn't looking at a pad all the time, trying to figure out what play to call. He was all involved in the game. He was either screaming something to somebody—something different to do or getting upset about something, but he was always a very active guy on the sidelines.
>
> A lot of coaches aren't, they just sort of put their headphones on and listen to what's going on upstairs; or some guys are looking at their notebook the whole time and seemingly not paying a lot of attention to the game. Others are walking up and down the sidelines, but everybody has a little bit of a different take on the way they run the team and who they assign responsibility to.

Writer Bill Lyon compared him to a strutting peacock/bantam patrolling the sidelines. Stram may have strutted in a rather self-important way, but he always cared about his players, and he made it a point to keep in touch with them years after their coach–player relationship ended. Kansas City's Bobby Bell said Stram would always help a former player in need any way he could, and that as many as 20 years after Bell retired, he and Stram spoke with one another roughly once a month.

Stram was on the frontier of racial equality, often seeking out talent from obscure black colleges. When the NFL had a tacit understanding that no team should have more than one-third of their team made up of African Americans, Stram was the first coach to actually have a majority of his roster composed of African American players. At times, eight of his 11 starters on defense were black.

Mike Ditka said, "He was a character. He was a little different than what you say the typical coach is. I thought he was good for the game. It was serious to him, but it wasn't life or death. He had some fun with [it]."

A profile of Stram tells a bit about what made him a man destined to become an NFL head coach. When Lamar Hunt, owner of the Chiefs (Dallas Texans originally), signed this man of many labels off the University of Miami campus as his first hiring, he was displaying his faith in someone who had never before been a head coach at any level. He had been an assistant coach at Southern Methodist University, Notre Dame, and his alma mater, as well as head baseball coach at Purdue.

Neither Hunt nor the self-confident Stram could have known it for sure, but they were about to embark on a dynasty. The AFL was born in 1960, and it became a part of the NFL in 1970. Stram was the only head coach whose tenure stretched throughout the entire history of the old AFL, running the same team throughout. During that span he won 87 times, more than any other AFL coach, and he also won more AFL championships than anyone.

Randy Covitz of the *Kansas City Star* wrote a story about the first training camp Stram held. It was run at the New Mexico Military Institute in, of all places, Roswell, the town better known for a 1947 alleged crashing of a UFO. Determined not to have his Texans plummet to earth, Stram toughened his troops in temperatures that soared into sweltering three-digit territory, working them out on a field made up of a lot of dust and grass, not exactly lush.[1]

No one even knew if the new AFL could survive, but Stram vowed to his players that they would later go on to win more games than any other team in the league. The immediate result of the team's efforts was an 8–6 record and a second-place finish in the West Division. The long-range result was that in the following 10 seasons, they were an elite team.

Like many of the Hall of Fame coaches, Stram was a superlative innovator, an inventor of new plays, schemes, and strategies on both offense and defense. Plus, he was even the first coach to employ a full-time strength coach throughout the year and the first to hold minicamps.

In about 1967, Stram's multiple offense, compared to the West Coast offense long before that term came into being, featured his tight end shifting out of the backfield and up onto the line. Oftentimes, he'd have tight end Fred Arbanas in his Tight-I formation lined up *behind* the quarterback before he would shift him to the left or right to cause, if only momentarily, some defensive indecision, as he loved deception. Another tight end look came about with his formation simply called the two-tight end offense.

Stram dubbed his offensive scheme the "Offense of the Seventies." Among other things, it featured men in motion, reverses, and his concept of the moving pocket, which featured men blocking for their quarterback while rolling away from the line, yet remaining in the formation of a traditional pocket. The quarterback would also roll out, staying inside the protective pocket until he spotted a receiver and heaved a pass. Stram made sure he had big but highly mobile linemen to work with. The moving pocket benefited quarterback Len Dawson, who, listed at 6 feet, often had trouble seeing receivers from the traditional pocket while mammoth defenders were bearing down on him.

The moving pocket, along with Dawson's prowess, helped him set a record, as he led his league a staggering eight times in quarterback completion percentage. He only had 10 seasons in which he started 12 or more games. Still, he almost had a lock on that statistical category, leading his league in eight of those 10 seasons. He led in 1962, finished second in 1963, and rattled off six straight seasons in which he again topped the league. He won that honor for the last time in 1975, in his 19th and final season. What made this even more astounding is he was 40 years old, and his 66.4 percent completion rate set a personal high. Dawson also boasted the highest quarterback rating six times in seven seasons between 1962 and 1968, and he had the most touchdowns thrown four times.

It was not at all unusual for Stram to take other teams' castoffs and turn them into contributors to the Kansas City cause. If foxes really are sly, Stram was truly vulpine. Going into the final game of the 1969 season, Kansas City played Oakland, a team they figured they'd face again, and soon, in the playoffs. So Stram called for basic plays and had Dawson throw just six passes, determined not to reveal anything that might later help the Raiders. Sure enough, despite losing that game to Oakland, three weeks later Stram won the AFL title, getting by the Raiders, 17–7.

Stram's stingy defense surrendered just 20 points in the three victories it took to capture the Super Bowl. They became the first AFL team to make it two Super Bowls (the next season the AFL became known as the AFC). They were also the first wild-card champ.

Normally, Stram liked to throw other new wrinkles at opponents, for example, having his offense line up in the Power I formation. After the season that was capped off with a Super Bowl IV win in January 1970, he was justifiably proud of his Power I, which had proved to be effective with receiver Otis Taylor lining up in different spots to fool the defense.

Stram contended the winning teams of the 1960s relied on simplicity, citing Green Bay's successful style of play, but his Offense of the Seventies was different. It would, he insisted, succeed by using many different offensive sets that would cause just enough confusion and hesitation on the part of their opponents to gain an edge.

Prior to his Super Bowl IV win, Stram even went so far as to say his Chiefs' upcoming encounter with the Vikings would be a confrontation between the old NFL offense and his, which contained a hernia-inducing playbook groaning with 300-plus plays that could be run off 18 different formations. Tex Maule's article in *Sports Illustrated* stated that mercy was the only thing Stram's team didn't show the Vikings in their easy Super Bowl victory. [2]

Pundits, however, joked that the so-called Offense of the Seventies and the Chiefs' success in general was really nothing more than two things (and they argued it had little to do with offense). First, there was Stram's suffocating defense. In their three postseason wins that had earned them the championship in January 1970, Kansas City gave up a microscopic amount of points: 6, 7, and 7, respectively. Secondly, that defense was coupled with a Hall of Fame kicker in Jan Stenerud. In an era in which fans clamored for fewer field goals and more touchdowns due to defenses that bent but often refused to break, Stenerud remained a Stram not-so-secret weapon.

In the opening playoff game on December 20, 1969, versus the Jets, Stenerud scored seven of the Chiefs 13 points, outscoring the Jets himself. In the Chiefs' three postseason victories, he was responsible for nearly half of his team's total points, scoring 23 of 53 points. In a rather boring, but thoroughly methodical, 23–7 Super Bowl IV dismantling of the Vikings, Stenerud booted three field goals and two extra points. In fact, the first three scores in that contest came on his field goals of 48, 32, and 25 yards.

Even after the Jets jolted the Colts in Super Bowl III, there were many fans who still believed the NFL was superior to the AFL. Stram and his Chiefs helped obliterate those thoughts when, as huge underdogs, they took on Minnesota and their awesome Purple People Eaters defense and thumped them. The old AFL finally, truly had gained parity.

A recap of Stram's biggest win is in order. The Chiefs had sailed to a 16–0 lead, highlighted by a five-yard jaunt by Mike Garrett in the second quarter. The 65 Toss Power Trap Stram had drawn up involved Dawson first faking a pitch to his fullback before spinning and handing off the ball to Garrett. The touchdown elated Stram and lifted Kansas City to what proved to be an insurmountable advantage.

The 16-point bulge was exactly the same lead as the Jets had constructed before the Colts futilely scored their first points in Super Bowl III. The Vikings' first score, a Dave Osborn four-yard run, didn't come until the third quarter. The game's final score, which came not long after the Osborn touchdown, was the result of a 46-yard throw from Len Dawson to the mercurial Otis Taylor.

No player on either team was able to put up sparkling statistics, except Taylor, who caught six passes for 81 yards—although the MVP went to Dawson, who went 12-of-17 for 142 yards. The leading rushers for the teams were Garrett, with just 39 yards, and Vikings fullback Bill Brown, who ground out a meager 26 yards. For the most part, Stram had Dawson emulating Joe Namath of one year earlier, tossing short passes. Upon his retirement, Dawson's lifetime pass completion rate was 57.1 percent; only Bart Starr, at 57.4 percent, was more on the money with his throws.

Kansas City had entered the game knowing the vaunted Vikings defense had yielded just 133 points all year long, the lowest total by an NFL team since 1946—and during that season teams played an 11-game schedule. Regardless, the Chiefs also knew their defense was strong. They had given up 177 points and owned the top defense in the AFL. Plus, they felt they could put up points against the Vikings because they also owned the second most prolific offense in their league, having exploded for 359 points.

One Viking who appeared in four Super Bowls under Bud Grant said he will never forget the one against Kansas City. He remains convinced Stram and his coaching staff outfoxed the Vikings in one respect. Minnesota breezed through a great regular season in 1969, posting a 12–2 record, losing only their season opener and finale. More than 40 years later, the player lamented his team's loss, saying,

> Let's just say this, [it] was lost by one of our coaches, and there's no doubt about it. It was a total lack of coaching—they ran a defense against us, and the first time we ever saw that defense was the day before the game.
>
> We had about four or five plays drawn up, and the first time we ran one of the plays, both of our guards pulled and ran into each other. It was because we had what we called role blocking—depending on what defense they ran, your blocking pattern would be different. In this particular case, if the guard was uncovered, he pulled. Well, both guards were uncovered and they pulled.
>
> Instead of dealing with it, [the coach] just basically said, "Wow. They're never going to run that any more. They only ran it about three times all year." Needless to say, in the second series of downs they jumped into that defense, and we had no plays to run against it. As a result, they stayed in that defense the whole game. We were totally unprepared; we had no plays to run. It killed us. It really did. And it was one of our best teams, but you can't win without plays.

Things got so bad for Minnesota that at one point a Vikings defensive player glanced at Grant on the sidelines and shrugged. Author Don Weiss writes that the gesture suggested Minnesota hadn't a clue what to do, while Stram, unfettered by today's concept of political correctness, gloated, "They didn't know where to go. [Karl] Kassulke was running around there like it was a Chinese fire drill!" He tossed in, "They can't cover that in a million years."[3]

Stram had come up with a game plan to deter the mighty Minnesota ground game, one that had registered a league-leading 1,850 yards. The average run by a Vikings ballcarrier only went for 3.8 yards (eighth in the NFL), but they pounded the ball into the end zone 15 times (fifth in the NFL) and controlled the football, gaining 102 first downs on rushes. Stram believed if they could force Minnesota into passing situations, their quarterback, Joe Kapp, would be unable to carry the offensive load.

Once Kansas City had built up a big lead, Kapp was indeed forced to pass often, which, of course, freed the Chiefs defenders to tee off on him. Stram's plans worked, as Kansas City's defense was superior that day, often hurrying Kapp's passes, picking off three of 28 Vikings passes, recovering two of Minnesota's three fumbles, and stifling the Vikings running game (67 yards). Minnesota didn't have a star runner, as Chuck Foreman had yet to arrive on the scene. Instead, they had four men who carried the ball 50 or more times on the year, with their leading rusher being Dave Osborn, who ran for a modest 643 yards.

Author Bob Carroll writes that Stram's key was arranging it so his middle linebacker, Willie Lanier, could roam around unhindered and make tackles all over the field.[4] To accomplish that, he had his 6-foot-7, 270-pound tackle Buck Buchanan, or Curley Culp, at 265 pounds, line up on Minnesota center Mick Tingelhoff, who weighed 237 pounds. That prevented him from being able to charge off the line of scrimmage and take direct aim at Lanier. Giving the Vikings different looks, ones they had never faced before, was also effective. In fact, Stram felt his defense was so effective, he only once called for a blitz.

Going into the game, Stram felt as if his Chiefs would win despite the line on the game spotting them two touchdowns. He believed that, with only one week off right before the Super Bowl, the Vikings would not be able to adequately prepare for what he had in store for them. He knew Bud Grant's Vikings were accustomed to the staider style of play seen in their league and that they would not have time to cope with the moving pocket and the Tight-I formation.

Not only did Stram prevail, but as the first coach to wear a microphone during a Super Bowl contest, his words and his crowing over a play he called which resulted in Kansas City's first score gained instant fame. Always on stage, Stram relished his role on his biggest stage ever.

Stram's opportunity to chortle at an NFL team served as a personal vindication, as he gazed back in his mind's eye at the humbling, devastating 35–10 loss to the Packers in the first Super Bowl. That season, Stram's offense normally was potent, averaging 32 points per game, while losing just once, but Green Bay overpowered them. Linebacker Bobby Bell believed once Stram's Chiefs gained a few years' experience after the loss to the Packers, they no longer made as many costly mistakes as they had in Super Bowl I, and they were no longer capable of being intimidated by an NFL team.

In fact, the year after their loss to the Packers, 1967, interleague preseason play started, and Stram opened up facing his boyhood Chicago idol, George Halas. Stram gained some retribution against the NFL by declawing the Bears, 66–24. The Chiefs' games featured a white horse that galloped around the field after each KC touchdown. In this game, some feared the exhausted horse might keel over and die right there in Kansas City Municipal Stadium. Len Dawson recalled that Stram psyched up his players by having them watch highlight film of their Super Bowl loss. It worked.

One job of any coach is to get his men to believe in him and what he tries to convey to his team. Once that's accomplished, another goal often is reached—the men begin to believe in themselves. Stram was able to get his Chiefs to buy into his plans, and the reward was a Super Bowl ring.

Now, with back-to-back wins by AFL teams, Stram had saved face for himself and his league. Many observers felt the old guard could no longer try to dismiss the Jets' win in the previous Super Bowl as merely a fluke. Stram's win came in the final Super Bowl played between the old AFL and the NFL.

By the way, Stram's fleecing of the Vikings wasn't the only time he caught an opponent off guard. In one game against the Chiefs' rival, the Raiders, Stram employed a three-man backfield and had Dawson throw the ball a mere three times all day long. Stram was unpredictable.

Naturally, Stram couldn't win without the horses, but, like so many great coaches, he knew a thoroughbred colt when he spotted one. That would certainly hold true when he acquired Len Dawson. Stram was an assistant at Purdue at the time Dawson starred there in 1956. Six years later, Dawson was no longer considered a bright prospect. He had been drafted by the Steelers as the fifth overall selection in 1957, but from then through the 1961 season, he started just two NFL games, a loss with Pittsburgh when he was a rookie and a win four years later when he was with the Browns, sent packing by the Steelers after three seasons.

Nevertheless, Stram, unlike Paul Brown, liked Dawson, and blessed with the rare ability to salvage talent buried in a scrapheap, he acquired the future Hall of Famer. He gave Dawson the starting nod in 1962, and was rewarded when Dawson, in his first year in the AFL, led the team, then the Dallas Texans, to a glittering 11–3 record and a first-place finish in the West Division.

The Texans wrapped up the season with a thrilling 20–17 overtime win against the Houston Oilers. That game ran just six seconds shy of 78 minutes and remained the longest game in pro football history until the Chiefs lost a double-overtime game in the 1971 playoffs—that contest ran more than 82 minutes.

Obviously, Stram knew talent and, therefore, craved certain players. Jackie Smith said he never really knew Stram but met him "in an airport one time, passing through." Smith added, "I acknowledged him and introduced myself, and he was in a hurry, but said, 'We tried like hell to trade for you, but they wouldn't do it.' I said, 'I wish you had told me. I would have joined in [on the discussion] and had a say so in it.'" The future Hall of Famer would have fit right in with the Chiefs.

Stram also wished he could have had Floyd Little on his team. Little recalled,

> I liked Hank. He was my coach in an all-star game. He used to always say, "I chased you around and I chased you around, and now I got you." Hank knew what kind of person I was as a player, and he always tried to get me. When he left Kansas City to go to New Orleans, he tried to trade for me to go there as his back.

Of course, being that good judge of talent, once he saw he would be unable to get Little, his Saints promptly drafted Chuck Muncie, a future 1,000-yard rusher, as the third overall pick in the 1976 draft.

Stram always tried to tailor his teams to his liking. Doug Crusan played left offensive tackle for the Dolphins, and in his seven seasons he went up against some tough Kansas City customers almost every year. He related, "People don't realize how big Kansas City was—they were the biggest team we played against. The offensive line, too. That's what Hank Stram wanted, a very powerful team."

Crusan continued, "The size of their defensive linemen was amazing. I had [to block] defensive end Aaron Brown, and I played across from Buck Buchanan, too, and he's in the Hall of Fame."

Throughout many of his seasons with the Chiefs, Stram possessed one of the best—and at times *the* best—defenses in the league. Don Maynard pointed out, "Stram [deserves] a big plus as far as ability goes, and for what he did with what he had. He got a lot of fame for his defensive alignments."

Stram's foundation included such men as Brown, Buchanan, Jerry Mays, and Culp, a fantastic front four, but there was more. Crusan said that under the colorful, excitable Stram, the Chiefs "funneled their defenses in what they ran—what we called the Kansas City Overstack." That defense sent a lot of traffic at middle linebacker Willie Lanier. Following Stram's plan, Lanier stymied many a running play.

Stram loved to have quick, multitalented linebackers, and what a crew he had when Jim Lynch, Bobby Bell, and Willie Lanier took the field as a unit. In addition, they were backed up with a great secondary featuring stars the likes of Emmitt Thomas, Johnny Robinson, Jim Kearney, and Bobby Hunt.

Bell remembered the stack defense, which was first used in 1962, as basically being what became known as the 3–4 defense. As a rookie with Kansas City, Bell would be told to drop back from what was then his position, left defensive end, and become a fourth linebacker. On such plays Stram also instructed left defensive tackle Jerry Mays to shift over to the defensive end slot. Variations on the defensive alignment could also feature Bell staying on the line before moving out to put pressure on a quarterback. Depending on what Stram called for, the stack defense could make it appear as if there were anywhere from three to seven down linemen.

Stram also loved the bump-and-run defense. That strategy features defensive backs lining up right in front of receivers. At the snap of the football, they'd make contact with the receiver in an attempt to throw off the timing of his pattern, to disrupt his route right off the bat. Bell was so talented and Stram so creative, Bell was once assigned to help double cover fleet receiver Lance Alworth even though Bell was a linebacker and not a defensive back. Stram instructed Bell to negate the receiver's blazing speed and skill by using bump-and-run tactics.

The cliche "You can't win 'em all" holds true for any coach, great or otherwise. While Stram's Super Bowl win was the gem of his coaching collection, the 1971 divisional round playoff game versus Miami was a classic, albeit one Stram didn't win. Held on Christmas Day, the game would not be decided until its second overtime period. The Chiefs opened things up with a field goal and a Dawson pass to Ed Podolak for a 10–0 lead, but two Miami scores tied it. The teams alternated on two more touchdowns each to raise the score at the end of regulation to 24–24, before a Garo Yepremian 37-yard field goal won the 82-minute-and-40-second marathon for Don Shula and his Dolphins.

Nevertheless, with a long and distinguished resume it would seem logical that Stram could write his own ticket in Kansas City and stay there as long as he wished; however, as men like Tom Landry found out, the NFL just isn't set up that way. In January 1975, Lamar Hunt fired Stram, who apparently was not in accord with the club president and general manager, Jack Steadman, concerning money matters.

In addition, after putting up nine consecutive winning seasons from 1965 to 1973, Stram's poor 5–9 record of 1974 didn't help, and attendance at Arrowhead Stadium was down. It was also suggested that a major problem was that Stram was unwilling to rid himself of his aging, veteran players. Faithful to those men, he had gradually allowed the team to become too old.

Later, the Chiefs certainly would regret the firing—after Stram had taken the team to its last playoff appearance in 1971, the team would not sniff another postseason game (other than two wild-card contests) for an eon, until 1991. Not only that, Kansas City's record in the subsequent four seasons after Stram was cut loose was 16–42, including a 2–12 showing in 1977. Without Stram, the team was headed in the wrong direction, finishing in last place three years in a row (1977–1979) and not producing a winning record until 1981, seven years after he was replaced.

Stram spent the 1975 season in the broadcast booth, working for CBS. The following season, he accepted the head coaching job with the New Orleans Saints, who finished the year at 4–10. In 1977, Stram took over the general manager job to go along with his head coaching duties for the Saints. This team was not even close to the caliber of team Stram was used to in Kansas City, and the Saints went 3–11. It would be his final season as an NFL coach.

Randy Covitz wrote that those final two seasons of futility tainted Stram's reputation enough that he had to wait more than a quarter-century before his 2003 induction into the Hall of Fame.[5] By then, at the age of 80, he was in poor health—he would live just two more years, passing away on Independence Day 2005. At one point during the day he appeared on the Canton, Ohio, stage, some of his former players and opponents encircled the seated Stram and unabashedly wept over him.

After his final coaching stint, Stram returned to CBS. He provided color analysis for *Monday Night Football* broadcasts on the radio for 17 seasons and became the first man to take part in the Super Bowl as both a broadcaster and a winning coach.

"Hank Stram was a great communicator," said Little. "He was always on the sidelines before a game, talking to the other players, not his own, trying to figure out if you were the kind of player that was somebody who could help his team, if you were somebody he could try to get in a trade."

Stram was known as a "player's coach" and fondly called "The Mentor" by his players and, using the third-person point of view, himself. Genial with opposing players, he was even friendlier with his own men. While he was the boss and, as must be the case with a leader, while he did have rules in place, he was very generous. Wide receiver Otis Taylor said Stram had been known to drive his men during a given practice with the zeal of a martinet, but then he would turn things around after they returned to the locker room and treat them to an expensive meal, topped off with a few kegs of beer.

He legitimately earned the nickname "The Mentor" as he became a diligent teacher for his players, imparting to them not only the fundamentals of the game, but also the proper techniques to be used for every position on the field. Armed with just four assistants, he was, either in reality or in effect, the offensive coordinator and the quarterback coach, while also being heavily involved, very hands-on, in his highly complex defense and special teams play.

Evidence vividly shows how well Stram taught his players. Hall of Famers and Stram went together like Crosby and Hope. Ten men who spent at least five seasons with the Chiefs are honored in Canton, Ohio. Stram coached seven of them: Lanier, Dawson, Stenerud, Thomas, Culp, Bell, and Buchanan.

Stram left behind a laudatory body of work. He was named NFL Coach of the Year in 1968, by *Pro Football Weekly*, and AFL Coach of the Year by United Press International that same season. He was also AFL or overall Coach of the Year in 1962, 1966, and 1969, as selected by other polls, and his Chiefs won the AFL title in those three seasons. Many say he is the greatest AFL coach ever, and Hunt argued Stram was probably the most important force behind the AFL's quest for parity with the NFL.

In Stram's Hall of Fame acceptance speech he revived one of his famous quotes (even though he once more misused one word), and his line took on a new meaning, summing up his approach to his sport and his life: "Just keep matriculating the ball down the field, boys."

11

DON SHULA

King of the Hill

Place of birth: Grand River, Ohio
Date of birth: January 4, 1930
Date of death: n/a
Lifetime wins, losses, and ties: 328–156–6
Career winning percentage: .677
Playoff wins and losses: 19–17
Playoff winning percentage: .528
NFL major titles won and years of championships: NFL champs 1968;
AFC champs 1971, 1982, 1984; Super Bowl champs 1972, 1973
Teams coached and years: Baltimore Colts 1963–1969; Miami Dolphins
1970–1995

Don Shula was born in Grand River, Ohio, and played high school ball in Painesville, Ohio, both towns not very far from the Pro Football Hall of Fame in Canton. As a senior halfback, he helped his team to its first season in which they racked up seven victories in almost 20 years. Had he not forged his parents' signatures to sign up for the football team, the name Shula may not have become a well-known moniker.

He attended John Carroll University in a Cleveland suburb, graduating in 1951. Shula started out on a one-year scholarship, but after running wild—in one game he rushed for 175 yards—the team wisely put him on a full scholarship. Incidentally, like Vince Lombardi, Shula didn't always aspire to make football his vocation. At John Carroll, a Jesuit school, he gave some serious consideration to becoming a priest.

Shula played pro ball at 5-foot-9 and 190 pounds. He spent two years as a defensive back with the Browns from 1951 to 1952, after being drafted in the ninth round. The following four seasons, he was with the Colts, before wrapping things up with one final season with the Redskins. He had a rather modest NFL career with no foreshadowing of his greatness to come.

However, Shula had at least an inkling of what his future held for him. He once said that even when he was playing, he felt as if he were a coach, relating,

> If the guy next to me didn't know what he was doing, I never hesitated to tell him. Sometimes he didn't appreciate it. I didn't want anybody to make a mistake. I was always [teaching] the guys around me what their responsibilities were. That's what coaching is all about—knowing what you're doing and executing in a pressure situation. [1]

Hall of Fame receiver Paul Warfield played for Shula from 1970 to 1974, and was with both of Shula's Dolphins Super Bowl–winning teams, including the undefeated 1972 team. Warfield provided some additional background on Shula, saying,

> He was drafted initially by the Browns. He did not have a long career with them, but he idolized Paul Brown and his innovations, and his philosophy as a head coach and the mental approach to the game. He was a part of that system, so he gained a feel for it. Although he did not have a long football career, he knew he wanted to remain involved with the game, and he wanted to go on to be a coach in pro football.
>
> As he started to go [up] the ladder in terms of coaching background and experience, one of his first and most important jobs was coaching at the University of Kentucky as an assistant coach. The head coach there was one Blanton Collier, who was steeped in the Cleveland Browns system also.
>
> So his background as a player was getting exposure and [then] understanding where he ultimately wanted to go to be a coach.

Then, said Warfield, there was Shula's admiration for Brown, the "very, very best coach in the game at that point, and being in that environment was helpful." He later coached on the same staff with Collier, Paul Brown's top assistant for many years with Cleveland. Warfield added,

> Don Shula is more of a coach of the Paul Brown genre. People have to fully understand what role they are to play, and they are to be highly disciplined and be able to execute their functions—using a model of 10—not three out of 10 times, not five out of 10 times, but as close to 10 out of 10 times as possible.

Shula said Brown was the man who had the largest influence on his life. He added that much of his attention to detail, to the importance of organizational skills, and his insistence on discipline came from Brown.

Charley Taylor said what he knew of Shula came from Warfield, a player he spoke with often. What it boiled down to, said Taylor, was, "Shula was easy to work with as long as you did your job."

Shula, continued Warfield, also insisted his players

> understand what one has to do and what his job is, be it offensively, defensively, special teams, whatever, and then have the discipline to do it every time. There is no excuse of not being able to do something if that strategy is right, or if that fundamental concept is correct every time. If one is disciplined and if one understands that he has a vital role because 10 others are depending on that one individual to do his job, [things work]. And once that one individual understands that, he will not let down in any situation, be it first play, last play, the most important play of the game, because he has been disciplined in that fashion, and he is able to function, able to do that with that mindset, and he should be able to get it done.

Warfield also said he appreciated the fact that Shula had been a part of the same Browns system that he had grown up with. The former wide receiver declared, "It was the very best system. It enabled me to have the career that I had."

Armed with a solid foundation, Shula became the defensive coordinator for the Detroit Lions. His first head coaching gig began when he was hired by the Colts in 1963. At the age of 33, he became the youngest NFL head coach ever. He initially gushed about the prospect of working with John Unitas, saying few coaches start off with such a great quarterback on hand. He even admitted to Unitas that how successful he would become as a head coach would depend heavily on how well Unitas, already a seven-year veteran, performed. Naturally, expecting the great Johnny U to excel was a given. The warmth, real or merely expressed for media consumption that day, would not last long.

It's no secret that Unitas and Shula, just three years older than his star quarterback and a former teammate of Unitas in 1956, did not get along. Unitas, brimming with the confidence that comes with consummate skill, was not about to have a rookie coach tell him how to execute his high-powered offense. Veteran Colts running back Tom Matte, who played under Shula and was a teammate of Unitas, said Shula's decision to stick with Earl Morrall too long in Super Bowl III deepened Unitas's unhappiness with his coach. The two coexisted, but with little harmony.

So, yes, it's true that even great coaches have their critics, and perhaps when the egos and wills of two all-time greats come into contact, sparks flying isn't a surprising outcome. Both Unitas and Shula, supremely confident in their talents, did produce glowing results throughout their careers; however, Unitas had been used to playing for Weeb Ewbank, and the transition to playing for a man who was so much different than Ewbank was not an easy one.

Matte stated,

> Weeb had a lot of respect for John. They had taken the '58, '59 championships. He got let go [by the Colts] after the '62 season and then he got the job with the Jets, and Shula came up here. That's when Shula and Unitas sort of went at it, and John said, "You take care of the defense, I'll take care of the offense." Shula, of course, didn't like that.

When Ewbank was fired, Don McCafferty, a well-liked offensive coordinator, survived the usual coaching purge. Matte, who played from 1961 to 1972, said,

> John had so much respect when McCafferty was here, and none of the coaching staff changed—hardly at all [when Shula came in], so we continued winning. We only had one losing season that I played in. That was when Robert Irsay got here in 1972, and that was the end of our [greatness].

Still, even an off season for Shula, 1969, his final year with the Colts, produced a winning record of 8–5–1—and the only other time his Colts flirted with not reaching the .500 plateau was in his rookie season as a coach, when Baltimore went 8–6.

Matte recalled instances when he trotted onto the field, shuttling in a play Shula had called only to hear Unitas tersely and scornfully dismiss it. Said Matte, "I'd run on the field to bring in a play that Shula wanted to run, and of course John would say, '[Blank] that play. It ain't going to work—I'm not calling it.'"

Shula's first NFL head coach, Paul Brown, called Shula a smart player and then said, "Had to be. He was one of the slowest players I ever saw."[2]

Unitas had known Shula's vulnerability as a player and exploited it. In a 1957 contest, the year after Shula departed the Colts, Unitas hooked up with Raymond Berry over and over again at Shula's expense. Shula, then playing for Washington, was assigned to cover Berry man-to-man. It was a miserable mismatch. Unitas hit Berry on a dozen passes to set a new Colts team record and establish Berry's personal best for his career (he would tie that reception total a year later, in the 1958 championship game). Those completions were good for 224 yards, another all-time high for Berry, as well as a new franchise high. That was Shula's last season before he went into coaching. It clearly was time for him to retire as a player, perhaps prodded by the quarterback he later would clash with.

Perhaps Shula wasn't the greatest defensive back, but Berry related,

> Shula's biggest strengths were many. He's one of the greatest competitors that you'll ever want to be around, and his teams played that way—a competitor bar none. And, he is tough and smart. He knew football, and he played defense. It's been my experience that a player who played professional football on defense that later goes into coaching has got a tremendous advantage over others. And Don Shula knew defense.

Berry recalled that after the Weeb Ewbank Colts won back-to-back NFL titles, the Colts records trailed off to 6–6, 8–6, and 7–7. The sinking into mediocrity, going from the top to finishing fourth, third, and fourth again from 1960 to 1962, led to Ewbank's firing, "despite his knowledge of the game and what he had brought to the city of Baltimore and to our team." Team owner Carroll Rosenbloom and general manager Don Kellett felt it was time for a change, and in came Shula, who was three years younger than two of his players, Gino Marchetti and Bill Pellington.

Shula's first year on the job in Baltimore resulted in an 8–6 record (third place), but in 1964, his Colts won the West Division, elevated to a 12–2 record, which included one stretch of 11 consecutive wins. The only downfall came in the title game versus the Cleveland Browns, a game they were heavily favored to win.

In addition to the previously discussed defeat at the hands of the Jets in Super Bowl III, another loss Shula has to regret was that shocking 27–0 defeat to the Browns in the 1964 NFL championship game. Shula, who had earned Coach of the Year honors for the fine showing of his Colts, entered the title game with what he felt was a solid strategy, but it simply didn't work out.

The first precept Shula stressed was ball control. He believed he had to keep the ball away from the Browns, who featured such weapons as the inimitable Jim Brown running, Frank Ryan throwing, and Gary Collins and Paul Warfield catching the football. Shula double-teamed Warfield and had Bobby Boyd cover Collins, who had five inches and 25 pounds on Boyd. Those moves proved costly, as Collins scored 18 of Cleveland's 27 points.

Shula had studied the film and came away with the belief his Colts could run directly at the Browns. After all, he reasoned, Cleveland had surrendered more yards per run than any other NFL team that season. He also felt that due to the Browns ends playing out wide, sweeps wouldn't yield much yardage. After studying the Cleveland linebackers, Shula noticed they dropped back deep, so he also was convinced screen passes would work.

Shula's playbook included 34 running plays and 27 passing plays, and each one could be carried out from four different formations. But this didn't matter, as the Browns wound up controlling the football, running off 70 plays to a mere 45 for the Colts. Cleveland gave Baltimore a few different looks Shula didn't expect, and by the time the score had soared to 17–0 in the third quarter, Shula had to scrap his game plan. It was a moot issue. The Browns never looked back.

The 1965 season proved that Shula had the ability to improvise when the necessity arose, and that occurred when two serious injuries took place. Tom Matte's career as a running back had a unique twist when his college quarterbacking background came in handy late in the year. His quarterback rating in college was 140, although with Woody Hayes as his Ohio State coach, Matte, an All-American option quarterback, didn't put the ball in the air a lot. By way of comparison, however, Bob Griese's career quarterback rating at Purdue stood at 123.5, and Dan Marion's at Pitt was 127.7.

The regular season was a successful one, as the Colts wound up at 10–3–1, tied with Green Bay atop their division. After 10 games, Baltimore was 9–1 under Shula, who had relied on Unitas to help put up the league's third-highest total for yards gained through the air. Winning it all with those two luminaries was a solid possibility.

The Matte saga began when the Colts were forced to use him in the role of an emergency quarterback. To set the stage, Unitas had started 11 games before sustaining a leg injury. His backup, Gary Cuozzo, then started two games, but he, too, got hurt, separating his shoulder late in the next-to-last game of the season versus Green Bay. That meant halfback Matte was unexpectedly thrust into the position of having to take on the role of quarterback against the Packers.

Matte stated, "When John Unitas got hurt and Gary Cuozzo got hurt—we only kept two quarterbacks then—I was the last man standing, the only guy who had experience except maybe Bobby Boyd. So I carried the responsibility of going out there as quarterback."

Baltimore was down by eight points to Green Bay when Matte took over in his first quarterback outing. He only threw three times, and one went for an interception in a 42–27 loss. Paul Hornung scored 30 of those points.

Marchetti remembered that prior to deciding to rely on Matte from that contest onward, "Don Shula called up Woody Hayes and asked him about Matte, and Hayes said, 'You know, he's pretty good, but you can't let him throw the ball.'" Matte would throw but sparingly.

Shula was smart enough, of course, to quickly pick up another true, experienced quarterback, Ed Brown; however, due to league rules, he could use Brown for the final game of the regular season against the Rams but not any postseason contests.

Another problem with Brown was he was accustomed to using the numbering system for the holes on the line, which his Steelers had used, but it was different from Baltimore's system. That led to some confusion, but Shula worked with both Brown and Matte on their duties, making adjustments to the way things had been done under Unitas. In Matte's first full game in relief of Cuozzo, Shula did allow Matte to throw the football but, once more, not very often.

Shula basically planned to put Brown in the game when he wanted to execute certain pass plays and Matte for all other occasions. Shula also decided he would use two tight ends when Matte was under center to provide more blocking for him in this crucial game.

Shula handled things masterfully. In the fourth quarter, with the Colts down by a score of 17–10, he opened a series with Brown throwing a four-yard completion. He shuttled Matte in, but a run went nowhere. Back in went Brown. Shula noticed the Rams had been playing a zone to the tight-end side of the field the entire game, so he believed a slant-in pass would get the job done. He was correct. Tight end John Mackey got open over the middle on the pattern, snared the pass, and tied things up on a 68-yard gallop.

Rejuvenated, the Colts marched the ball down the field on their next possession, got in field goal range, and made good on a game-winning Lou Michaels 23-yard kick. Aside from the 68-yard throw, Brown threw for only 13 yards, going 3-for-5, but that one pass helped propel the Colts to their stunning victory.

Nonetheless, another big story line in the win against the Rams had actually come about before the game. That's when Shula proved the old line about necessity being the mother of invention. With some help, he devised a wristband (later on display at the Pro Football Hall of Fame) that listed the plays he wanted Matte to run that day. Matte wore his cheat sheet, a predecessor to what quarterbacks often use today, on his forearm and referred to it in the huddle throughout the day.

At game's end, the Colts had defeated the Rams, 20–17, with Matte going to the air just twice, both incompletions. Shula wanted him to run the ball, and Matte did what came naturally, and he did it well, gaining 99 yards on 16 carries.

Matte praised Shula's offensive line, saying,

> This is something that people have to understand; nothing happens unless the guys in the trenches are doing the good job. And when I went out and played my first [full] game as a quarterback against the Rams, I never got touched in the backfield once. And this is Deacon Jones and Merlin Olsen and all those guys. My offensive line did such a tremendous job, it was unbelievable.

Berry observed, "His performance was absolutely one of the most remarkable things I think anybody's ever seen in the NFL."

Shula had the Colts pound the ball on the ground for 214 yards to 57 for the Rams. The win launched Baltimore into a divisional tie with Green Bay. This time Shula would have to go with Matte all the way in the win-or-go-home contest. Sadly, on this day, the Matte magic ran out. He did hit on five of 12 passes on a blustery day at Lambeau Field, but that was good for just 40 yards.

Still, it turned out Shula was one bad call away from advancing to the NFL championship game. With two ticks less than two minutes to go in regulation, Don Chandler booted a 22-yard field goal that would soon force the game into overtime. Many observers contend the kick sailed high and wide of the uprights, which, back then, did not extend as high as they do now. In fact, the following season, poles were lengthened due to the controversy that swirled after this kick. Shula felt the "Baltimore extensions" made to goal posts supported his contention that the kick wasn't good. The play proved an old saying to be true: Close only counts in horse shoes and hand grenades.

About 30 years later, Chandler himself admitted his kick was no good, and replays proved he did miss; however, the game did forge on, into overtime, where a legitimate 25-yard Chandler kick won it for the Packers, 13–10.

Shula and the Colts had come oh-so-close to winning despite overwhelming and odd circumstances. If the correct call had been made on the 22-yard kick, the Colts would have advanced to meet the Browns in the NFL championship game, a game Green Bay won, 23–12, giving Lombardi his third of five NFL titles.

Shula's hands had been manacled in the loss to Green Bay, as the Colts netted a mere 32 yards passing. Baltimore threw the ball just 12 times, while rushing 47 times. Berry remembered, "Going into the game head coach Vince Lombardi and his players knew we had to run the ball a lot. Planning accordingly, they held us to three yards per carry."

Matte did a serviceable job against Green Bay with little offensive support. Lenny Moore, normally a dynamo, provided just 48 yards of total offense, and Matte and Jerry Hill tied as the leading Baltimore runners, each carrying the ball for 57 yards.

The Colts ended the season at 10–4–1, cursing the Packers' skill and luck, as three of those four losses came against Green Bay (two of them by a combined six points).

Shula had known it would take a great master plan to have even a wisp of a chance to knock off Lombardi's mighty team. His planning almost culminated in a dazzling upset. It was little consolation, but Shula kept his underdog Colts in the game until the very end.

Berry stated,

> When he first decided to go with Matte, Shula addressed us. "This is what we are going to do," he said. "Defense, you shut them out. Tom is going to be our quarterback, and I want the offense to get the ball in field goal range." He turned to our kicker, Lou Michaels and said, "Lou, you kick the field goals." That was the essence of it.
>
> Our plan had worked until the Packers game, and, remember, the three-point margin of their win came on a missed field goal. A referee later admitted he blew the call. So we came within three points of playing for the world's title with a running back as our quarterback. Our defense, in particular, took it to another level. Shula's refusal to be deterred by adversity was the catalyst. It's just a shame we fell a bit short.
>
> I still think that what happened over those several weeks was probably the most improbable scenario I have ever seen in my years in the game. No doubt this had to be Shula's finest hour, including his 17–0 season with the Dolphins.

Many years later, Matte joked,

> And I cheated my way into [the] Hall of Fame with the wristband. If I had of patented that thing, I'd have made a fortune because now everybody uses it. It was the first time anyone had ever used it, and that came from Don McCafferty, the backfield coach, and Don Shula. They found this little wristband that had a plastic thing on it, and you slid the plays inside of it, and I had my whole game plan right there.

Matte further analyzed Shula's strategies, stating,

> What he executed just about followed the same philosophy of running the wishbone, but I was under center—we didn't do the direct snap, but I wish we would have. I'd just take off around the corner, or we'd fake a sweep going one way and I'd do a bootleg going the other way, a naked bootleg. I always had one of the receivers, a tight end would come across—if I was going to the left, he'd line up on the right-hand side—and we used to come across and I'd sort of roll out that way, and

if he was open, I'd pop it. If they came up to get me, most of the time, what Shula said, was run the ball. It was what Woody says, "Run the ball. Get what you can get." In a way, the Colts nickel-dimed their opponents.

The best play we had in our repertoire was a quarterback draw where I'd just take a stab, go back, set up in the pocket, the receivers would clear out the area and get the middle open, and I'd pop, run up the inside. The first game we played against the Rams, which had a great defense—the Fearsome Foursome back then—hell, I had 99 yards rushing as quarterback, so that wasn't too bad a deal.

We kept them honest so they had to wait, they couldn't put that full court press on you because they were afraid I might take off up the middle, which I had done. And the other teams, when I played them, did the same thing. They had to respect the fact that I could shoot the gaps and get through there to pick up big yardage.

I tell you, the team rallied around me, and Unitas said, "Tom, do the things you do best," and that's where Mac, Shula, Unitas, and I came up with a game plan where they took advantage of what my abilities were—get outside the pocket, put the pressure on the line-backer and defensive back, and if they come up to get you, drop it off.

Shula was like an improv comedian, working with what he had on hand and in his brain.

Now, any coach, no matter how successful, experiences his share of failure; however, only a misguided critic would carp that Shula became the first coach to lose a Super Bowl in both NFL conferences. Shula himself negatively critiqued at least one of his failures. He has blamed himself for the loss to the Jets in Super Bowl III at the conclusion of the 1968 season, saying he permitted his Colts to treat the time leading up to the game as a vacation, with kids and wives tagging along.

Of course, it takes a man of character and self-confidence to be willing to accept blame. Furthermore, such a man learns from his errors. He would later have his men lead a Spartan existence, whipping them into shape mentally and physically on their drive to championships.

Departing briefly from the golden age, let's skip ahead to the 1970s, to further illustrate Shula's greatness. The Dolphins became instant winners at Shula's urging. In 1969, Miami slogged their way through an anguish-ing 3–10–1 season, plunging them into fifth place. Enter Shula. Presto chango. In his first season, he flipped things around by winning, not losing, 10 times (10–4) and hoisting the Dolphins into postseason play for the first time.

During the next three years, Shula annually took Miami to the Super Bowl, and they'd win it twice. His string of excellence continued in his fifth and sixth seasons in Miami (and beyond, actually), as he posted records of 11–3 and 10–4. That gave him a six-year record of 67–16–1, which works out to a sizzling winning percentage of .807, not counting the tie.

By the way, in his first six seasons as a head coach, in Baltimore, he put together a glistening regular-season record of 63–18–3, good for the best start of a coach's career—better than such greats as Vince Lombardi and George Halas had done in their first six years.

The only thing the Dolphins regretted about Shula's first season in Miami was their loss to Oakland in the divisional round of the playoffs. The next year, their record was almost identical to their 1970 showing, at 10–3–1, but more significantly, Shula secured his first AFC title as Miami rolled over Kansas City and Baltimore en route to the Super Bowl. Only a loss there to Dallas marred the season.

Then came a two-year explosion. First, in 1972, football fans witnessed something unprecedented in the annals of the NFL: a team that won the championship with an unblemished record. Shula's Dolphins put a notch in the win column 17 times, without a single loss or tie.

They relegated their nearest AFC East Division contender to a mere flyspeck in their rearview mirror, winning the division by seven games over the Jets, who went 7–7. Having wrapped up the division early, some observers feared rust might set in, or maybe complacency. Shula's men showed no sign of either flaw, although their three wins on the path to the NFL title did feature close games. They dispatched the Browns, 20–14; got by the Steelers, 21–17; and wrapped it up with their brilliant defense in a 14–7 victory against the Redskins.

Even if the media slapped the label "No-Name Defense" on the Dolphins, that unit helped Miami become a perennial winner under Shula. One key was the fact that Shula was so good at spotting latent talent. He often grabbed no-name players off other teams' scrap piles and used them for building blocks.

Nick Buoniconti serves as a solid example of how Shula could spot talent (and how Shula believed versatile linebackers were the key to winning football games), often where other coaches were myopic. Buoniconti, a middle linebacker, was drafted out of Notre Dame by the old Boston Patriots in 1962, but not until the 13th round. By 1968, they saw him as someone to cast off unceremoniously. Shula, on the other hand, saw potential—perhaps not realizing he had a future Hall of Famer on his hands, but he certainly saw a budding All-Pro.

Buoniconti said Shula's defense may have toiled in relative anonymity at first, but it was a cerebral group. After the unit helped Miami secure the Super Bowl win against Washington, defensive coordinator Bill Arnsparger approached Buoniconti and informed him that the defense was guilty of a mere 13 mental miscues in their 17-game run of excellence.

The next season began with the Dolphins record standing at an uninspiring 1–1 early on, but the relentless team would lose only one more time all year long. They may not have run the table again, but the season was hardly anticlimactic. They went from September 30 until December 9 before losing a game, tearing off 10 straight wins. This time they waltzed through the postseason, crushing Cincinnati by 18, blowing by Oakland by 17 points, and turning the Super Bowl into a romp, topping Minnesota, 24–7, and shutting out the Vikings until the final quarter.

Shula took his Dolphins to the playoffs again in 1974, 1978, 1979, and 1981, but it wasn't until 1982 that he'd win another AFC championship. Just two years later, he repeated that accomplishment. He wasn't done. He took five more teams to the playoffs from then through 1995, his final season.

After his 1982 success, Shula was approached by Donald Trump, who tried to lure him to coach his United States Football League team, the New Jersey Generals. According to the book *Rozelle* by Jeff Davis, Trump, having fired the team's coach as one of his first moves as owner, offered $700,000 to sign Shula. Initially, Shula expressed no interest in the job, but when the pot was upped to $1 million, Shula considered the offer, first wanting to know more about Trump.

At one point, Shula's business manager asked Trump if Shula was ever in New York and needed somewhere to stay, could he use a Trump Tower apartment? The answer from Trump was yes. A deal was imminent.

However, when Shula heard that Trump had told the media that the only thing holding up the deal was that Shula had made a *demand* to be given a suite in Trump Tower, Shula felt he was being used to gain publicity for the Trump property. So, he called Trump and expressed his consternation about Trump's comment. He then called off the deal and said what Trump had done was typical of his character. Trump, he said, had broken a confidence and made Shula look greedy, like some kind of hooker willing to abandon Miami in quest of an apartment in New York. When Trump was told the negotiations were over, instead of showing dismay, he shook it off as still being positive publicity for his building.

Shula, now entrenched in Miami, continued to show how he could adapt to many different situations. Some professional managers/coaches set out to build a team through drafts and trades that fit their personality and style. Others are flexible enough to win with the personnel they have and adjust their style of coaching to fit.

Shula had won with the Colts with a great passing attack, and he was able to keep winning as a ball control type of coach when he first went to Miami. Later still, when he lost key running backs, he told Bob Griese to let the ball fly. Before long, Griese led the NFL in touchdown passes and quarterback rating for the first and only time in his career.

The year after the Trump fiasco, Shula again won the AFC title, this time with a second-year quarterback named Dan Marino, who was good enough to outshine Griese in many ways. Shula showed again and again that he could win even with an ever-changing cast of characters, not unlike a popular, long-running soap opera.

It had taken until 1976 before Shula suffered his first of just two seasons with a record below .500. The 6–8 season was due to his Dolphins being decimated by injuries and 11 starters having to undergo surgery. Still, half of his losses came when Miami was outscored by four points, three on two occasions, and once by one point. Somehow Shula found a way to be competitive, and that held true even when, a mere two months after Miami had won its second straight Super Bowl, Larry Csonka, Paul Warfield, and Jim Kiick signed deals with the new World Football League. In 1975, the first season without those three men, miraculously and without the aid of smoke or mirrors, Shula still managed to go 10–4.

Doug Crusan played on the offensive line for the Dolphins his entire career (1968–1974). He arrived in Miami the year before Shula, enduring a 3–10–1 season. Then he reaped the benefits of playing the left tackle position for Shula, especially being part of the undefeated team and two Super Bowl wins.

Crusan had a great deal of admiration for Shula and his methods. "He demanded respect," Crusan began. He added,

> You respected him because he won. He worked you hard, but one of the stories I always tell people is before practice he'd stand up there and go through what we were going to do. And practice was, we'll say, an hour and 30 minutes. He'd say that was how long it would run, and, not like stories you hear about one coach, "Oh, you guys look so terrible, we're going to start all over again." He never did that. He was true to his word, and you respected him for that.

Shula no doubt picked that up from his former coach, Paul Brown, who ran short but precise practices.

Crusan continued,

> Our training camp was forever, and we had two, three practices a day. We went at it, and in that heat of Miami for us to boot. That's the way Coach Shula did it. We had none of that one-against-two stuff. Now they only have so many practices in pads and so many in shorts and helmets. We never had that—it was all in full pads.
>
> We repeated things so many times, literally step-by-step, and he felt that we'd go into a game and know exactly what to do and do it automatically. He was repetitious precision. He was a good guy.

Manny Fernandez was also on the 17–0 team and knows many facets of Shula. Asked if he had any good Shula stories, he began with a story he heard from Colts star Art Donovan.

> He had a great sense of humor and was one heckuva' football player. He came down and spoke for us at the Miami Touchdown Club. I was on the board of directors, and he was one of the guys we tried to get every year if we could because he would just pack the house.
>
> One story he told had to do with when Don Shula was a young player for the Colts. He came to a team party, brought a girlfriend, and I guess everybody was mingling. The next thing you know, Shula looks over and his date is smoking a cigar with one of the players. Shula read her the riot act, ran her off, put her in a cab, and sent her home.

There was no tolerance regarding the violation of his value system.

Fernandez followed up with a tale he said was "something we did to him in, I want to say in 1973." He elaborated,

> I had a swamp buggy, and Bill Stanfill and I were out deer hunting one Friday morning. Meetings on Fridays didn't start until 1:00 in the afternoon, so we'd go out in the morning to deer hunt in the Everglades. And Bill happened to catch an alligator. Just a small one, I don't know, four foot, nothing spectacular.
>
> I asked him what he was going to do with it and he said, "You'll see." So we put him in the tool box, put him in the trunk of my car, and went back to camp. Then, after practice I got Larry Csonka to give me a hand—it was Bill's idea, but he was tied up with something so it was up to me to get it to where it needed to go. I enlisted Larry because I knew he could keep the secretary distracted. While he did that, I slipped into Shula's private office and put the alligator in his shower and closed the door.
>
> We got the heck out of there, and I guess it would be about, oh, 7:00 when Dorothy, Don's wife, would come pick him up on Friday evenings and go to dinner—it was a ritual. Don always had his schedule, and the schedule never changed.
>
> It was about 6:30, a quarter to seven, and he was going in to take a shower. He found that gator and ran all the way out of the building stark naked, screaming and yelling for the equipment manager. He sent him in there to catch it and get it the hell out of there.
>
> Needless to say, at the next meeting he brought the incident up to the team. He says, "I'm pretty sure I know who did it." And Jim Kiick raised his hand and said, "Hey, Coach, you ought to be thankful. We took a team vote and it was by just one player that we voted to tape the gator's mouth shut."
>
> Shula knew it was me and Larry. That night we came back to the equipment room about 7:30, thinking he'd be gone. We drank a beer with Darin Dowe, our equipment manager. Darin was telling us how it went down, Shula running out of there. We were sitting there just laughing our asses off when all of a sudden Shula's standing in the doorway looking at us. "I knew it was you. I knew it was you." We said, "We don't know what you're talking about." He asked what we were still doing there and we said, "We just stopped by to have a beer with Darin." He said, "Bullshit."
>
> We never did admit to it, but the whole story was that [Coach] Bill Arnsparger had actually gone in to take a shower in Shula's office rather than walk all the way through the building to the players' show-

er. He saw the gator, closed the door, and just left it there—never told Shula a thing.

When I finally admitted to Shula, many, many years later, we were roasting Bill at the Miami Touchdown Club. I got up. I told the alligator story and said, "Coach, I'm going to admit you were right, it was Larry and me. We did it. But what you don't know is the rest of the story—your trusted head assistant coach, your defensive coordinator, your best buddy, went in and saw that gator before you ever did and never told you a thing." Oh, boy, did Bill turn red. It was a very closely guarded secret. It was a good 15 or 20 years before it came out.

The story may surprise some who wonder, "Wasn't Shula a taskmaster? Didn't he fine the players involved or make the entire team suffer with a grueling practice session?" Fernandez laughed, relating,

He couldn't prove anything. Good luck. What was he going to do to Csonka and me? But he *was* a tough disciplinarian, oh, yeah. We just needed to loosen him up a little bit. We thought he was getting too tight.

It was his fourth year there and we had gotten to know each other pretty well, and he knew I didn't give a damn. Just let me go out on Sundays and create mayhem. As long as I could do what I was doing on Sunday he wasn't going to do nothing to me.

Still, it's true that Shula was unafraid of reaming out a player who didn't put out full effort, and he did drive his players. Early in his career, some of his men called him a dictator. In his first training camp in Miami, he held unprecedented four-a-day workout sessions. His approach must have worked, as he took a cellar-dwelling team with a 3–10–1 record and turned them into a playoff bound, 10–3 unit.

He didn't want to instill fear in his players and said he genuinely wanted their respect, but he also believed he had to be *the* authority figure, subscribing, at times, to the trite phrase, "My way or the highway." Donovan, a former teammate of Shula's, writes of his wild ways and toughness as a player. Shula, he recalls, was one who didn't think twice about thrusting an elbow to a receiver's eye, and later, as the Miami coach, he did instill fear in those around him, even the media.

Donovan adds that even during some mediocre Miami seasons in about 1986, Shula was a miracle worker considering his personnel, always getting the max out of his players. Donovan says that as a player,

Shula was always the smartest guy on the field, and it was rather like having an extra coach out there playing.[3]

As Miami's coach, Shula used his wits to gain any possible advantage. It's been said he purposely had a long pregame invocation done during home games to make his opponents have to stand under the sweltering Florida sun.

Shula knew the importance of teamwork. Paul Warfield noted,

> To be a part of a team sport requires, in this case, 11 individuals in the team concept with a focus of having great success. In that we're talking about football, having 11 individuals, whether it's offense, defense, or special teams, it's a whole *team* when you include them all. Being able to consistently produce success at a high level and staying focused—for all 11 team members to, as the often-used concept [has it], to buy into that concept and understand that it's all 11 people who have contributed to a touchdown or contributed to a major win or going undefeated in a season—is the essence of who we are and what we are as a society today.

Warfield went on, "The more you have individualism or the 'I' that comes to the table in sports, you won't see those organizations have that kind of success." He said he was fortunate that his coaches—Woody Hayes at Ohio State and Blanton Collier of the Browns—stressed cohesive team play over individualism, adding, "And Don Shula essentially stressed that, and [his] people bought into that. That's why we had that kind of success."

Having his players believe in his philosophy, coupled with his ability to motivate his men to go beyond what seemingly was their top effort, led to eye-popping results.

Naturally, while his defenses, those with no name and otherwise, were important to Shula, offense mattered, too. One key element of Shula's offense was bruising fullback Larry Csonka. Crusan said, "I know he's officially listed at 237 pounds, but I guarantee by game day he was up to 250 again."

That relates to the way the week leading up to a game worked under Shula. Crusan stated that Mondays were days off, and, "Tuesdays were shorts, and it was film day, and getting the kinks out because you were banged up." He continued, "Wednesdays and Thursdays were what I call the heavy days, in full pads. Wednesdays stressed the offense, the next day focused on defense, and Fridays were a combination of the two. It was a cycle thing." For Csonka, the cycle included dropping some weight by the Thursday weigh-ins, then putting it back on, repeating the entire process.

Csonka had plenty of time to bulk up again, especially with Fridays being a light day, with workouts in shorts and helmets, and Saturdays being reserved for travel or, for home dates, a 45-minute workout in T-shirts and shorts in the heat of the blazing Miami sun. Needless to say, Csonka used every ounce of his body weight to pound the ball at and through defenders. From 1971 to 1973, he amassed 1,000-plus yards yearly, and he was always dependable when Miami needed tough, short yardage for first downs and/or touchdowns.

Rick Volk spent three seasons with Shula in Baltimore, from 1967 to 1969. Touching on the subject of Shula's practices, the defensive back said most of the time practices involved working on such things as seven-on-seven passing drills. Volk commented,

> The ones we always tried to do every practice. You want to tackle people you're covering, you're trying to work within your offensive or defensive system, and you're trying to improve yourself as a team.
>
> So if guy catches the ball on you, you're not going to whack him [under practice conditions]. Every now and then it might happen, but if John Unitas goes back to pass, they're not going to go sack him, that's for sure. You could get close to him and touch him, something like that, but we know who butters our bread. You're not going to go out and hurt somebody in practice. You want to be ready to play on Sunday, that's when I had to be ready to go, but most of it's just timing during the week.
>
> We did have hitting, offense line, defensive line, we'd do hitting, and we would do a little bit as defensive backs here and there, but we didn't have tackling drills and stuff like that in scrimmages, not really *during* the season, but getting ready for it during preseason. That is where you'd have intrasquad scrimmage and then preseason games where you're getting ready to hit and ready to play the game, but you don't want to get anybody hurt before a season or before a game.

So Shula's practices were, in some ways, typical of all NFL coaches, but in other ways he had his own approach.

Baltimore great Gino Marchetti feels there is a big difference between the head coaches of his era and those of today, and he cited one strong example, declaring,

> Don Shula was a tough coach, he was a mean coach. He would cuss you out, but you know what, after it was over, he'd shake your hand. A lot of these coaches [today] are buddy buddy, but they'll stab you in the back. When it comes to push and shove, they won't stand up for you. You want a guy that's going to stand up and fight for you because it's too tough to play the game if everybody's going to kick the hell out of you one way or the other.

Tom Matte said Shula demanded a lot of his players. For example, Matte was supposed to know not only his duties on pass and run plays, but also what the Colts' entire offense was going to execute. And that wasn't all. Remembered Matte, "On defense, Shula said I had to understand what *everybody's* doing on every play—whether they're using man-to-man, a combo, a zone, whatever defense [they use]. You have to understand what the other guys are looking for, too."

Yet another former Colt, Sam Havrilak, provided the following take on his coach:

> The first meeting that we had as rookies, he said to everybody, "You know, everybody in this room has a lot of talent. I do not tolerate mental mistakes. If there are two people in here that have the same ability, I'm going to choose the one that makes the fewer mental mistakes because everybody gets beat physically, but you can't beat yourself by making mental mistakes." I saw a lot of good athletes come and go because either they couldn't learn the system or they kept making mental mistakes. That would hurt their chances.
>
> I remember in 1969, my first year, they must have brought 40 or 50 people in that were cut from other teams—this was Shula who brought them in—and what the Colts would do is they would sign them to a contract in the morning after they flew them in, issue them equipment, then they would go out for the afternoon practice—probably not even practice because they didn't know any of the plays, but they would run them through a couple of drills, throw the ball to them, see how they ran. If they liked them, he'd keep them. If he didn't, that night they'd be on their way out.

Shula had that kind of clout to spend the time and money to fly players in to look them over even though such efforts weren't very productive. Many football teams would not have supported or even attempted such an experiment. Havrilak continued, "Of all those people in 1969 that Shula brought in, he only kept one. That was a guy named Perry Lee Dunn from Mississippi." Shula was quite willing to seek the proverbial lightning in the bottle. For the record, Dunn spent his final NFL season (of six) with the Colts. More accurately, he spent five games with Baltimore, where he would gain only 45 yards on just 13 carries.

Shula coached 33 seasons and a truckload of big games, but there was a contest that, although insignificant when compared to, say, postseason games, nevertheless stood out for Shula. On October 2, 1994, Shula's Dolphins blew out the Cincinnati Bengals, 23–7. What made the lopsided game memorable was the fact that it marked the first time ever that two NFL head coaches who went head to head in a game were father and son. Dave Shula had begun his head coaching days two years earlier, and he held that job for five years, through the 1996 season. He only chalked up a career coaching record of 19–52, but add those 19 wins to his father's 328, and you come up with the answer to a trivia question: "What father–son duo owns the most lifetime NFL wins?" Dave's brother Mike has also coached football at the college and pro levels, beginning in 1988.

There seems to be two theories on how to define a truly *great* season in sports. Some feel that having reached, say, the Super Bowl, anything can happen. Perhaps a pass that should have been caught glances off a receiver's fingertips and is picked off and returned for a cheap touchdown, causing the better team to lose. Or a missed field goal costs a team the title, as was the case with the Buffalo Bills in Super Bowl XXV. The first theory, therefore, holds that just getting to a title game means a team has had an outstanding season.

A much less forgiving concept argues that there can be no excuses— you either win it all or you are a loser. In 1984, Hall of Fame baseball manager Sparky Anderson's Detroit Tigers cruised to a scorching start, going 18–2 in April. At that point, going to the playoffs was virtually guaranteed. Anderson stated he believed nothing short of winning the World Series would satisfy fans and the media. To lose in the Series, he felt, meant failure regardless of the huge success the Tigers had experienced throughout the long haul of the regular season of 162 games. Incidentally, Detroit won 104 games and coasted through the World Series in five games over San Diego.

Shula felt the same as Anderson as he approached the Super Bowl, sporting a 16–0 record. He realized that a loss in that contest would have turned him into a loser in the eyes of many critics.

Shula felt that if his team executed the way he felt and believed they *should*, they should win every time. That's the ideal, but Shula coached in 37 playoff games and won just two more than he lost. His record in the Super Bowl is 2–4. Does that really diminish his greatness? Floyd Little promptly shrugged off such a suggestion, saying, "You can't say enough about Don Shula and how he has taken his teams, over a period of time, to Super Bowls. Anytime you get to the Super Bowl, it's a success." Shula, by that definition, is an absolute success. He was the first of just two coaches to take a team to six Super Bowls—the record now belongs to Bill Belichick alone, with eight trips through the 2017 season.

Little added,

> A lot of coaches say you just can't hope to get to the Super Bowl—you got to hope you get to the Super Bowl and *win*. That's the difference. [Some] guys just play to get to the Super Bowl, but they never think about winning. But it's just an honor and a privilege and a pleasure to have the opportunity to get there and play in it.
>
> [There's] a mindset that you have to have as a player and a coach— that we're going to the Super Bowl and we're going to win it. You just can't say, "We're going to the Super Bowl," and not really have in your consciousness that you're going to win it.

Make no mistake, Shula never settled for winning the AFC or NFL title, but sometimes outside factors beyond his control dictated who won a given game, even a Super Bowl.

Clearly, Shula's overall credentials are impeccable. Plus, in 1972 and 1973, he truly did have the attitude Little said was so important—Shula and his Dolphins were positive they were going to win it all, and nothing would stop them.

In those two seasons when Shula won back-to-back Super Bowls, his Dolphins' overall record, counting postseason play, stood at 32–2. That works out to an unbelievable, blistering win–loss percentage of .941. That also means if the record from the 1971 Dolphins team (10–3–1) was added into the mix, as great a record as they had that season, the winning percentage of the 1972 and 1973 seasons alone would drop. Still, what a three-year span that was! For that matter, from 1970 through 1975, Shula won in double digits each and every year.

His undefeated 1972 season helped him build another record. No coach in the annals of the NFL has ever won as many games as Shula, who logged a career record of 328–156–6. He's still king of the hill with that win total. When he was about halfway through his coaching days, he had already shot up the list of career wins to the number-three slot, behind only George Halas and Curly Lambeau.

Shula went 257–133–2 as the Dolphins coach, and entering the 2017 season, the Miami franchise had won a grand total of 439 games. That means that single-handedly, coaching-wise, Shula accounted for an exceptionally high percentage (almost 60 percent) of the total wins in the team's history, which dates back to 1966. Not only that, Shula experienced just two losing seasons as an NFL head coach. He also holds the record for having coached the most consecutive seasons, with 33.

However, in 1978, he said he didn't feel he ranked up there with men like Halas because he believed his success came simply from determining what had to be done, getting down to the task, and attacking the job.

Some of his success comes from his working with great quarterbacks. Shula once said, only partly in jest, "Sure, luck means a lot in football. Not having a good quarterback is bad luck." One could easily argue Shula had two of, say, the top five quarterbacks in NFL history in John Unitas and Dan Marino, both coming from the Pittsburgh vicinity, to help him compile his record-setting win total—and don't forget Bob Griese.

By the way, Raymond Berry said Shula was not a total stranger to the quarterback position. Stated Berry, "Few people remember this, but once in an exhibition game, he had to serve as our emergency quarterback, even though he was normally a defensive back. He got in for one play, the only time he ever played that position in the NFL—and he got sacked." Hardly the historic stuff of a Tom Matte.

Clearly, however, Shula has left his fingerprint on the NFL. Floyd Little was suitably impressed with Shula, stating,

> He shows up in Miami and puts together an undefeated team. He did that with my [college] teammate Larry Csonka and some of the other guys I played with over the years in all-star games, like Bob Griese.
>
> Don Shula is a Hall of Fame coach, a recognizable coach who's done great things for the Dolphins—more so than he did for the Balti-

more Colts. Don's a friend of mine as well, not only as a Hall of Famer, but as a coach that I've admired for the work he's done in building a team with players with character. All of his players, for the most part, are considered to be serious, dedicated athletes, unlike some of today's players—and they've had their problems with the Miami Dolphins, but if they had any problems under Don Shula [they didn't last]; he had complete control of his team and his players.

"He's produced great players and many Hall of Famers," said Little, who then, with a liberal dose of hyperbole, said most of the Hall of Famers have played under Shula. Perhaps not, but Shula has coached numerous Canton honorees, including John Unitas, Lenny Moore, John Mackey, Gino Marchetti, Dan Marino, Paul Warfield, Raymond Berry, Larry Csonka, Bob Griese, and so on, seemingly ad infinitum.

"So," Little continued, "I admire him for what's he's done for the Dolphins—he's made their name synonymous with success, having the only undefeated season in all of pro football." Actually, Shula didn't have the only undefeated season in *pro football*, but he put together the only untainted season in the NFL. Paul Brown took Cleveland to a perfect championship season as well, but that was in the old All-American Football Conference (AAFC).

Shula, then, has done it all in the world of pro football. He will no doubt be remembered most for two achievements—his 17–0 season and his 328 career regular season coaching wins. Through the 2017 season, that win total is 10 more than the coach with the second-most wins, George Halas, more than Tom Landry and 78 more than the highest-ranked active coach, Bill Belichick. Naming the greatest coach of all is a subjective matter, but the winningest one of all is indisputable. Shula reigns as king of them all.

12

GEORGE ALLEN

"He Wanted to Win at All Costs"

Place of birth: Grosse Point Woods, Michigan
Date of birth: April 29, 1922
Date of death: December 31, 1990
Lifetime wins, losses, and ties: 116–47–5
Career winning percentage: .712
Playoff wins and losses: 2–7
Playoff winning percentage: .222
NFL major titles won and years of championships: NFL champions 1972
Teams coached and years: Los Angeles Rams 1966–1970; Washington Redskins 1971–1977

George Allen was born to be a coach. He possessed a laser-like focus on winning and paid such attention to every little detail he could almost be taken for a man diagnosed with obsessive-compulsive disorder.

Some say he would do almost anything to win, or at least to get an edge. Asked for his take on Allen, Mel Renfro of the Cowboys quickly replied,

> George was fiery. I mean, he *was* the rah-rah guy. He pulled out all the stops to win. He did things that were unusual to try to win. He encouraged his players to do things that nowadays you'd probably get fined heavily for doing. Very competitive coach. We had our battles with him. He wanted to win at all costs.

Tex Schramm, Cowboys general manager, said one day he noticed a car that looked suspicious parked by the Dallas practice field. When he had the car's license plate traced, he discovered the car had, in fact, been rented by the head of Allen's scouting system.

Renfro remembered the incident, relating,

> He spied on our practice—one of his coaches was across the street in a tree and got chased down and caught—traced back to [Allen's team], but they didn't do anything about it at the time. But he always was encouraging his players and coaches to do things that just weren't quite normal.
>
> It was no secret that he did some things that I don't think were ethical. I know one of our linebackers got blocked from behind, below the knee one time by one of Allen's wide receivers, and I think that was because of George Allen's encouragement. I think the league changed the rules on blocking because of that.

Like Renfro, Jackie Smith heard of Allen's cloak-and-dagger episodes. Said Smith,

> We always were suspect of what he was doing as far as how he was gathering his information. He made a lot of coaches, like Don Coryell, nutty, thinking that they saw him behind every tree or riding by our workout place in a car or something. He had everybody paranoid. He would just make coaching staffs go to a lot more work—we'd go to a different workout site every day during the week we were playing his teams a couple of years. You'd think you saw somebody in a building who looked like they were watching—and he'd look like George Allen or somebody obviously working for him. They'd send somebody up there to check out who the guy was.

Once Allen's son was with him on the sidelines and shouted out an insult to a referee, who then was ready to toss a penalty flag. The win-at-any-cost Allen prevented the penalty by telling the ref the young man near him was not associated with the team. He disowned his own son, perhaps claiming he was a ball boy assigned to work the game, and avoided a penalty. Any little edge. *That* was George Allen.

He was so obsessive about his occupation that Otto Graham once said Allen basically sequestered himself in a room, away from friends and family, each season. Graham further said he didn't feel that price was a fair one to pay for success. Allen, destined for Hall of Fame recognition, did.

Dave Robinson, who spent his final two NFL seasons playing under Allen, observed,

> He was a very emotional guy. You know how guys [huddle] together and shout, "One, two, three. Hey," before a game? George started that. Every game he got in the middle, got the whole team together, and we'd shout, "One, two, three. Go Redskins," or something like that. He was the first coach I ever saw do that. Now every coach does that.

Many coaches have famous idiosyncrasies, little habits like NCAA basketball coach Jerry Tarkanian's biting on a towel during games. Robinson said Allen's trademark was "licking his fingers all the time when he was talking to you." Pacing along the sidelines, licking his fingers, applauding good plays, and exhorting his men on, Allen was probably as enthusiastic, or even more so, than any NFL coach ever, a veritable extra cheerleader.

Author Robert Smith didn't think Allen looked like a prototypical football coach. He compares him to a "rising young manager of a thriving branch of your local chain store. He has a faintly diffident air, always looking somewhat tousled." He adds Allen "seldom raises his voice, seldom says a bad word, and never berates a player in public," and writes that Allen may have run the "most tightly organized practice in all of pro football."[1]

The way Allen obtained his first head coaching job in the NFL with the Rams is an interesting story. When he heard Harland Svare had been dismissed as the Rams coach shortly before Christmas 1965, Allen took it upon himself to call the Rams, seeking the gift of a head coaching job. When principal team owner Dan Reeves learned of this, he was interested, but he knew Allen was still under contract for two more years to George Halas as an assistant coach. Plus, Allen had done such a great job with the Bears defense, especially his work with the 1963 defensive unit, which helped win a championship. Reeves also realized Papa Bear might get surly and become ursine if asked to release Allen from his obligation.

At one point, Allen told the Rams that Halas had said it was fine for him to work out a deal with the Rams, so they hired him; however, it was reported that after Halas had given his approval to Allen, he changed his mind and insisted he considered the signing of Allen to be a case of tampering. More confusion and litigation ensued, but eventually Halas, after actually winning a court judgment, apparently was satisfied he had made his point. Now a contented bear settling in to hibernate, he dropped his lawsuit and allowed Allen to depart. The first time Allen's Rams played the Bears during the second week of the season, Halas absorbed a galling 31–17 defeat.

The industrious Allen churned out many more wins as the Rams coach, ignoring such criticism as what author Bob Carroll dealt out. He writes that Los Angeles, led by quarterback Roman Gabriel, was a boring team due to its reliance on ball control. Fans who craved long passes, dazzling runs, and trick plays would be disappointed after taking in a Rams contest.[2] Typically, the Rams kept possession of the football with short stuff, while employing a magnificent, heavy-on-the-veterans defense to keep points at a minimum and frequently give Gabriel fine field position.

The Rams defense, unlike their offense, was far from being somniferous. Fans were kept wide eyed and delighted by the play of the Fearsome Foursome, led by "Deacon" Jones, Merlin Olsen, Lamar Lundy, and Rosey Grier (who was replaced by Roger Brown in 1967). This was a unit Dick Butkus called the most dominant one in NFL annals. Obviously, Allen had inherited some fine players.

As a rookie head coach in 1966, Allen took a team that had finished at 4–10 the previous season and transformed it into an 8–6 unit, good for the Rams' first winning season since 1958. The next year, the team's learning curve went berserk, off the charts, and the Rams began a spree, winning 92 percent of their games (again, not counting ties), going 11–1–2. Their trek to the playoffs was the first for a Rams team since 1955; however, the Packers of Vince Lombardi handed Allen a 28–7 spanking to eliminate them from the postseason. Green Bay went on to win Super Bowl II versus Oakland, so losing to them after winning the division was still extremely impressive for a coach in just his second season.

The next two seasons, 1968 and 1969, Allen led Los Angeles to records of 10–3–1 and 11–3. The 10–3–1 mark wasn't good enough to qualify for postseason play, as Don Shula's Colts won the Coastal Division at 13–1. Then the '69 Rams dropped a tough one in the playoffs to Bud Grant's Vikings. In 1970, Allen's final year with the Rams, he went 9–4–1, finishing in second place.

It's been said that Allen was fired by the Rams because he wanted more power and/or independence from the ownership/front office, including his desire to pay his players more generously. Allen may have deserved what he demanded based on his record with the Rams, at 49–17–4, and the fact that in the season prior to Allen's arrival in Los Angeles, 1965, the team had finished in the cellar, buried in seventh place. Allen steered them to third-, first-, second-, first-, and second-place finishes, respectively, in his five seasons as their coach.

Actually, Reeves had fired Allen after just three seasons, disagreeing with Allen's philosophy of discarding draft picks to obtain veterans. In 1967, for example, Grier was injured in the preseason. Allen traded three draft picks to the Lions for a leviathan replacement, 6-foot-5, 300-pound Roger Brown (back when a 300-pound player was very, very rare). The swap was yet another example of Allen casting off future draft picks.

Reeves did not believe, as Allen most certainly did, that the future is now, disdaining any talk of figurative time travel. Reeves did not want to later find himself and his Rams having to pull off an Old Mother Hubbard act, discovering he was bare of draft picks. That helped him decide to fire Allen.

Incidentally, Allen was once fined $5,000 for, get this, trading away some draft picks he didn't even own. Allen's self-destructing tendency to alienate his bosses, for example, Reeves, once led the Rams owner, right after the team had gone 11–3, to mutter he had more fun losing than winning with Allen.

The firing of Allen did not stick. After 38 of 40 Rams signed a petition in support of Allen, Reeves rehired him less than two weeks after he was axed, not even enough time for him to collect unemployment benefits.

After Allen finally was cut loose from the Rams for good, he still didn't qualify for an unemployment check. The story would prove different for his replacement, Tommy Prothro. After going 8–5–1 and 6–7–1 with the Rams, Prothro joined the unemployment lines. As for Allen, just two years after Lombardi left his job as head coach of the Redskins, Allen, like Lombardi, a great motivator of men, moved right in. A talented coach is always in demand, and after departing from Los Angeles, Allen had found a new team right away.

The Redskins had finished 5–7–2 under Lombardi in 1969, and 6–8 the next season under Bill Austin; however, in his first season with Washington, the demonstrative Allen turned things around with his 9–4–1 record and a playoff berth. In fact, Allen took his team to the playoffs then and for the next three seasons, even winning the NFC championship in just his second year on the job.

With the Redskins, he added 67 wins, versus just 30 losses, to his resume. He also again proved he won a lot more often than most coaches. With the Rams, his winning percentage was .742, and with the Redskins, it again deserved acclaim, almost hitting .700.

In Washington, Allen showed once more just how fervent his reliance on and trusting of veterans was. He missed his experienced players from his days with the Rams so much he made it a point to obtain some of them soon after he took over the Redskins.

One of them was Myron Pottios, who recalled,

> George's philosophy was, "Winning is everything," and he'd do what it took. He liked veteran ballplayers. He liked guys that knew his system. And what he hated the most was people that made mistakes on the field.
>
> So that's why I never worried about young guys or most veterans coming in taking my spot because it's tough for a guy to learn a system and go there [to a new team] and do all the changes in defenses that we did right at the line of scrimmage. You don't have time to think—it's something you do automatically. You don't think about doing it, *then do it*, it's got to be a natural move after you hear the defense called. A new guy coming in has to learn all the defenses, all the terminology, and do things in a split second. That's why George preferred the veterans.

It's also why Allen came up with that catch phrase, "The future is now."

If he valued veterans (as long as they kept in shape), it follows that he didn't trust rookies. He felt rookie mistakes, forgiven in some systems and written off as a learning experience, would hurt a team over and over again, and in so many ways. Allen knew the phrase "rookie mistakes" didn't enter the football lexicon by accident, and his faith in veterans ultimately helped make him a Hall of Fame coach.

Bob Carroll writes that Allen's Rams "had more veterans than a Memorial Day parade. Allen disliked playing anyone who couldn't remember Truman's presidency."[3]

Floyd Little had an interesting take on Allen and his players. Said Little, with a chuckle,

> I liked him because all of his players liked him. He liked a lot of the older players, so he had them on a schedule where they didn't burn themselves out. So George was the guy that everybody would love to play for because he was a coach who saved his players. With George, you didn't beat yourself up during practice because you saved yourself for the game because you were an experienced, or a veteran, player. George liked all of the veteran players, and the veteran players loved George because they didn't have to work so hard.

Adding a final, most pertinent comment, Little declared, "And he *won*."

Due to Allen's propensity for putting together an elderly team, a nickname was attached to the Redskins—the Over-the-Hill Gang. They could just as easily have been dubbed the Geriatric Gang. In the 1971 NFL draft, Allen used just one of his first five picks (and the player he did draft never played a game for Washington). Allen traded away the other four top slots prior to the draft to obtain veterans in the ultimate carpe diem move.

He began his machinations by trading two picks to the New Orleans Saints to get 32-year-old Billy Kilmer, hardly a hot prospect but a cagey veteran of eight seasons. His talent had been wasted with the Saints. In his final year with New Orleans, his record as a starter was a miserable 2–8. With the Redskins, however, he went six consecutive years with records of 7–3 or better, and he led the NFL in touchdown passes in his second season under Allen. He also helped Washington make it to post-season play five out of six seasons from 1971 to 1976. In 1972, he became the first Redskins quarterback ever to start in a Super Bowl game, although they would lose a tight one, 14–7, to Shula's flawless Dolphins.

In addition to Kilmer, Allen soon filled his shopping cart with other vets, many from Los Angeles. He shocked everyone when he sent a whopping seven draft picks, including a first- and a third-round pick in 1971, along with Marlin McKeever, to the Rams in return for Pottios, fellow linebacker Jack Pardee, Diron Talbert, John Wilbur, and Jeff Jordan. It was almost as if Allen was trying to reconstruct his Rams team in the nation's capital—either that or hold a Rams reunion there.

Allen wound up gaining seven veterans on draft day, and he wasn't through. He later obtained another Ram in strong safety Richie Petitbon and Ron McDole, a defensive end from Buffalo. Allen would start the season with three-fourths of his starting defensive line being new to the team—Ron McDole, Vernon Biggs (from the Jets), and Diron Talbert.

Only Bill Brundige was a holdover from 1970. When Allen's Over-the-Hill Gang won nine games in 1971, that total represented their highest amount in almost exactly three decades, 29 seasons in all.

There was some frustration, however. Allen's first three visits to post-season play resulted in an 0–3 record, as did his final three playoff games; however, in 1972, he was not to be denied. His Redskins won the NFC championship at 11–3, relying on a 33-year-old Kilmer and a 38-year-old quarterback in Sonny Jurgensen, who went 4–0 as a starter that season.

Despite his overall winning ways, Allen was dismissed by Redskins president Edward Bennett Williams after Allen rejected a contract that called for him to be paid $1 million for four seasons' work, which would have begun with the 1978 season. Williams felt he had ample reason to reject Allen—he once famously said, "I gave George an unlimited budget, and he exceeded it."

Still, no one can deny Allen's success, and Dave Robinson pointed out one contributing factor for that: He was good at using psychology on his players. Robinson recalled,

> I remember one week we're playing, I think it was Denver, and we're in the locker room before the game. In his pregame talk he said, "You had a lousy week in practice. It didn't seem like you were there. I don't know what to do this week. You know what? I'm ready for this game. I wish that I could just go up to the 50-yard line and go one-on-one with the Denver coach. Winner take all." I think it was John Ralston that year. He said, "But they won't pay to see that. They want to see *you* play the Denver Broncos. You guys have got to go out there and play." We went out and won the game, handily, too.

Later, said Robinson, his teammates shook their heads and joked about their elderly coach, saying, "Can you imagine George going out there? John would have kicked George's butt." He continued his tale, adding, "We had Monday off. We came in Tuesday morning, and George gives a little talk on the game. Then he brings this little Asian guy in, the guy that ran a karate class in Washington, DC.

> George had been taking karate lessons and nobody knew it. George started breaking boards with his hand, and, I'm not sure, but maybe a cinder block, and he said, "I would have killed John," and the whole team gave him a big standing ovation.

Robinson feels Allen's strongest point was probably his relationship with his players. When Allen left the Rams, Jack Pardee said he liked and respected Allen so much that if a trade couldn't be worked out that would reunite the two, he would retire—he simply didn't want to play for anyone else.

As Robinson stated, "The guys loved him. He was just a great guy." Allen told his players that losing a game was "like dying a little bit.' He continued, "I can't wait for the next week to be reborn." During many a Tuesday team meeting after a defeat, he'd grumble, "I wish we could play today." Robinson said, "That's just how he was. I liked him; we should've won for him, but we didn't and I felt bad about that."

His sympathetic feeling for Allen, and his teammates' distaste for disappointing their coach, probably stemmed from the fact that Allen instilled a sense of pride and family in his players. He even felt owners shouldn't scrimp on salaries, that a well-rewarded player will toil harder for his team. What, he reasoned, was more important, saving several thousand dollars on paychecks or winning?

Allen certainly was unique. For instance, All-Pro Myron Pottios said Allen reminded his players when they were on the road that they were strictly on a business trip. Stated Pottios,

> We're going there for business. And he tied [up players' time] as much as he could. For instance, if we're on the West Coast, going back to the East Coast, you leave on a Friday, get there Friday night. He made sure you had dinner, most of the time together as a team, get up in the morning, and have breakfast together.
>
> Go to the field and work out, come back to the hotel on a bus around 3:00 to 5:00, in that range, and you had to be at a meeting at 7:00. You had maybe a three-hour [free time] period in there. The meetings would be over at about 9:00, and you had a bed check at 11. The next morning, you get up, have a pregame meal, and go to the stadium. Right from the stadium the busses took you to the airfield and you were on your way back.

There was virtually no sightseeing or visiting relatives for these players. Even when Pottios was playing in Pittsburgh as a visitor, he had no time to make the short trip to his hometown. His relatives had to come to his hotel to see him.

Pottios played under just two coaches in the NFL, Buddy Parker at Pittsburgh and George Allen in Washington and Los Angeles. He revealed,

> I loved Buddy and thought he did a good job. He was well versed, knew the game well. You're only as good as your players. We had a lot of good players, but not enough to get us up to the top. We were a little short. We played good football, but after a couple of guys got hurt, we dropped off.
>
> George was different. He was the kind of guy who wanted to win every game. He wanted to go about doing that by giving you every phase of the game—all the information you would need to win the game. Paying attention to detail was his strong point.

When it came to playing a crucial game Allen was even more intent on covering every contingency. Before his Redskins took on Shula's undefeated Dolphins in Super Bowl VII, Allen sent some coaches to the game's venue to take note of what the various angles of the sun and shadows would be like in Los Angeles Coliseum during the same hours the game would be staged.

However, his laborious ways could also be a drawback. His tight end, Jerry Smith, said that during the two-week hiatus between winning the NFC title and the Super Bowl, Allen had his players in a condition where they "were so sick of each other and sick of the whole situation, it wasn't fun." Smith added, "We dreaded what we were having to do. We were poorly prepared and way overprepared."[4] Smith suggested that the players were reflecting the wound-too-tight demeanor of Allen.

Hall of Famer Charley Taylor played for George Allen in Washington from 1971 to 1977. Asked about Allen, Taylor chuckled before saying, "George was one of a kind."

But, like Smith, Taylor did mention one aspect of Allen that didn't draw a laugh: "He just felt that the more work you put in, the better off you were going to be, but we found out against Miami that we wore ourselves out before the game; I think so, and a lot of guys probably feel the same." That Super Bowl, contested at the end of the 1982 season, resulted in a Redskins loss, 14–7. Miami jumped on top, 14–0, by halftime, and Washington didn't manage to score until the final quarter—and that score came not from a fatigued offense, but on a special teams fumble return.

Nevertheless, Allen's diligence usually paid off, as did his coaching philosophy. Pottios said,

> He loved defense and put more emphasis on it. So he loved it when we'd go out there and have a so-called field day. Loved it when the guys would fly in there and get the quarterback. Then that became a part of our publicity, promoting the defense, pushing the defense.
>
> The pass rush wasn't the big thing until the middle 1960s, when Deacon Jones played for George Allen with the Rams. Prior to that, the only guy that was really physical and would destroy the quarterbacks was Doug Atkins.
>
> The publicity for the big pass rush began with the Fearsome Four-some when Allen came to Los Angeles in 1966. *Then* they emphasized the sacks. Before that, nobody talked about sacking the quarterback or kept records—that came later. What we linebackers, Maxie Baughan, Jack Pardee, and myself, did was let the front four rush, go destroy.

Taylor said Allen wasn't really a risk-taker, and while he was very involved with both the Redskins offense and defense, "He was more into defense, absolutely." Taylor continued, "He'd pick out one play a week that he knew [our opponent] would run. He knew they were going to run it. A play that he thought that they couldn't change, or wouldn't change. We just didn't know when. We knew they were going to run it, so the defense would be there."

Taylor said once against Green Bay, Allen unveiled a five-man line. "They hadn't seen it, and it worked out fine for us. He loved defense, and we had Rich Petitbon—those two guys together, man! They took our defense and made a great team out of guys like Pat Fisher, Kenny Houston, Mike Bass—we had some players. We were tough."

The stress on "D" was perhaps never more evident than in 1963, when Allen was serving as the Bears defensive coordinator. While Allen's first NFL assistant coaching job had lasted just one year, in 1957, with the Rams, the next year he became an assistant under Halas in Chicago, doing a fantastic job.

He felt the team would benefit from a zone defense and proved it when the Bears won the '63 championship, halting the Packers' bid for their third-straight championship. In fact, the Bears handed Green Bay their only defeats of the season. In doing so, Chicago won their division over Lombardi by a thin margin of one game in the loss column, at

11–1–2, versus Green Bay's 11–2–1. In those two victories, Allen's defense held Lombardi's offense to 10 total points, a field goal in one game and a lone touchdown in another, limited to what was easily their lowest outputs on the year.

Allen made the Bears defense unpredictable. His linebackers, Larry Morris, Joe Fortunato, and Bill George in the middle, mixed things up, sometimes coming with a blitz, sometimes staying home to defend the run, while also being competent enough to occasionally drop back and cover receivers.

The secondary was impenetrable, led by Rosey Taylor and Petitbon, with nine and eight interceptions, respectively. Toss in six interceptions apiece from Dave Whitsell and Bennie McRae, and teams were loath to pass on Allen's number-one-rated defense. The Bears gave up 144 points, representing the lowest total since the 1950 season, which ran just 12 games. No question, the defense carried the bulk of the load, as the Bears offense came in 10th out of 14 teams.

Pottios, referring to Allen's years spent after he was with the Bears, continued,

> Allen would blitz, not a lot, but under certain situations. We would do our film breakdown, and our defense was surprising [in that] I would say that 85 percent of our defenses were called at the line of scrimmage because we had good defensive quarterbacks—like Pardee, who called our defense, the signals.
>
> We'd go out there and call our defense after we'd studied the film, where offenses would come out in certain formations, on a certain down, on a certain part of the field, and you'd be surprised how many times they'd run the same play that they had in the past. So, in the game, we'd see the formation and we'd know the down and distance, and he'd put us in a defense that was the strongest for that particular play. If we thought the blitz was necessary, he'd run the all-out blitz, or whatever.

Allen also emphasized football intelligence. Pardee, for instance, was so wise, so defensively minded, he would go on to become the head coach of the Bears, Redskins, and Oilers for a total of 11 years. In five of those seasons, his team went at least four games over .500. They won 10 to 12 games on four occasions, and Allen secured two division championships as well.

Pottios continued, "What was amazing about George is how he wanted his players to understand everything that was going on. His philosophy was—he always used this: 'No detail is too small.' Whatever you knew about the other team was to your advantage."

Pottios remembered a playoff game in the late 1960s, which his team had to play in frigid Minnesota. Allen took the squad there a week early to get acclimated to the weather. Recalled the former linebacker,

> We went there on a Monday and figured we were going to practice the whole week there. Well, we went to practice on Tuesday and Wednesday, and we couldn't practice because the snow was [coming down so hard], we couldn't keep the field clean. And in a clear area, the wind was blowing. It was just a bad break. It was a good idea, but the weather didn't cooperate.
>
> Like I said before, when he talked to you, he'd always would use this phrase: "No detail is too small," so anything, whether it was picking up paper on the sideline to not having a distraction to the key plays, it was all important to George because he felt they were going to enhance your chances of winning the game. He didn't want anything to distract from your thinking about nothing but the game always.

Fred Cox also pointed out,

> People don't understand that coaches get paid for winning football games. He knew one thing—that coaches got paid for winning. Their success was winning, and George didn't want anything to get in his way, to stop him from winning football games. George understood that, and he wanted to make sure that his players were going to do everything that he needed them to do to win the ball game.
>
> He kept emphasizing no detail being too small, so a lot of guys studied film. They'd take it home and have breakdowns. Prior to George, there was very little film breakdown as to what we were going to do defensively or what the other team was going to give us and how we were going to play it.
>
> And I think it's a great approach. That's what you're there for. To go out there, do all you can, do your best. And we all get satisfied, get our accolades, our notoriety, to do what we're there for. Another phrase he always used was, "There's more to this game than just collecting a paycheck."

Allen also placed high value on his special teams, realizing a blocked kick or a long kick return could turn games around. One of his better players on such squads was Bill Malinchak. Once, during a two-week span, he blocked a punt versus Minnesota, retrieved it, and rambled in for a score, then blocked a New England Patriots punt, which resulted in a safety. Unlike most players, Malinchak split his hands when they neared kickers' feet, blocking the ball before it began its ascent. Malinchak called Allen a "great communicator and a great teacher," and one who knew and appreciated the importance of special teams. A blocked field goal or punt can, in fact, be the difference between victory and defeat.

Pottios, who later coached at the professional level with the Philadelphia Bell of the World Football League, said playing under Allen gave him a taste of what coaching was all about. He stated,

> You got a kind of feeling for it because you got involved in a lot of meetings and breakdowns. So the transition was easy, but to get with the guys and be able to communicate what you wanted, and to get them to do it, became, not a problem, but it was the hardest part of the deal. You'd show them and at game time they'd do something different.

Dave Robinson, who played linebacker for both Vince Lombardi and Allen, observed,

> They both would say something a thousand times, so, come Sunday, it was just automatic—your reaction—you didn't have to think about it.
>
> The difference between them was Vince would tell you something a thousand times in a thousand different ways. He'd build it up over and over until it sunk in. George would tell you the same thing a thousand times and that was week in and week out. And the difference was when you got through the 16-game schedule and went to the playoffs, George's message tended to be stale, it didn't seem to be as fresh as Vince's. His was new and fresh, and could fire you up. Consequently, you didn't get as fired up with Allen in the playoffs as we got with Lombardi.

Robinson's praise for Allen was probably tempered only by the fact that he had been coached by a master in Lombardi. Robinson remembered,

I had a very, very good high school coach who taught us all the fundamentals, but I knew that when I went to college at Penn State that the coaching would be better. And, sure enough, I played under Rip Engle, and our assistant coach was Joe Paterno, and, lo and behold, I was right, the coaching was much better.

Then I said, "When I go to pro ball, the coaching has got to get better." And what do you know, I went to Green Bay, and the coaching was superb, much better in every sense of the word. I stayed there for 10 years and I thought, "This is how pro football is."

I left there and went to the Washington Redskins, and played for a very fine coach, George Allen. All of a sudden I realized I had been to the summit, I had been to the top of the heap. Allen, as fine as he was, was not Vince Lombardi. He was above and beyond the finest coach I was ever affiliated with. That was just it. I don't mean to disparage George Allen, I loved him. He was a defensive coach; Lombardi was an offensive coach. But Allen was just no Vince Lombardi. That's the only way I can put it.

Perhaps not, but Charley Taylor observed, "He was a player's coach in a way, and in a way he was a little strict. As long as you were working [hard you were fine with George], but if you didn't work out extra, you'd wish you [had]. He expected a lot out of us. He did."

For a dedicated player like Taylor, he said it was very easy to play for Allen "because George wanted to win." Taylor continued, "We both wanted the same thing in that way." He also said players who made special plays were rewarded, another example of Allen's motivational methods.

Mike Ditka, who goes way back with Allen, was even more positive in his view of the coach. He recalled,

George signed me to my first pro contract. He was the defensive coordinator for the Bears, and he was also kind of an assistant general manager, so he signed me. George Allen was a helluva coach. The job he did with the Rams was outstanding. He had great defenses.

He was the architect of the '63 Bears defense, which was every bit as good as the '85 Bears defense.

That says a lot, as Ditka was head coach of the 1985 Bears, and his defensive unit helped him win the Super Bowl. That defense was loaded with talent, including a handful of men who are now honored in the Hall of Fame.

Deacon Jones had a great talent for throwing quarterbacks for a loss. He is said to have coined the term *sack*. Jones heaped more praise on Allen, calling him the best coach he ever played for, saying Allen was smart and dedicated, stressing conditioning and discipline, and watching more film than movie critic Roger Ebert and then coming up with some tactic to defeat his foes.

On a negative note, Allen torched enough relationships with his teams' owners, men whose authority he often challenged, that after he left the Redskins he never again coached in the NFL, even though he had never languished through a single losing season. He did have stints with Chicago and Phoenix in the United States Football League (USFL) for two years (1983 and 1984), and a one-year college gig at Long Beach State at the age of 72. Allen and Marv Levy are the only NFL Hall of Fame coaches to have head coached in the USFL.

Actually, Carroll Rosenbloom did hire Allen to return to the NFL in Los Angeles to coach his Rams in 1978, which would have completed an uninterrupted cycle of coaching in Los Angeles, Washington, and back to LA; however, a rare thing took place. Rosenbloom fired him after just two *preseason games* because Allen couldn't work within the framework of the team, which, after all, belonged to Rosenbloom, not Allen.

A final note: The workaholic Allen, who frequently put in 16-hour days and sometimes slept at the Redskins complex instead of going home, loved football, and he adored winning, doing so at a phenomenal rate. Pro Football Reference lists Allen's lifetime winning percentage in his 12 seasons as an NFL head coach at .712.[5] Few people realize this, but that's better than Landry, Brown, Shula, Halas, and, in fact, all of the other coaches featured in this book, save Lombardi (.738).

13

BUD GRANT

"He Understood Every Player"

Place of birth: Superior, Wisconsin
Date of birth: May 20, 1927
Date of death: n/a
Lifetime wins, losses, and ties: 158–96–5
Career winning percentage: .621
Playoff wins and losses: 10–12
Playoff winning percentage: .455
NFL major titles won and years of championships: NFL/NFC champs 1969, 1973, 1974, 1976
Teams coached and years: Minnesota Vikings 1967–1983, 1985

Harry "Bud" Grant wasn't just a coach with an image as icy as Minnesota itself. This man was a fine player many years before he became an NFL coach. In his two seasons as a versatile player in the NFL (1951 and 1952), Grant led his Philadelphia Eagles in sacks as a rookie, then switched over to offense and led the team in receptions and receiving yardage. In fact, his 56 receptions placed him second in the entire NFL, as did his 997 yards on catches. His longest reception went for 84 yards, second best in the league that season.

As a trivia sidenote, he is even considered to be the first man in NFL history to play out his option—doing that when he defected from Philadelphia and moved north to join the Winnipeg Blue Bombers for a heftier ($11,000 to $8,000) contract.

Starting in 1953, Grant played four seasons with Winnipeg of the Canadian Football League (CFL), where he set records as a receiver and defensive halfback. Impressed with his know-how, the team hired him to coach the Blue Bombers, which he did for 10 seasons, from 1957 to 1966. Along the way, his teams took part in six Grey Cup games (Canada's equivalent of our Super Bowl) and won four, in a five-year period. The team honored Grant, erecting a statue of him outside their new stadium in 2014.

In 1967, Grant became head coach of the Minnesota Vikings, replacing their first-ever coach, Norm Van Brocklin, a legendary quarterback who had run the team since its inaugural season, 1961. Expansion teams are not expected to bolt out of the chute and win in the NFL, and for the Vikings' first three seasons, they didn't—more accurately, they stumbled and crumpled in a heap. Their record stood at a lowly 10–30–2. In their next three seasons, they went 19–21–2, not good enough. Van Brocklin and the Vikings parted ways.

Grant was then hired by general manager Jim Finks, who, like Grant, had spent time in the CFL. Football was in Grant's blood, as his father played for the Duluth Eskimos back when helmets were made of leather.

Assuming the job as the Vikings coach, Grant quickly took stock of his personnel and opted to stress defense, realizing he already had a good group of linemen on his hands in Carl Eller, Jim Marshall, Paul Dickson (who would be replaced by Gary Larsen in 1968), and a highly touted rookie in Alan Page. Grant knew he could build a dynamic defense around those linemen, which included two, Page and Eller, who would become Hall of Famers.

Grant didn't work his magic in his first season, as the Vikings went 3–8–3, but he took the team to the playoffs, at 8–6, the very next year, a franchise first. He was off and running, a formidable force on his way to the Hall of Fame.

Dave Robinson of the Packers had a great deal of respect for the Vikings of Grant. His memories of them go way back.

> My first year was 1963, and when they introduced us in Metropolitan Stadium, the baseball field, the Green Bay Packers got a bigger round of applause than the Minnesota Vikings did. It had been Green Bay territory—there was no other team up that way. Green Bay had all the

television [coverage] until they cut that section up when the Vikings came into the league and they gave that territory to Minnesota.

But you can't just change fans, draw a line and, "Now you're Minnesota fans." But, slowly, over the years, they're all Minnesota fans, and we're the enemy, the archenemy when we go up there.

Grant and his successful ways became responsible for the fans shifting their allegiance to the Vikings, no small task given Green Bay's tradition and winning ways.

Charley Taylor said, "He was a great leader, and players loved to play for him because he put good players around good players. They were happy about that."

Years later, other coaches would pay Grant a compliment by using the system he had come up with for Minnesota. Tony Benjamin, an NFL running back from 1977 to 1979, said his Seattle Seahawks head coach, Jack Patera, had been the "defensive line coach for the Purple People Eaters." Added Benjamin,

So he was a protege of Bud Grant, and a lot of what we did with the Seahawks was a replica of what was being done at Minnesota at that time. Even guys at the end of their career, like Carl Eller, came to the Seahawks for one year, and he had been coached by Patera at Minnesota. So, from a defensive standpoint, Patera brought over the system from the Vikings and Bud Grant.

The results were pretty clear. You don't win football games without defense. So the early success that we had with the Seahawks during my tenure there can be attributed to the effectiveness of Grant's system. It was a 4–3 system. At that time Grant and the Vikings may have been a little ahead of their times in terms of the level of athleticism that they wanted on the defensive line. Not big guys, but guys who were good athletes.

If you look at those guys, from Eller and Marshall and Page, they were athletes. They weren't 320-pound guys. These were guys that were quick off the ball. But, because they weren't going to necessarily take up a lot of space in terms of kicking offensive linemen off of the linebackers, you also had to have athletic linebackers. There has to be logic in the type of athletes that you're blending, so, again, if you're going to have athleticism on your defensive line, you also need linebackers who could move and not allow the offensive linemen to lock up on them.

So Grant had a very athletic defensive scheme—the *entire* defense.
They focused on good athletes.

And that included, of course, a corps of talented defensive backs. The top
coverage man was safety Paul Krause, yet another Hall of Famer. Having
Karl Kassulke and Bobby Bryant, who both made it to the Pro Bowl,
helped as well.

Grant, like Tom Landry, had a reputation for being stoical, stone-
faced. During a *Monday Night Football* contest, broadcaster and former
Dallas quarterback Don Meredith said over the airwaves, "In a personality contest between Tom Landry and Bud Grant, there would be no winner." Funny perhaps, but not fair.

While Grant, with his piercing blue eyes, may have come across as
rather stern, cold, and unemotional, there was a thoughtful, caring side of
him that only insiders may have seen. Grant's finest quarterback, Fran
Tarkenton, said his coach was not at all what people thought he was.

Minnesota kicker Fred Cox supplied a comparison between Grant and
another great coach, and this comparison dealt with compassion.

> He was very much like Paul Brown—you have to remember that Grant
> played for Brown when Grant was in the military. He coached a lot
> like Paul Brown. They had this interesting little quirk about them.
> They just absolutely despised when they would have to cut somebody.
> Brown wouldn't even cut anybody [in person]. He'd put letters in a
> mailbox. Bud would tell them, but he admitted that it was the one thing
> he disliked the most about football.

Grant was so sensitive about his players' feelings, he saw himself as
being the antithesis of Lombardi and said he never got along with him
because he was a dictator who relied on fear as a tool. Grant's first NFL
win came against the Packers, and after the game, when he extended his
hand to Lombardi, he refused to shake hands. Grant said that was it, and
he never again spoke with him.

Unlike some coaches, for instance, George Allen, Grant was not ob-
sessed with football, having many other interests. He even viewed football as entertainment rather than the center of the world, and he once said
that, because of that, when his coaching days ended, it would not be the
end of the world for him.

Jackie Smith was inducted into the Hall of Fame along with Grant. According to Smith,

> That's really where I got to know him the best. He always impressed me as a Coach Landry-type coach. He did a lot with not much effort, and everybody respected him the same way they did with Coach Landry. One of the highlights of my getting into the Hall of Fame was being able to sit down and visit with Grant—he's really a wonderful man and an entertaining guy.

Mike Ditka played and coached in the same division as Grant and called him a "great coach," further stating, "He was kind of stoic, but he had a great personality when I met him at a coaches' convention. He was a good guy. I liked Bud. I got along with Bud very well, and we had good competition against Minnesota—it was all good stuff." Under such coaches as Grant, Lombardi, and later Ditka, the "good stuff" spawned a division packed with hard-hitting, take-no-prisoners defenses.

A serious man on the field, Grant wanted his players to be serious about the game, too. Fred Cox was so skilled that when he retired, only George Blanda and Lou "The Toe" Groza had scored more career points. Cox said, "When you played for Bud Grant, you didn't talk to anybody before the game, and you didn't talk to anybody on the field after the game. If you wanted to talk to them, you took a shower and went out to their bus and talked. That's the way it was with Bud Grant."

Cox spoke about Grant's philosophy of having his Vikings not make hard, full contact during practice sessions, saying he was one of the first coaches to "figure out that when you went all out against your own team, all you were doing was hurting your own people. We never, ever had more than half-line scrimmages."

That meant only "either the right side or the left side of the line was 'live,' and could tackle somebody," said Cox, who kicked and played halfback for Pitt. He continued,

> Everybody else just grabbed their person and held them in place. That's what he always did, and we did that very seldom. We did not hit very much. Bud had the same theory that I do—guys that will hit, will hit, and you're not going to teach them how to hit. What you want to do is teach them what they're supposed to be doing, who to hit.

Oh, there were a lot of pro teams that went full contact all week. And, of course, when I was in college we did that all the time. I never could quite understand it. That's why I had a reputation of being such a terrible practice player. I never understood beating on my friends. It doesn't make sense.

Grant had a reason for everything he did as a coach. The media made a big deal of Grant's refusing his players to have heating devices near the Vikings bench during games, no matter how harsh the Minnesota weather turned. Some critics felt he was hindering his team by doing that. A few said his ban on heat fit in with his cold, tough ways. Cox refuted such thoughts, reflecting,

It didn't bother us, but it was funny because as rigid as Bud was, he was not an ogre by any means. You could talk to him; and if you asked him why we're doing this, he would tell you why we're doing it.

For instance, why we didn't have heat—guys would ask about heaters, and "How come we can't have gloves?" He said, "Well, it's real simple. If we put heaters out here, everybody would be running over there trying to get warm. The problem with that is it's so cold up here, there's no way for you to get warm. But you would lose your focus on the game because you'd be so worried about trying to get warm. What we want you to do is remember one thing: I know you're cold, you know you're cold, and I know you can play cold and you know it. That's all that matters." And he was right about that.

No hypocrite, Grant didn't, for example, have a personal heater on the sidelines. In fact, for one playoff game when the thermometer itself shivered at six below, Grant showed up wearing a short sleeve shirt.

Another player from the Vikings' Black and Blue Division (so named for the bruise-inducing, rugged defensive play of the teams that made up the NFC West Division) chimed in on the heater issue. Dave Robinson played most of his career with Green Bay, and his Packers teams went head-to-head with Grant's Vikings twice a year from 1967 to 1972. He observed,

All I remember about him is he didn't like me. We beat them in '72 to win the division in Minnesota—they had beaten us in Milwaukee earlier.

I was the defensive captain, so they interviewed me after the game and a reporter said to me, I'm paraphrasing, "Well, they beat you down there in Milwaukee. What was different about today's game?" And I said, "Well, we had heaters and they didn't." They put that in the paper, and Bud Grant read it. I don't think he's spoken to me since. That really upset him. He had a big thing going on about heaters on the sidelines. But he was a Hall of Fame coach, of course. Went to four Super Bowls. I know his teams were always prepared.

Robinson concluded, "People talk about the Ice Bowl, and the first thing they say is how cold it was. I tell them that's BS there. It's mental. The mental thing is a big thing." Grant apparently felt the same way.

Somehow Grant had the rare ability few coaches ever attain. Cox remembered,

He loved to hunt, and we used to go hunting with him a lot of times. And you could hunt with him and then come back and get dressed and go out on the field to practice, and he had the uncanny ability to, so to speak, be one of the guys when he was hunting, come back, walk out on the field, and when he put that whistle on, somehow, everybody knew that he was running the show. Nobody ever questioned him.

It's difficult to imagine that many of today's coaches would employ some of the actions of men like Grant because football today is more businesslike than it was long ago. Thus, coaches today might not be as understanding or forgiving as Grant comes across in the revelatory stories Cox relates.

"Bud's first year with the Vikings, I had a really good year until we played the last game against Detroit," began Cox, continuing,

We played indoors, and I missed three field goals out of four. After the game I was sitting in front of my locker, needless to say distraught about the whole thing, and this guy walks up and puts his hand on my shoulder. I look up and it's Bud Grant. All he ever said—he never said anything after that—was, "Bet you never had a game like that before." That's the kind of guy he was.

The other thing he never did was if he chastised somebody for what they did, he would never, ever bring it up again. Now if you kept doing it, you'd be gone in a second, but he would never bring it up again.

Naturally, there were some situations where coaches the likes of Grant might not be so patient. "One thing about Bud, you better not have to have him come looking for you, so whenever we got to midfield, I always stood beside him," said Cox. "If we needed to kick a field goal, I wanted to be there."

What would Grant do, however, if a player made an absurdly stupid play, for example, getting called for being offside in a key spot in a game—was he forgiving in those circumstances? Cox said,

> That happened very seldom with us. He would call it what it was, though. He would say in a meeting, "That's a really bonehead play."
>
> Now the only time I've seen him do anything else was when we were playing the Cleveland Browns in the last exhibition game of the year and it was the last play of the game. We were winning by, like, three points, and we had a defensive back named Dale Hackbart, a former quarterback at Wisconsin. They threw a pass to a big wide receiver named Gary Collins, who was around a long time, and Hackbart comes across the end zone and just nails Gary after the ball was gone.

Cox called the bush league late hit an "absolute stupid play." He further stated,

> He clotheslined him, but in those days you could do that.
>
> They threw a flag, the Browns got the ball on the one, and scored and beat us. And this is the kind of stuff that Bud would [criticize] once, but he would never bring it up again. When we were watching the film the next day, Bud stopped the film and said, "Dale, this is for you and everybody else in this room. If I ever see anybody ever make a dumb play like that again in that kind of a situation, you won't be here on Monday."
>
> Dale Hackbart played five years for us after that, and that play was never, ever brought up again.

Cox smiled then added, "Nobody ever did that again, either."

Another touchy situation came up in early 1966, when Vikings wide receiver Lance Rentzel got in trouble for driving to a playground and exposing himself to several young girls. In just his second season, Rentzel had yet to catch a pass in the NFL. He underwent psychiatric treatment, avoided jail time, and stayed with the team. But one question was,

How he would be accepted by his Vikings teammates? Would they react, on a smaller scale, of course, like hardened inmates who don't tolerate new prisoners who are, for instance, sexual predators?

Cox responded,

> When you had Bud Grant as a coach, you didn't have very many [awkward, difficult] situations happen. He would take care of everything. He was not a guy that let things fester long. He would take care of it; he would talk to people because he was so open. He was not afraid to step up and tell everybody what he thought.
>
> He might not mention the name or where the problem was coming from, but you knew there was a problem and it better go away. We never had problems.

Grant used Rentzel sparingly that season. He did play in nine games but caught just two passes for 10 yards. He was gone the following season, traded to Dallas. There he blossomed, snagging a career-high 58 passes for more than 900 yards for the first of three straight seasons in which he approached or hit the 1,000-yard mark; however, in 1970, his career began to hit the skids when he was arrested, charged for indecent exposure after he had "flashed" a 10-year-old girl. This time it was not Grant's headache.

Simply put, Grant knew his Psychology 101; he knew how to handle each of his players the best he could, and, said Cox, "Bud handled everybody different." Cox recalled another example, mentioning one of Minnesota's bruising fullbacks, Bill Brown, reflecting,

> He was a real character, a great football player, but Bud Grant would yell at Bill all the way across the field, call him a rock head, and Bill Brown just reveled in it—he loved it. He loved the notoriety of Bud doing that. How did Bud know that? I have no idea—he understood every player.

Grant often showed great faith in his players, and it paid off. Cox recalled one such instance as follows:

> Someone may have broken it, but up until a couple of years ago every time I'd watch football and somebody was playing Green Bay after the first of November, and the announcer would always stick in there the fact that I kicked the longest field goal at Lambeau Field. I kicked a

52-yard field goal sometime in the middle of November, which almost any time in Minnesota or Green Bay when you did that, it was a major feat because it was like kicking an ice chunk. I have no idea what possessed Bud Grant to tell me to kick [under such conditions].

Well, the reason Grant sent him out there that day to drill the long field goal was that Grant knew his personnel. He was aware of what Cox himself once said about his skill set and his mindset. Cox commented on how he always believed he was able to focus even more than normal during a big game. He stated, "My mentality is that to be a great kicker or a great quarterback, you're going to play much better against the great teams."

Another instance of Grant's ability to understand people and get the most out of them deals with Ahmad Rashad, who twice exceeded the 1,000-yard mark on receptions for Minnesota after spending his first three NFL seasons with St. Louis and Buffalo. Cox remembered,

> I really became good friends with Ahmad Rashad. He's a perfect example of what happened when people came to a Bud Grant-coached team. We got Ahmad for nothing. He was known as a troublemaker, but from the day he came to our team until he left, he was nothing but a team man. You just wonder how a guy gets a reputation like that.

Rashad felt as if he had finally found *the* place where he belonged, citing the atmosphere, the personnel, and the right man to coach—a man who found a way to win and who was totally honest.

Cox continued,

> For some reason, Bud had this innate ability to know what people needed. As a result, Bud never raised his voice to Ahmad Rashad *ever*. In fact, almost never talked to him in front of any other players. The man became, probably, at that time for a few years, the premier wide receiver in football. Yet, everybody said he was a troublemaker, and to this day I have no idea why they thought that, but on our team he was an absolute model citizen. To me, that's what great coaching is all about. It's not about Xs and Os.

Maybe not, but Grant was also a clever coach. Cox, a straight-on kicker, typical of most kickers of his day, says Grant was responsible for a strategic move that has since been imitated by many other coaches.

> I used to kick off soccer-style on occasion whenever [head coach] Bud
> Grant would want me to. When he was coaching football in Canada, he
> had a soccer kicker.
>
> During practice one day he said, "Is there any chance that you
> could kick the ball low, driving [the ball] down into the corner?" The
> idea was to get the ball down on the ground so the other team couldn't
> make a long return. I told him, "No problem. I played soccer. If you
> want me to, when I kick off I will kick the ball like I'm kicking a
> soccer ball."
>
> We were the first one in the NFL to do that. After that a lot of
> teams started doing that. I would literally use a soccer-style kick and
> [boot] a line drive that probably never got over eight feet high. The
> idea was to kick it hard and get it to roll and bounce—hopefully it
> would take crazy bounces so people had a hard time picking it up.

It was a new idea and one that reaffirmed the old line about imitation and
flattery.

Unfortunately, Grant has one everlasting blemish on his coaching resume. If someone played the word association game and was asked to
respond to Grant's name, there's a good chance the reply would be something along the lines of, "Lost four Super Bowls."

Buffalo quarterback Jim Kelly took his Bills to four consecutive Super
Bowls, and each time he left the field he was under a cloud of gloom, on
the losing end. "I know the losses in the Super Bowl killed him," said
Kelly's high school coach, Terry Henry, "but on the outside you wouldn't
know it."

By and large, the same was probably true with Grant. Authors Don
Weiss and Chuck Day point out that Grant "let things bother him that
really shouldn't have. He just never seemed to accept all that went on at
the Super Bowl."[1] Grant could be uptight, which, to be fair, is under-
standable given his circumstances.

Although it's true that a Super Bowl crown remained elusive throughout his otherwise illustrious career, consider what others thought of him.
In December 2012, a street near the Vikings home facility was named
Bud Grant Way in his honor. Incidentally, despite temperatures that
didn't break into double digits, Grant appeared at the event gloveless, true
to form.

Dallas Cowboys great Mel Renfro commented, "He was stoic, kind of
like Landry, but a good coach. He wasn't the rah-rah coach. He was to the

point, a businesslike coach. He coached his team well. They had great players. We had some problems with the Vikings—I know of one time they kicked us out of the championship game."

Floyd Little felt that Grant was a "quiet coach," adding,

> You didn't hear too much about him. He wasn't a hollerer or a screamer. He was just a consistent coach that got to the Super Bowl many times. Bud was a players' coach. His players loved him. I never had a chance to play for him, but only to watch him and what he did as a coach, and he brought a lot of confidence and respectability to the Minnesota Vikings. Unfortunately, they never won the Super Bowl. Still, if you can get there, *that's* a big accomplishment.

Again, that's what everyone remembers: Grant went 0–4 in the Super Bowl. Calling a coach like Grant a loser or claiming, "He can't win the big one," is sheer folly. Just getting there, as Little touched on, is a daunting, monumental task, deserving commendation, not criticism, after a defeat.

Cox also addressed the subject many Vikings and their fans find odious, commenting, "The only thing that stands out in my career is we lost four Super Bowl games." When reminded that just getting there four times was a great feat, he replied,

> Well, I agree with that, I understand that, and it doesn't bother me. To be honest with you, it doesn't bother me as it always bothers the Minnesota fans. But when you're playing, you know that you gave it everything you had, and if you lost, you lost. There is nothing much you can do about it. You only have to live with yourself, and I know that we worked hard and we gave it our best shot.

Whatever Grant endeavored, he also gave it his best shot. Coming out of college, where he won nine letters, he was so highly rated, the Eagles made him the 12th overall pick in the 1950 draft; however, having starred for the Minnesota Golden Gophers in both football and basketball, he opted to play for the Minneapolis Lakers in the NBA, making him the only man to play in the NFL and NBA. There, during his rookie season (1949–1950), he won his first professional world championship, and he won another the following season—with a little help from a guy named George Mikan. As mentioned, in Canada he was responsible for carving out a dynasty with his four championships in five seasons.

If all of that doesn't suffice to prove Grant was a winner, consider the following: Under Grant, Minnesota once had a stranglehold on the NFC title—he prowled the Vikings sidelines for 18 seasons and took his team to the playoffs 12 times, including a half-dozen times in a row. His Vikings were also the first modern expansion team to make it to the Super Bowl.

They not only made it to the Super Bowl, but also did it four times in a short and spectacular eight-year span. In 1969, in just his third year at the helm, Grant won the NFL title—the Vikings record was a lofty 14–2 after their 27–7 win against Cleveland to capture that championship.

Take away an aberration of a season (7–7 in 1972) during his great eight-year run, and Grant's win–loss record proudly stood at 80–17–1. Fran Tarkenton once spoke of how consistent Minnesota was under Grant, observing that in his last seven seasons playing for the steely-eyed Grant the team won six division crowns and went on to play in three Super Bowls. Extending that, Grant won 10 Central Division titles in 11 years—*and* he began that streak in just his second season on the job.

Upon his retirement, only seven men owned more career wins (counting postseason play) than Grant's 168: George Halas, Don Shula, Tom Landry, Curly Lambeau, Chuck Noll, Chuck Knox, and Paul Brown—elite company. Grant is also the only coach to be inducted into both the NFL and CFL's Hall of Fame. As a matter of fact, his combined win total is higher than any football coach except Shula and Halas.

In short, Bud Grant was an incredible man, and, once more, it is ridiculous to measure him based exclusively on what his teams did in four contests. A champion in many ways, this great coach was born in a Wisconsin town fittingly named Superior.

NOTES

THE GREATEST GAMES OF THE GLORY YEARS

    1. Jack Cavanaugh, *Giants among Men* (New York: Random House, 2008), 21.

2. THE ICE BOWL

    1. Jerry Kramer and Dick Schaap, *Instant Replay* (New York: Doubleday, 1968), 71.

    2. Kramer and Schaap, *Instant Replay*, 248.

    3. Tom Landry, with Gregg Lewis, *Tom Landry: An Autobiography* (New York: Harper Paperbacks, 1990), 167.

    4. Richard Whittingham, *Sunday's Heroes* (Chicago: Triumph, 2003), 45.

    5. Ed Gruver, *The Ice Bowl* (Ithaca, NY: McBooks Press, 1998), 222.

    6. Gruver, *The Ice Bowl*, 217.

    7. William Povletich, *Green Bay Packers: Trials, Triumphs, and Tradition* (Madison, WI: Wisconsin Historical Society Press, 2012), 155.

3. THE HEIDI GAME

    1. Hank Hersch, *Greatest Football Games of All Time* (New York: Time Home Entertainment, 1997), 117.

2. Bob Carroll, *When the Grass Was Real* (New York: Simon & Schuster, 1993), 232.

4. SUPER BOWL III

1. Bob Carroll, *When the Grass Was Real* (New York: Simon & Schuster, 1993), 252.

5. GEORGE HALAS

1. Dave Anderson, ed., *Red Smith Reader* (New York: Random House, 1982), 103.

2. *The Tim McCarver Show*, guest Mike Ditka. JMJ Films, Inc. Executive producer Jim Moskovitz. Original air date August 22, 2016.

3. Brad Herzog, *The Sports 100* (New York: Macmillan, 1996), 71.

8. VINCE LOMBARDI

1. Ed Gruver, *The Ice Bowl* (Ithaca, NY: McBooks Press, 1998), 75.

2. Gruver, *The Ice Bowl*, 77.

3. Jerry Kramer and Dick Schaap, *Instant Replay* (New York: Doubleday, 1968), 4.

4. Kramer and Schaap, *Instant Replay*, 97.

5. Alex Karras, with Herb Gluck, *Even Big Guys Cry* (New York: Signet, 1977), 139.

6. Karras, with Gluck, *Even Big Guys Cry*, 139.

7. Gruver, *The Ice Bowl*, 36.

8. Don Weiss, with Chuck Day, *The Making of the Super Bowl* (New York: McGraw-Hill, 2003), 211.

9. Lee Green, *Sportswit* (New York: Fawcett Crest Book, 1984), 114.

10. Gruver, *The Ice Bowl*, 13.

11. David Maraniss, *When Pride Still Mattered* (New York: Simon & Schuster, 1999), 274.

12. "The Buzz: Football Follies," *Virginia Pilot*, January 18, 2008, http://pilotonline.com/sports/the-buzz-football-follies/article_f79ad569-2828-5424-9c2b-d5d9c825fafe.html.

13. Kramer and Schaap, *Instant Replay*, 273.

9. TOM LANDRY

1. Ed Gruver, *The Ice Bowl* (Ithaca, NY: McBooks Press, 1998), 73.

2. Joe Nick Patoski, *The Dallas Cowboys* (New York: Little, Brown and Company, 2012), 120.

3. *The Tim McCarver Show*, guest Mike Ditka. JMJ Films, Inc. Executive producer Jim Moskovitz. Original air date August 22, 2016.

4. Patoski, *The Dallas Cowboys*, 144.

5. Lee Green, *Sportswit* (New York: Ballantine, 1984), 113.

6. *The Tim McCarver Show*, guests Nick Buoniconti and Tony Dorsett. JMJ Films, Inc. Executive producer Jim Moskovitz. Original air date January 21, 2017.

7. Robert Smith, *Illustrated History of Pro Football* (New York: Grosset & Dunlap, 1972), 280.

8. *The Tim McCarver Show*, guests Nick Buoniconti and Tony Dorsett.

9. *The Tim McCarver Show*, guests Nick Buoniconti and Tony Dorsett.

10. *The Tim McCarver Show*, guest Mike Ditka.

10. HANK STRAM

1. Randy Covitz, "Stram Takes His Winning Ways to Pro Football Hall of Fame," *Kansas City Star*, August 3, 2003.

2. Tex Maule, "Wham, Bam, Stram!" *Sports Illustrated*, January 19, 1970, https://www.si.com/vault/1970/01/19/542176/wham-bam-stram.

3. Don Weiss, with Chuck Day, *The Making of the Super Bowl* (New York: McGraw-Hill, 2003), 179.

4. Bob Carroll, *When the Grass Was Real* (New York: Simon & Schuster, 1993).

5. Covitz, "Stram Takes His Winning Ways."

11. DON SHULA

1. Tim Warsinskey, "Don Shula Comes Home and Reconnects with Cleveland: Pro Football Hall of Fame Fan Fest," *Plain Dealer*, May 3, 2014, http://www.cleveland.com/browns/index.ssf/2014/05/don_shula_comes_home_and_recon.html.

2. Don Weiss, with Chuck Day, *The Making of the Super Bowl* (New York: McGraw-Hill, 2003), 332.

3. Arthur J. Donovan Jr. and Bob Drury, *Fatso* (New York: William Morrow and Company, 1987).

12. GEORGE ALLEN

1. Robert Smith, *Illustrated History of Pro Football* (New York: Grosset & Dunlap, 1972), 280.

2. Bob Carroll, *When the Grass Was Real* (New York: Simon & Schuster, 1993).

3. Carroll, *When the Grass Was Real*, 263.

4. Don Weiss, with Chuck Day, *The Making of the Super Bowl* (New York: McGraw-Hill, 2003), 214.

5. "George Allen," *Pro Football Reference*, www.pro-football-reference.com/coaches/AlleGe0.htm.

13. BUD GRANT

1. Don Weiss, with Chuck Day, *The Making of the Super Bowl* (New York: McGraw-Hill, 2003), 212.

BIBLIOGRAPHY

BOOKS

Anderson, Dave, ed. *Red Smith Reader*. New York: Random House, 1982.

August, Bob. *Fun and Games*. Hinckley, OH: Moonlight Publishing, 2001.

Beilenson, Peter, ed. *The Sports Page*. White Plains, NY: Peter Pauper Press, 1989.

Berry, Raymond, with Wayne Stewart. *All the Moves I Had: A Football Life*. Guilford, CT: Lyons Press, 2016.

Buckley, James, Jr. *The NFL's Top 100*. Berkeley, CA: Thunder Bay Press, 2011.

Canfield, Jack, Mark Victor Hansen, Mark Donnelly, Chrissy Donnelly, and Jim Tunney. *Chicken Soup for the Sports Fan's Soul*. Deerfield Beach, FL: Health Communications, 2000.

Carroll, Bob. *When the Grass Was Real*. New York: Simon & Schuster, 1993.

Cavanaugh, Jack. *Giants among Men*. New York: Random House, 2008.

Creative Staff of National Football League Properties. *The First Fifty Years*. New York: Simon & Schuster, 1969.

Curtis, Mike, with Bill Gilbert. *Keep Off My Turf*. Philadelphia, PA: J. B. Lippincott, 1972.

Davis, Jeff. *Rozelle: Czar of the NFL*. New York: McGraw-Hill, 2008.

———. *Papa Bear: The Life and Legacy of George Halas*. New York: McGraw-Hill, 2005.

Donovan, Arthur J., Jr., and Bob Drury. *Fatso*. New York: William Morrow and Company, 1987.

Green, Lee. *Sportswit*. New York: Ballantine, 1984.

Gruver, Ed. *The Ice Bowl*. Ithaca, NY: McBooks Press, 1998.

Hersch, Hank. *Greatest Football Games of All Time*. New York: Time Home Entertainment, 1997.

Herzog, Brad. *The Sports 100*. New York: Macmillan, 1996.

Jenkins, Dan. *Saturday's America*. New York: Berkley Books, 1973.

Karras, Alex, with Herb Gluck. *Even Big Guys Cry*. New York: Signet, 1977.

Kramer, Jerry, and Dick Schaap. *Instant Replay*. New York: Doubleday, 1968.

Landry, Tom, with Gregg Lewis. *Tom Landry: An Autobiography*. New York: Harper Paperbacks, 1990.

MacCambridge, Michael, ed. *ESPN Sports Century*. New York: ESPN, 1999.

Maki, Allan. *Football's Greatest Stars*. Buffalo, NY: Firefly Books, 2008.

Maraniss, David. *When Pride Still Mattered*. New York: Simon & Schuster, 1999.

Olderman, Murray. *The Pro Quarterback*. Englewood Cliffs, NJ: Prentice-Hall, 1966.

———. *The Running Backs*. Englewood Cliffs, NJ: Prentice-Hall, 1969.

Patoski, Joe Nick. *The Dallas Cowboys*. New York: Little, Brown and Company, 2012.

Pearlman, Jeff. *Boys Will Be Boys*. New York: HarperCollins, 2008.

Pluto, Terry. *When All the World Was Browns Town*. New York: Simon & Schuster, 1997.

Povletich, William. *Green Bay Packers: Trials, Triumphs, and Tradition*. Madison: Wisconsin Historical Society Press, 2012.

Smith, Red. *The Red Smith Reader*. New York: Random House, 1982.

Smith, Robert. *Illustrated History of Pro Football*. New York: Grosset & Dunlap, 1972.

Smith, Ron. *Pro Football's Heroes of the Hall*. St. Louis, MO: Sporting News St. Louis, 2003.

Sports Illustrated Books. *Football's Greatest*. New York: Time Home Entertainment, 2012.

Stewart, Wayne. *America's Cradle of Quarterbacks*. Carlisle, PA: Tuxedo Press, 2014.

Weiss, Don, with Chuck Day. *The Making of the Super Bowl*. New York: McGraw-Hill, 2003.

Whittingham, Richard. *Sunday's Heroes*. Chicago: Triumph, 2003.

MAGAZINES/NEWSPAPERS

Covitz, Randy. "Stram Takes His Winning Ways to Pro Football Hall of Fame." *Kansas City Star* (August 3, 2003).

Herskowitz, Mickey. "Papa Bear." *Pro* 3, no. 5 (January 1984): 22–26.

Klobuchar, Jim. "The Man behind the Iceberg Myth." *Pro* 2, no. 2 (December 1982): 80–88.

Ribowsky, Mark. "Shula Pride." *Sport* 67, no. 6 (December 1978): 26–32.

TELEVISION SHOWS

Beyond the Game: Green Bay Packers: The Ice Bowl and More. Executive producer John Vorperian. Directed by Keith Baker. Original air date July 28, 2015.

A Football Life: Dick Butkus and Gale Sayers. NFL Network. Produced by NFL Films. Original air date November 28, 2014.

Paul Brown: Ohio's Head Coach. Executive producers Jason Pheister and Alison Momeyer. Original air date January 31, 2016.

The Tim McCarver Show, guests Nick Buoniconti and Tony Dorsett. JMJ Films, Inc. Executive producer Jim Moskovitz. Original air date January 21, 2017.

The Tim McCarver Show, guest Mike Ditka. JMJ Films, Inc. Executive producer Jim Moskovitz. Original air date August 22, 2016.

The Tim McCarver Show, guest Paul Hornung. JMJ Films, Inc. Executive producer Jim Moskovitz. Original air date December 24, 2016.

DVD

Go Tigers! A film by Kenneth A. Carlson. Producer Sidney Sherman. IFC Films, 2001–2002.

WEB ARTICLES

Anderson, Dave. "Sports of the Times: George Allen: Won Games, Lost Jobs." *New York Times*, January 4, 1991, http://www.nytimes.com/1991/01/04/sports/sports-of-the-times-george-allen-won-games-lost-jobs.html.

"The Buzz: Football Follies." *Virginia Pilot*, January 18, 2008, http://pilotonline.com/sports/the-buzz-football-follies/article_f79ad569-2828-5424-9c2b-d5d9c825fafe.html.

Covitz, Randy. "Remembering Hank Stram: Stram Takes His Winning Ways to Pro Football Hall of Fame." *Sun*, August 3, 2003, http://prod.static.chiefs.clubs.nfl.com/assets/images/imported/media/misc/hank_stram_hall_of_fame%20_nduction.pdf.

Farmer, Sam. "Wild Super Bowl Stories from Steve Sabol: Death and Robbery in New Orleans." *Los Angeles Times*, February 24, 2016, http://www.latimes.com/sports/nfl/la-sp-wild-super-bowl-stories-from-steve-sabol-20160203-story.html.

Gehman, Jim. "Pardee: Redskins Fans "A Breath of Fresh Air.'" *Redskins.com*, April 2, 2013, http://www.redskins.com/news-and-events/article-1/Pardee-Redskins-Fans-A-Breath-Of-Fresh-Air/e154ed60-3385-4eb2-8ec5-a3010f17041d.

"History: Bud Grant." *Scout.com*, http://www.scout.com/nfl/vikings/story/11606-history-bud-grant.

Klein, Christopher. "The Bizarre History of the NFL's First Title Game." *History.com*, January 29, 2015, http://www.history.com/news/the-bizarre-history-of-the-nfls-first-title-game.

Klemko, Robert. "If Winning or Losing Is Going to Define You, You're on a Rough Road." *SI.com*, January 31, 2016, https://www.si.com/mmqb/2016/01/31/nfl-mmqb-bud-grant-minnesota-vikings-super-bowl-losses-vince-lombardi-disklike.

Maule, Tex. "Wham, Bam, Stram!" *Sports Illustrated*, January 19, 1970, https://www.si.com/vault/1970/01/19/542176/wham-bam-stram.

Penner, Mike. "Allen: Best Coach Rams Ever Fired." *Los Angeles Times*, January 2, 1991, http://articles.latimes.com/1991-01-02/sports/sp-6982_1_george-allen.

Rand, Michael. "A Fitting Day for Bud Grant." *Star Tribune*, December 2, 2014, http://www.startribune.com/a-fitting-day-for-bud-grant-way/284413781/.

Rentzel, Lance. "When All the Laughter Died in Sorrow." *Wikinut*, https://reviews.wikinut.com/When-All-the-Laughter-Died-in-Sorrow-by-Lance-Rentzel:-A-Sports-Book-Review/2fgnfedo/.

Warsinskey, Tim. "Don Shula Comes Home and Reconnects with Cleveland: Pro Football Hall of Fame Fan Fest," *Plain Dealer*, May 3, 2014, http://www.cleveland.com/browns/index.ssf/2014/05/don_shula_comes_home_and_recon.html.

Young, Chris. "The 'Fearsome Foursome' of the Los Angeles Rams." *Bleacher Report*, July 25, 2010, http://bleacherreport.com/articles/424715-the-fearsome-foursome-of-the-los-angeles-rams.

WEBSITES

Pro Football Reference, http://www.pro-football-reference.com.

INDEX

Adderley, Herb, 29, 132, 139, 141, 148
All-American Football Conference
    (AAFC), 99, 102, 112, 156, 157, 216
Allen, George, 79, 90, 92, 217–232, 236;
    as Bears assistant coach, 219, 227–228;
    film, use of, 229, 232; fired from Rams,
    221; players, relationship with, 225; as
    Rams head coach, 219–220; as
    Redskins head coach, 221–222, 227;
    special teams, regard for, 230; spying
    on teams, 218; US Football League,
    coaching in, 232; veteran players,
    preference for, 222–224. *See also* Los
    Angeles Rams; Washington Redskins
All-Pro Team honors, 6, 24, 90, 151, 157,
    158, 205, 225
Alworth, Lance, 51, 189
Ameche, Alan "The Horse", 8–9, 15–16,
    113
American Professional Football
    Association, 81–82, 84
Anderson, Donny, 31, 37–39, 41, 45
Andrie, George, 25, 35
Arbanas, Fred, 182
Arnsparger, Bill, 208–209
Arrowhead Stadium, 190
Atkins, Doug, 90, 94, 227
Atlanta Falcons, 56, 162
Austin, Bill, 221

Baker, Ralph, 66

Baltimore Colts, 2, 111, 143, 161–163,
    193, 220; All-Time Team players, 6;
    fans, 5, 67; offensive unit, 7; two-
    minute drill, 11, 12–13. *See also*
    Greatest Game Ever Played; Eubank,
    Weeb; Shula, Don; Super Bowl III
Bass, Dick, 141
Baugh, Sammy, 87–88
Bears. *See* Chicago Bears
Belichick, Bill, 3, 136, 164, 216
Bell, Bobby, 181, 186, 189, 191
Belu, George, 42
Bengals. *See* Cincinnati Bengals
Bengston, Phil, 140, 150–151
Benjamin, Tony, 235
Berry, Raymond, 7–17, 19, 21, 216; on
    Brown, Paul, 103, 109; on the Colts, 6,
    113–114; on Ewbank, 109, 113–114,
    116–117, 122, 149, 197; on Landry,
    157–158, 159–160, 162, 163, 169–170,
    178; on Lombardi, 142, 149, 201; on
    Shula, 197, 215; on slant plays, 11–12;
    on sweep plays, 128; Unitas, plays
    with, 8, 11–13, 15–16, 19–20, 163, 197
Beverly, Randy, 65
Biggs, Vernon, 223
Biletnikoff, Fred, 54–55
Bills. *See* Buffalo Bills
Blanda, George, 55, 100, 237
Boozer, Emerson, 52, 66, 121
Bowman, Ken, 34–35, 41–42

Boyd, Bobby, 198, 199
Braase, Ordell, 61, 62, 72
Bratkowski, Zeke, 34
Brown, Aaron, 188
Brown, Bill, 241
Brown, Ed, 199–200
Brown, Jim, 100–101, 108, 109, 162, 198
Brown, Paul, 79, 112, 116, 160, 194, 216, 236, 245; as Bengals coach, 102–103; as Browns coach, 98–102; calling plays, 105–106; Coach of the Year honors, 110; contributions to modern football, 103–106; as high school and college coach, 98; playbook, 103, 106; players, relationship with, 106–108; transmissions to quarterback, 105; two-minute drill, use of, 103. *See also* Cleveland Browns
Brown, Roger, 220, 221
Brown, Tom, 45, 145
Browns. *See* Cleveland Browns
Brundige, Bill, 224
Bryant, Chuck, 75
Bryant, Paul "Bear", 60, 102
Buchanan, Buck, 186, 188, 191
Buffalo Bills, 57, 110, 213, 243
Buoniconti, Nick, 175; on Landry, 175; on Shula, 175, 204–205
Busch Memorial Stadium, 167
Butkus, Dick, 90, 94, 220

Caffey, Lee Roy, 139
Camp, Walter, 103
Canadian Football League, 234, 244, 245
Cannon, Billy, 54
CBS Superbowl III broadcast, 63
Chamberlin, Guy, 27, 79, 152
Chandler, Don, 201
Chicago Bears, 81–82, 83–94, 126, 127, 143–152, 187, 227–228. *See also* Halas, George
Chicago Cardinals, 82
Chicago Stadium, 85
Chiefs. *See* Kansas City Chiefs
Christy, Earl, 56
Cincinnati Bengals, 97, 102–103, 213
Clark, Earl "Dutch", 85
Cleveland Browns, 28, 61, 73, 97–102, 143, 162, 198; fans, 101–102; team

name, 108. *See also* Brown, Paul
Cleveland Municipal Stadium, 101
Cline, Dick, 55
Collier, Blanton, 8, 102, 109, 194, 210
Collins, Gary, 198
Colts. *See* Baltimore Colts
Columbus Panhandles, 84
Conerly, Charlie, 9
Conzelman, Jimmy, 79
Coryell, Don, 171
Cowboys. *See* Dallas Cowboys
Cox, Fred, 35, 130, 229, 236; on Grant, 237–238, 239–243, 244
Crusan, Doug, 188, 206–207, 210–211
Csonka, Larry, 206, 208–209, 210–211, 215, 216
Culp, Curley, 186, 189, 191
Cuozzo, Gary, 199
Curtis, Mike, 72, 77

Dallas Cowboys, 23, 102, 142, 155, 218; as new team, 157–158. *See also* Ice Bowl; Landry, Tom
Dallas Texans, 179, 181, 188. *See also* Kansas City Chiefs
D'Amato, Mike, 56
Davidson, Ben, 50–51, 55
Davis, Willie, 136, 141, 148
Dawson, Len, 53, 109, 122, 182–183, 184, 187–188, 189, 191; on Hank Stram, 187
Dayton Triangles, 84
Decatur Staleys, 81–84. *See also* Chicago Bears
Detroit Lions, 164, 195
Detroit Tigers, 164, 213–214
Dickson, Paul, 234
Ditka, Mike, 90, 92–93, 94, 177; on Allen, 231–232; on Brown, Paul, 106; on Grant, 237; on Halas, 82, 90, 92–93, 94–95; on Landry, 157, 167, 177–178; on Lombardi, 151; on Namath, 75; on Stram, 181
Dixon, Hewritt, 54
Dolphins. *See* Miami Dolphins
Donovan, Art, 9, 21, 119, 120, 122, 207; on Shula, 209–210
Doomsday Defense, 35, 172, 175
Dorsett, Toney, 168, 175–176
Dowler, Boyd, 32, 35–37

Duluth Eskimos, 84
Dungy, Tony, 79
Dunn, Perry Lee, 213
Dupre, L.G. "Long Gone", 15
Durfee, Jim, 90–91

Eagles. *See* Philadelphia Eagles
Eischeid, Mike, 56
Eller, Carl, 234, 235
Ewbank, Wilbur Charles (Weeb): as
    assistant Browns coach, 112, 116;
    calling plays, 117–118; college career,
    112; as Colts head coach, 62–63,
    112–114, 115–120; fired by the Colts,
    2, 123, 197; Greatest Game, role in, 1,
    5, 6–8, 9, 17–18, 22; Heidi game,
    coaching in, 3, 49–50, 57; as high
    school and college coach, 112; as Jets
    head coach, 58, 61, 113, 114–115, 116,
    119, 120–123; Namath, relationship
    with, 116, 119; playbook, 116; pregame
    talk, 7–8; responses to alleged spying,
    50; Super Bowl III, coaching in, 2,
    60–63, 67, 72, 74; Unitas, relationship
    with, 114, 116, 117. *See also* Baltimore
    Colts; Heidi game; New York Jets

Falcons. *See* Atlanta Falcons
Feathers, Beattie, 86
Fernandez, Manny, on Shula, 207–209
Finder, Chuck, 91
Finks, Jim, 234
Flaherty, Ray, 79
Flanigan, Jim, 25
Fortunato, Joe, 90, 228
Frankford Yellow Jackets, 83

Gabriel, Roman, 220
Garrett, Mike, 184
Garrison, Walt, 166, 173
George, Bill, 90, 94, 139, 228
Giants. *See* New York Giants
Gibbs, Joe, 79
Gifford, Frank, 6, 9–10
Gillingham, Gale, 44–45
Gillman, Sid, 79
Golden Era of the NFL, 1–4, 24
Goodman, Julian, 57

Graham, Otto, 99–100, 105–106, 135, 156;
    on Allen, 218–219
Grange, Red, 85, 94
Grant, Harry "Bud", 3, 35, 79, 185, 245;
    Canadian Football League, coaching in,
    234; college career, 244; dislike of
    Lombardi, 236; players, relationship
    with, 236–237, 239–242; pro basketball
    career, 244; pro football career,
    233–234, 244; Super Bowl losses,
    243–244; as Vikings head coach,
    234–236, 237–245. *See also* Minnesota
    Vikings
Greatest Game Ever Played (1958 NFL
    title game), 1, 5–22, 113; overtime play
    in, 13–19. *See also* Baltimore Colts;
    New York Giants
Green Bay Packers, 23–47, 88, 125–152,
    164, 199, 201–202, 220; fans, 32;
    sweep play, 117, 128. *See also* Ice
    Bowl; Lombardi, Vince; Super Bowl I;
    Super Bowl II
Green, Cornell, 161
Gregg, Forrest, 149, 151
Grier, Rosey, 7, 220, 221
Griese, Bob, 206, 215, 216
Groza, Lou, 162, 237

Hackbart, Dale, 240
Hadl, John, 53
Halas, George "Papa Bear", 79, 84, 94, 95,
    187, 204, 215, 216, 219–220, 245; as
    Bears coach, 83, 84, 85–94; Coach of
    the Year honors, 94; counter plays, 88;
    high school and college career, 82;
    NFL, creation of, 81–82, 83; nickname,
    84; pro baseball career, 82–83; pro
    football career, 82; relationship with
    other coaches, 91–92; role in NFL
    rulemaking, 86–87; Sneakers Game,
    85–86. *See also* Chicago Bears
Hall of Fame. *See* Pro Football Hall of
    Fame
Havrilak, Sam, 33–34, 62, 72, 76–77, 164,
    172; on Shula, 212–213
Hayes, Bob "Bullet Bob", 29–30, 36, 40
Hayes, Woody, 198, 199, 210
Heidi (television movie), 50, 55–57

Heidi game (1968 Giants-Raiders game), 3, 49–58; NBC broadcast of, 50, 55–57

Henderson, Thomas "Hollywood", 174, 175

Herzog, Brad, 95

Higgins, Steve, 77

Hill, Calvin, 173

Hill, Jerry, 62, 67, 70, 201

Hill, Tony, 175

Hill, Winston, 61

Hilton, Roy, 72

Hornung, Paul, 24, 27, 118, 127, 135, 151, 199

Houston Oilers, 51, 122, 188

Howell, Jim Lee, 1–2, 14, 126

Howley, Chuck, 37, 45

Hudson, Jim, 53, 56, 70

Huff, Sam, 6, 9, 14, 16, 162

Hunt, Lamar, 181, 190

Hyland, Bob, 147–148; on flex defense, 172–173; on Ice Bowl, 25–26, 29–31, 33–35, 42–43; on Lombardi, 137, 148, 150, 151; on race in the NFL, 132–133

Ice Bowl (1967 NFL title game), 3, 23–47, 147, 164, 239; referees in, 33, 39; use of gloves in, 29–30; quarterback sneak play in, 39–41, 137

Isenbarger, John, 133–134

Jeter, Bob, 29, 136

Jets. See New York Jets

Johnsos, Luke, 88, 92

Jones, David "Deacon", 220, 227

Jones, Jerry, 165–166

Jones, Ralph, 84, 87

Jordan, Henry, 28, 134, 148

Jordan, Jeff, 223

Jordan, Lee Roy, 45

Jurgensen, Sonny, 224

Kansas City Chiefs, 57, 59, 122, 146, 179. See also Stram, Hank

Kapp, Joe, 186

Karilivacz, Carl, 16

Kassulke, Karl, 185, 236

Kelly, Jim, 243

Kiick, Jim, 206, 208

Kilmer, Billy, 223, 224

Knox, Chuck, 245

Kramer, Jerry, 39–40, 41–43, 46, 128, 129–130, 133, 138–139, 142

Krause, Paul, 236

Kuharich, Joe, 119

Lambeau, Earl "Curly", 79, 83, 152, 215, 245

Lambeau Field, 23, 26, 32, 35, 46–47, 241

Lamonica, Daryle "The Mad Bomber", 49, 50, 53–55, 56

Landry, Tom, 3, 79, 102, 176, 216, 220, 237, 245; autobiography, 165; Coach of the Year honors, 178; computers, use of, 160; as Cowboys head coach, 24, 157–162, 164–165, 167–176, 178; defense, emphasis on, 157, 159, 162–163; fired from Cowboys, 165–166, 176; flex defense, 171–173; as Giants assistant coach, 1–2, 6, 16, 21, 157, 162–163; high school and college career, 155–156; Ice Bowl, coaching in, 29, 36–38, 40–41; playbook, 159–160, 174–175; players, relationship with, 166–168; pro football career, 156–157; shotgun formation, use of, 160, 161; as World War II pilot, 155–156. See also Dallas Cowboys; Ice Bowl

Lanier, Willie, 186, 189, 191

Larson, Gary, 234

Lassiter, Ike, 51

Layne, Bobby, 89, 156

LeBaron, Eddie, 169

Levy, Marv, 79, 232

Lilly, Bob, 39, 44–45, 166–167

Lipscomb, Gene "Big Daddy", 10

Little, Floyd, 55–56; on Allen, 222–223; on Brown, Paul, 108–109; on Ewbank, 114–115; on Grant, 244; on Halas, 95; on Landry, 176; on Shula, 214, 215–216; on Stram, 180, 191

Livingston, Cliff, 16

Lombardi, Marie, 133

Lombardi, Vince, 3, 21, 79, 204, 221, 236; Coach of the Year honors, 127; as college coach, 126, 128; as Giants assistant coach, 1–2, 6, 9, 100, 126; as high school coach, 125; Ice Bowl, coaching in, 26, 38–40, 43–44; as Packers head coach, 23, 28, 44, 126–152; playbook, 27, 39–40, 91–92, 142; players, relationship with, 126, 130–131, 134–137, 151–152; quotes, 131–132, 150; as Redskins head coach, 44, 145; response to alleged spying, 91–92, 138; sweep play, use of, 27, 44, 128; T formation, use of, 125–126. *See also* Greatest Game; Green Bay Packers; Ice Bowl

Long, Bob, 145

Los Angeles Coliseum, 226

Los Angeles Rams, 26, 128, 140–141, 200–201, 217, 219–221. *See also* Allen, George

Luckman, Sid, 87, 89, 94

Lujack, Johnny, 89

Lundy, Lamar, 112, 220

Lyles, Lenny, 62

Mack, Connie, 83

Mackey, John, 216

Madden, John, 3, 79, 152

Malinchak, Bill, 230

Malone, Charlie, 87

Marchetti, Gino, 6, 115, 197, 216; on Ewbank, 118–119; Greatest Game, playing in, 9, 10, 12–13, 18, 20–21, 113; on Namath, 60; on Shula, 199, 212; on Unitas, 16–17, 60

Marino, Dan, 215, 216

Marshall, George Preston, 86–87

Marshall, Jim, 234, 235

Mathis, Bill, 54, 121

Matte, Tom, 65, 69, 70–71, 73, 118, 196, 198–199, 201, 215; on Ewbank, 72, 118; quarterback sub for Colts, 199–200, 202–203; on Shula, 68, 118, 196–197, 200, 202, 212

Maynard, Don, 30, 51–52, 58, 64–65, 69, 74, 116; on Ewbank, 2, 62, 120–122; Greatest Game, playing in, 14, 21–22; Heidi game, playing in, 53, 54, 56; on Landry, 2, 21; on Lombardi, 2, 21, 126–142; on Stram, 189

Mays, Jerry, 189

McBride, Arthur, 108

McCafferty, Don, 196

McDole, Ron, 223

McGee, Max, 134, 144

McKeever, Marlin, 223

McRae, Bennie, 228

Mercein, Chuck, 37; Ice Bowl, playing in, 24–26, 28–33, 37–39, 43, 44–47; on Lombardi, 137

Meredith, Don, 30–31, 168, 169, 236

Miami Dolphins, 102, 189, 193, 194, 203–216; playoff games, 205; undefeated season, 194, 204, 215. *See also* Shula, Don

Miami Touchdown Club, 63, 207, 209

Miami University of Ohio, 112

Michaels, Lou, 65

Mikan, George, 244

Milwaukee Badgers, 84

Minnesota Vikings, 73, 165, 183, 220, 233, 234–236, 243, 245; fans, 244. *See also* Grant, Harry "Bud"

Mitchell, Tom, 65

Modell, Art, 101–102

Modzelewski, Dick, 7, 15–16

Moore, Lenny, 6–7, 11, 12, 14–17, 21, 113, 115, 163, 201, 216; on Ewbank, 115–116, 118

Morrall, Earl, 65–66, 69–72, 164

Morris, Johnny, 93

Morton, Craig, 169

Motley, Marion, 108

Muncie, Chuck, 188

Murchison, Clint, 41, 166

Murray, Jim, 43

Mutscheller, Jim, 15–17, 163

Myhra, Steve, 12–13, 17–18

Nagurski, Bronko, 85–86, 94

Namath, Joe, 49, 73, 121; Heidi game, play in, 50–51, 52–54; Ewbank, relationship with, 63, 116, 121; Super Bowl III, play in, 59–64, 67, 72, 73–75, 77

NBC broadcasts, 16, 50, 55–57

Neale, Alfred Earl "Greasy", 79

Nelson, Andy, 9, 14; on Lombardi, 151; on Unitas, 18–19

New England Patriots, 107, 205

New Orleans Saints, 179, 188, 190–191, 223

New York Daily Herald, 58

New York Giants, 2, 85–86, 88, 90, 144,
    149, 157; defense, 7, 162–163. *See also*
    Greatest Game Ever Played
New York Jets, 2, 3, 111, 184; name
    change, 50, 58; 1968 AFL title game,
    57–58, 59. *See also* Ewbank, Weeb;
    Heidi game; Super Bowl III
New York Times , 57
1958 NFL title game. *See* Greatest Game
    Ever Played
1967 NFL title game. *See* Ice Bowl
1968 Jets-Raiders game. *See* Heidi game
Nitschke, Ray, 42, 129, 141, 148, 150
Noll, Chuck, 3, 79, 104, 245

Oakland Raiders, 44; in Heidi game,
    49–57; 1968 AFL title game, 57–58,
    59; in Super Bowl II, 59, 147
Oakland-Alameda County Coliseum, 52
O'Brien, Jim, 164
O'Connell, Tommy, 100
Oilers. *See* Houston Oilers
Olsen, Merlin, 200, 220
Oorang Indians, 84
Orange Bowl, 70
Orr, Jimmy, 65, 67, 69–70
Osborn, Dave, 184, 186
Over-the-Hill Gang, 223–224
overtime play rules, 13–14, 83
Owen, Steve, 79, 85, 162

Packers. *See* Green Bay Packers
Page, Alan, 234, 235
Parcels, Bill, 79
Pardee, Jack, 223, 225, 227, 228
Parker, Buddy, 226
Parrish, Bernie, 101
Patera, Jack, 235
Patriots. *See* New England Patriots
Patton, Jimmy, 8, 12, 16
Paul Brown Stadium, 108
Pearson, Drew, 165, 175
Petitbon, Rich, 223, 227, 228
Philadelphia Eagles, 99, 130, 152, 233
Pitts, Elijah, 136
Pittsburgh Steelers, 114, 143, 165,
    174–175
playoff tie rules, 13–14
Plum, Milt, 100

Porter, Ron, 65
Portsmouth Spartans, 84–85
Pottios, Myron, 148–149, 223, 230; on
    Allen, 222, 225–227, 228–229
Pro Bowl, 8, 24, 108, 148, 161, 170, 175,
    236
Pro Football Hall of Fame, 3, 79, 84, 95,
    148, 193
Prothro, Tommy, 221
Pugh, Jethro, 39, 41–42, 160

Racine Legion, 83
Raiders. *See* Oakland Raiders
Ralston, John, 224
Rams. *See* Los Angeles Rams
Rashad, Ahmad, 242
Rauch, John, 3, 49–50
Redskins. *See* Washington Redskins
Reeves, Dan, 36, 174, 219, 221
Renfro, Mel, 108, 132, 136, 161; on Allen,
    217–218; on Grant, 243–244; on
    Landry, 158–159, 161, 167–169,
    174–175, 176–177; on Stram, 179; on
    Thomas, Duane, 174
Rentzel, Lance, 36, 240–241
Richardson, Willie, 65
Ridlehuber, Preston, 56
Ringo, Jim, 130
Robinson, Dave, 148–149, 238; on Allen,
    219, 224–225, 230–231; on Grant,
    238–239; on Halas, 91–92, 95; Ice
    Bowl, playing in, 38–39, 45, 239; on
    Lombardi, 91–92, 129, 130–131, 132,
    134–141, 143–147, 153, 230–231; on
    the Vikings, 234–235
Robustelli, Andy, 6
Rock Island Independents, 83–84
Rosenbloom, Carroll, 76, 197, 232
Rote, Kyle, 9
Ryan, Frank, 198

Sample, Johnny, 65
San Diego Chargers, 57
San Francisco 49ers, 164
Sauer, George, 51, 53, 61–62, 72–73, 74,
    121
Sayers, Gale, 90, 94
Schnelker, Bob, 9
Schramm, Tex, 218

Seattle Seahawks, 235
Shea Stadium, 57, 122
Shinnick, Don, 62
Shula, Dave, 213
Shula, Don, 79, 215–216, 245; blitz plays, use of, 61–62, 72; Brown, Paul, influence of, 194–195, 207; Coach of the Year honors, 198; college football career, 193–194; as Colts head coach, 61, 76, 195–203; as Dolphins head coach, 102, 202, 203–216; high school football career, 193; Lions, coordinator for, 195; playbook, 198; pro football career, 194, 197; players, relationship with, 207–210; Super Bowl III, coaching for, 2–3, 7, 61, 66–68, 203; Unitas, relationship with, 12, 195–197; US Football League offer, 205–206; wristband for quarterbacks, use of, 200, 202. See also Baltimore Colts; Miami Dolphins; Super Bowl III
Shula, Dorothy, 208
Shula, Mike, 213
65-Give play, 38, 44–45
Skoronski, Bob, 38
Smith, Bubba, 70, 72
Smith, Charlie, 54, 56
Smith, Jackie, 151–152, 161–162; on Allen, 218; on Grant, 237; on Landry, 170–171; on Stram, 180, 188
Smith, Jerry, 226
Smith, Red, 90–91
Snell, Matt, 52, 75, 122; in Super Bowl III, 60–61, 62, 65, 71, 72–73
Speedie, Mac, 156
St. Louis Cardinals, 140, 167
Stagg, Amos Alonzo, 87
Staley, A.E., 83
Stanfill, Bill, 208
Starr, Bart, 27–28, 149, 151, 184; Ice Bowl, playing in, 28, 31, 34–35, 36–41, 45–46, 142
Staubach, Roger, 161, 165, 169, 175
Steelers. See Pittsburgh Steelers
Stenerud, Jan, 122, 184, 191
Stram, Hank, 79, 182, 190, 192; as CBS announcer, 190, 191; as Chiefs head coach, 181–188; Coach of the Year honors, 191; defensive plays, 189; fired

by Chiefs, 190; high school and college career, 180, 181; on Lombardi, 142; microphone, use of, 186; Offense of the Seventies, 182–183; playbook, 180, 183; players, relationship with, 191; Power I formation, use of, 183; race equity, promoting, 181; as Saints head coach, 188, 190–191; Tight I formation, use of, 182, 186. See also Kansas City Chiefs
Super Bowl I, 126, 142
Super Bowl II, 44, 59, 147, 220
Super Bowl III, 59–77, 99, 122, 184, 198
Super Bowl IV, 183–186
Super Bowl V, 76
Super Bowl VI, 159, 175
Super Bowl VII, 226
Super Bowl X, 174–175
Super Bowl XII, 174
Super Bowl XV, 133
Super Bowl XXV, 213
Super Bowl LI, 14
Summerall, Pat, 8
Svare, Harland, 11–12, 16, 219

Talbert, Diron, 223
Tarkanian, Jerry, 219
Tarkenton, Fran, 139, 236, 245
Taseff, Carl, 9
Taylor, Charley, 151, 231; on Allen, 226–227, 231; on Grant, 235; on Landry, 176; on Lombardi, 151; on Shula, 195
Taylor, Jim, 24, 128, 150
Taylor, Otis, 183, 184, 191
Taylor, Rosey, 90, 228
T formation, 87, 125–126
31-Wedge play, 39–41
Thomas, Duane, 173–174
Thomas, Emmitt, 189, 191
Thorpe, Jim, 81, 83, 84
Thrower, Willie, 91
Thurston, Frederick "Fuzzy", 128, 133, 145
Tomlinson, LaDainian, 24
Townes, Willie, 37
Triplett, Mel, 9
Trump, Donald, 137, 205–206
Tunnell, Emlen, 8, 146

Turner, Cecil, 148
Turner, Jim, 53, 54–55, 66–67, 74, 122

Unitas, Joe, 19, 66, 89
Unitas, John, 113, 114, 143, 199, 215, 216;
    Berry, coordinating plays with, 8,
    11–13, 15–16, 19–20, 163; Ewbank,
    relationship with, 114, 121; Greatest
    Game, playing in, 6–8, 11–13, 15–20;
    on Namath, 59–60; Shula, relationship
    with, 67–68, 196–197; Super Bowl III,
    playing in, 65–69
Unitas, Leonard, 19
Unitas, Paige, 18–19
Unitas, Sandy, 59

Van Brocklin, Norm, 234
Villanueva, Danny, 35
Vince Lombardi Trophy, 153
Volk, Rick, 13, 211; on Ewbank, 62; on
    Morrall, 68; on Namath, 63–64, 68–69;
    on Shula, 211; Super Bowl III, playing
    in, 68–69, 71, 76

Walsh, Bill, 79

Walton, Joe, 21
Warfield, Paul, 109, 195, 198, 206, 216; on
    Brown, Paul, 97, 103–105, 106–107; on
    Shula, 194–195, 210
Washington Redskins, 44, 86–89, 125,
    178, 217; veteran players and, 222–224.
    See also Allen, George
Webster, Alex, 9
Wells, Warren, 53–54
Werblin, Sonny, 114
White, Danny, 162
Whitsell, Dave, 228
Wiggin, Paul, 107
Wilbur, John, 223
Williams, Edward Bennett, 224
Williams, Travis, 147–148
Willis, Bill, 108
Winnepeg Blue Bombers, 234
Wood, Willie, 35, 46, 141, 148
World Football League, 206, 230
Wrigley Field, 84–85, 92
Wright, Neil, 165

Yankee Stadium, 5–6, 20, 86, 144

ABOUT THE AUTHOR

Wayne Stewart was born in Pittsburgh and raised in Donora, Pennsylvania, a small town that has produced four big-league baseball players, including Stan Musial and the father–son Griffeys. In fact, Stewart was a member of the same Donora High School baseball team as Donora High School classmate Griffey Sr. Stewart, who retired from teaching after 31 years, now lives in Amherst, a suburb of Cleveland, Ohio.

Stewart began covering the sports world as a writer in 1978, freelancing for such publications as *Baseball Digest*, *Beckett Baseball Card Monthly*, *Baseball Bulletin*, and *Boys' Life*, and for official team publications of 10 major-league clubs, including the Atlanta Braves, Baltimore Orioles, Boston Red Sox, and Los Angeles Dodgers.

He has interviewed and profiled many stars from several sports, including Larry Bird, George Gervin, Robert Parish, Nolan Ryan, Bob Gibson, Rickey Henderson, and Ken Griffey Jr., and written biographies of Babe Ruth, Stan Musial, and Alex Rodriguez. In addition, he has written on a wide range of topics, resulting in the titles *Baseball Oddities*, *Fathers, Sons, and Baseball*, and *You're the Umpire*. His most recent books are *All the Moves I Had*, the autobiography he cowrote with NFL Hall of Fame wide receiver Raymond Berry, and *Remembering All the Stars of the NFL Glory Years*.

This is his 33rd book to date. Stewart has also appeared, as a baseball expert/historian, on numerous radio and television shows, including an ESPN Classic program on Bob Feller, ESPN radio, and the *Pat Williams Show* (a radio program). He also hosted several radio shows for a small Lorain, Ohio, station including pregame reports prior to Notre Dame football games and Cleveland Indians baseball games, and a call-in talk show. He has written for several Ohio newspapers, and some of his works have been used in eight anthologies.